HEALED BY THE Stripes OF JESUS

A TRUE STORY OF GOD'S UNCONDITIONAL LOVE & GRACE

My Story! My Miracle!
How I Overcame Metastasis Colon Cancer:
You Can Be Healed Too!

BY DR. RUTH TANYI

Reviews and Endorsements

"If only you knew how close you were towards your healing and the Healer; you will be stunned. Dr Tanyi's story is a true life's non-technical narrative of God's miraculous healing in our modern day and time.

God's continual love, mercy and miraculous healing power was demonstrated in the life of Dr. Ruth Tanyi. This is when those who do not only believe in the Lord Jesus Christ as their personal Lord and Savior, but equally believe in the living and healing Word of God's unchanging promises through the finished work of Jesus Christ by whose stripes we were and are being healed, if only we believe. Dr. Ruth shows us how through her true life's testimony, the Almighty God brings in the power and leadership of the Holy Spirit miraculous healing of diverse sort to anyone who truly believes and wants to live believing.

She is a living testimony of one more story in our modern day of God's mighty acts of healing through his son Jesus Christ, over cancer. **Her testimony will not only challenge you to put your faith in God as you take him for His Word but also for you to realize this wasn't meant for her alone, but for all who put their faith in God through Jesus Christ.** Can this be your experience too and how?

And finally, if you have ever wondered about God's miraculous healing power in today's world; then, Dr. Ruth Tanyi's book is a **must read** for you and all. I recommend you get a copy of Dr. Ruth Tanyi's book. Read her story and engage the Living and Almighty God through Jesus Christ".

Rev. Dr. Lobe Bernard Metombe; Biola University, Southern California.

"This book is an amazing real life story from the heart of Dr. Ruth Tanyi. Her testimony of steadfast faith to experience the miraculous healing of her Metastasis Colon Cancer is a **must read for Pastors, Christians, Medical people who know someone or is dealing with any medical dilemma.** **This book will inspire and encourage you to rethink any of** your previous beliefs about the healing the Lord has provided, and to pursue the Ultimate Healer, Jesus Christ, the One and Only True Living Lord".

Pastor Harry Bratton; Greater Faith Grace Bible Church
Rialto, CA.

"I applaud Dr. Ruth in her courage for penning down this amazing testimony of healing through the amazing work of God. This book will unbelievably bring the reader to an understanding of the man Jesus and His healing ministry through the word that became flesh (John 1:14). As a minister of the Gospel of Jesus Christ, my focus in reading Dr. Tanyi's testimony is that, **I became empowered, my Scripture knowledge in healing was rekindled, my faith as a child of God was affirmed and it took away all doubts about healing.**

Indeed, as stated in (Matthew 8:17), that it might be fulfilled which was spoken by Isaiah the prophet, who said, "He Himself took our infirmities and bore our sicknesses". **This book is an excellent resource to not just those struggling with cancer, but anyone with any affliction to the saving knowledge of Jesus Christ. It tells of the fact that, God is still a miracle soul saving Father to those who believe.**

In conclusion, as you read this powerful work of God's healing through an amazing vessel of God, Dr. Ruth Tanyi who believed, held God to His Word, put away all doubt, be open minded to God's work through the healing ministry of Christ Jesus, and receive your healing."

Rev. Mrs. Fatima Deku; Holy Spirit Power Ministries
Fontana, CA.

"Dr. Ruth is one of the most prolific speakers and writers I have ever met. Her story is not only riveting, but revelatory through shifting mindsets on healing. In her book, she not only tells her story, but gives us insights into how a person can be doing all of the right things, yet still be "attacked" in their body. **What I love most about this writing is that she not only tells her story, but equips the reader with spiritual insights and practical tools to ensure they are informed of, comprehend, and are living in the victory promised through Christ. Every reader, whether sick or well, will leave this reading refreshed, revived, and ready to receive every promise from The Lord."**

Pastor Torrian Scott, Harvest International Church
Brea, CA.

"I haven't known Dr Ruth real long. I must say, that after reading her book I felt like I have known her forever! I was riveted to each page wondering when will this trial be over. Each page you see her slipping deeper and deeper into the darkness. Her whole life was planned out and coming together like planned; then the whole world crashed in on her. I must admit I was waiting for it to level off, but it didn't. Her life line was her love and trust for God her Father. Man hit the end of what they could do, and Dr Ruth hit the end of what she could do — that left one last participant — Her Heavenly Father. He didn't hit the end for there is no end to His love and provision through Christ! **This book should be read with a Bible at hand. Look up each scripture reference and don't be in a hurry to get through this book. If you are in need of healing; this book is for you! If you want to know how to bring healing to others; this book is for you!** Dr Ruth answers so many questions about God's will to heal and lovingly reveals God's Grace and

Compassion for everyone that is suffering with any sickness or disease. It is so important that we don't let someone else's opinion jeopardize our health or healing. Thank you so much Dr Ruth for laying a plan, not just a book, that will elevate suffering for all that embrace and believe the TRUTH lying in these pages."

Pastor, Dr. Dan Thompson, PhD, Faith Builders Family Church
Banning, CA.

Healed by the stripes of Jesus. A true story of God's unconditional love & grace. My Story! My Miracle! How I Overcame Metastasis Colon Cancer! You Can Be Healed Too!

Copyright © 2018 by Dr Ruth Tanyi.
Published by   Dr Ruth Tanyi Ministries, Inc
                 P O BOX 1806
                 Loma Linda, CA, 92354, USA.
                 www.DrRuthtanyi.org

Cover design and Interior layout by: AJ Design

Additional copies of this book can be obtained from:
                 Online: www.DrRuthtanyi.org
                 Email: Info@DrRuthtanyi.org

All Scripture quotations, unless otherwise indicated, are taken from the *Holy Bible, New International Version®, NIV®*. Copyright ©1973, 1978, 1984, 2011 by Biblica, Inc.™ Used by permission of Zondervan. All rights reserved worldwide.

Scripture quotations marked NLT are taken from the Holy Bible, New Living Translation, copyright ©1996, 2004, 2007, 2013, 2015 by Tyndale House Foundation. Used by permission of Tyndale House Publishers, Inc., Carol Stream, Illinois 60188. All rights reserved.

Scriptures marked NKJV are taken from the NEW KING JAMES VERSION (NKJV): Scripture taken from the NEW KING JAMES VERSION®. Copyright© 1982 by Thomas Nelson, Inc. Used by permission. All rights reserved.

Scripture quotations marked MSG are taken from THE MESSAGE, copyright © 1993, 1994, 1995, 1996, 2000, 2001, 2002 by Eugene H. Peterson. Used by permission of NavPress. All rights reserved. Represented by Tyndale House Publishers, Inc.

Scriptures marked AMP are taken from the AMPLIFIED BIBLE (AMP): Scripture taken from the AMPLIFIED® BIBLE, Copyright © 1954, 1958, 1962, 1964, 1965, 1987 by the Lockman Foundation Used by Permission.

We want to hear from you. Please send your comments and/or testimonies about this book to: Info@DrRuthTanyi.org or write to:

                 Dr. Ruth Tanyi Ministries, Inc
                 P O BOX 1806
                 Loma Linda, CA, 92354, USA.

If you find any error in the citation of Scripture anywhere in this book, kindly contact us so we can make the necessary corrections, thank you.

ISBN 978-0-9986689-6-3
Library of Congress Control Number: 2018911160

All rights Reserved. No part of this book may be reproduced in any form without written permission from Dr. Ruth Tanyi Ministries Inc.
Printed in the Unites States of America.

CONTENTS

Introduction 9
Preface 14
Acknowledgments 21

SECTION 1
The Journey To The Real Diagnosis!

Chapter 1	The Subtle Symptoms!	27
Chapter 2	How Can I Be Sick?	35
Chapter 3	The Misdiagnosis!	43
Chapter 4	The Surgery: The First Miracle!	53
Chapter 5	The Real Diagnosis!	63
Chapter 6	Unbelievably Shocking!	75

SECTION 2
The Fight For My Life!

Chapter 7	What Just Happened To Me?	85
Chapter 8	And God Spoke!	97
Chapter 9	The Spirit of "Death!"	107
Chapter 10	"I Can't Let Jesus Down!": The Healing Ministry of Jesus (PART A)	117
Chapter 11	"I Can't Let Jesus Down!": The Healing Ministry of Jesus (PART B)	129
Chapter 12	Receiving My Healing: Changing My Thinking Processes	149
Chapter 13	Receiving My Healing: Reducing Unbelief	159
Chapter 14	Receiving My Healing: Strengthening My Faith Through Meditation	171
Chapter 15	I Received My Healing in My Spirit and Soul!	187

SECTION 3
Waiting For The Visible Manifestation of My Healing!

Chapter 16	The Mental Torture of Waiting	197
Chapter 17	Only Jesus!	209
Chapter 18	Endurance Through the Scriptures While Waiting	221
Chapter 19	No More Medications!	237
Chapter 20	Christ-Like Perspective In Suffering	249
Chapter 21	The Visible Evidence: Cancer Free!	261

SECTION 4
You Can Be Healed Too!

Chapter 22	Barriers To Receiving Your Healing: "Physical" Barriers (PART A)	279
Chapter 23	Barriers To Receiving Your Healing: "Hidden" Barriers (PART B)	287
Chapter 24	Receive Your Healing: Foundational Truths About Healing (PART A)	301
Chapter 25	Receive Your Healing: You Can Be Healed Too! (PART B)	309
Chapter 26	Resting in the Lord	325
Chapter 27	Some "Do's and Don'ts" When Ministering Healing to Others	333
Chapter 28	Moving Forward with Jesus: Concluding Remarks	343

About Jesus	349
Appendix A	354
Bibliography	355
Ministry Resources	356
About The Author	361

Introduction

Dear friend, I pray that you may enjoy good health and that all may go well with you, even as your soul is getting along well.

(3 John 2; New International Version, NIV).

As the above Scripture clearly teaches, God wishes that we, His children, enjoy good health physically, just as much as He wants us to prosper in our souls (i.e., in our emotions, mannerisms, mental processes, intellect, behaviors, etc). God is pleased when His children prosper in every area of life! The God of the Bible is a good God, and there is no evil in Him (James 1:17; Psalm 92:15; 1 John 1:5). As such, I know beyond a shadow of doubt, that God is very pleased because today, after 9 years, I am 100% Cancer Free— healed by the "Stripes" (i.e., the beatings and floggings on the sinless body) of the Lord Jesus!

I am one of the thousands of cancer statistics in July of 2009. But today, in 2018, I am alive! I am a living testimony that if I can receive my healing from God, you can be healed as well of any disease that you are dealing with right now, because God is no respecter of persons! This book is about my story! It is about my miracle, and the unconditional love, grace and compassion I experienced from God through Christ Jesus, and the enabling of the Holy Spirit when I was facing a "death sentence" —metastasis Colon cancer. You can be healed too! Be encouraged!

Thousands of people worldwide are affected by cancer daily, either personally or through a family member or friend. And in spite of advancement in medicine and technology, cancers remain on the list as one of the top 10 killers of people worldwide. Notwithstanding, many individuals are surviving with the diagnosis of all types of cancers today compared to just three or four decades ago. For some individuals living with various types of cancers today, they have probably been told that the "cancer is in remission," which may mean that (1) a person may stop certain types of treatments for sometime because the cancer is no longer growing; or (2) there is no laboratory, diagnostic or clinical/physical evidence of cancer in the individual's body. While the phraseology "remission" might be comforting to many, I do not accept this phraseology for myself; because in my view, it gives the impression that the "cancer is still present although imperceptible." Rather, as a cancer survivor, I consider myself 100% "Cured" of cancer by the "Stripes" of Jesus Christ.

I believe 100% that, when the Lord Jesus, my Redeemer, died on that Cross over 2000 years ago for my personal sins, He also died so that I could experience healing in my physical body and soul, as well as prosperity in every area of my life; and He has also delivered me from the Kingdom of darkness belonging to Satan, and from the fear of death. So No, the cancer I was diagnosed with in 2009 is not in "remission" —I received my healing from the Lord Jesus.

Not About Medicine

If you are looking for a book with medical explanations and details about cancer, I am sorry to tell you right now that, this is not the focus of this book. However, in some chapters, I discuss, very reluctantly and briefly, certain medical aspects pertaining to the cancer journey I experienced, in order to give you a richer perspective and understanding of my story. I intentionally left the majority of the medical details out of this book, so as to focus on my journey with Christ Jesus through my healing process, that way you can learn from my experience and receive your healing likewise, if you so desire. **Also, I purposefully left out most of the medical details and focused more on the spiritual aspect of my journey so as to encourage you, the reader, to focus on Christ Jesus, Who is the Only Faithful, True, and Ultimate Healer of all types of cancers for those who believe!** To this end, the purposes of this book are fourfold. To:

1. Share with you, the reader, how I received my healing from Christ Jesus, hopefully strengthening and encouraging you not to "give up", regardless of the doctors' diagnosis and prognosis ;

2. Teach you, if you are still doubting whether or not you can receive your healing from God through Christ, that Jesus

indeed wants you to be healed today;

3. Teach you, through the Scriptures, the absolute Truth that, when our Savior Christ Jesus died for our sins over 2000 years ago, He also died for us to walk in "divine health" as well;

4. Teach you, through the Scriptures that, God does not choose whom to heal and whom not to heal (this is a very wrong and unscriptural notion that is going around).

I am very aware that the topic of healing is very controversial around certain Christian circles. There are many Godly Christians, who unfortunately, have been taught wrong, and as such are believing that it is not God's will to heal His children today. There are Christians who do not even believe that miracles of healings and other miracles as discussed in the Bible are still in operation today! Friend, I am here to say that since God is the same yesterday, today and forever (Hebrews 13:8), all of the miracles discussed in the Bible are still happening in the body of Christ (i.e., a collection of all Christians globally, regardless of geographical location or denominational preference) today.

The Bible teaches that faith comes by hearing the Word of God and the testimonies of others (Revelation 12:11; Romans 10:17). Thus, I am hoping that as you read about my experience and how God was with me through each step of the way, your faith will be strengthened to fight against cancer or any other disease. It is my belief that the lessons you will learn from my experience will position you to overcome any disease, trial, dire circumstance, etc — Nothing is impossible with God. Many individuals, including many Godly Christians "cower" when they hear the "C" word, that is to say — Cancer. But as you will learn from this book, your first reaction to any crisis will probably determine the outcome: whether or not you will win or lose the battle.

As you read along, this book will strengthen you to come to the realization that while the medical field may capitalize and magnify the "C" word, that is —Cancer; to God —Cancer is just as easy to treat as the common cold, when you stand strong in faith and focus on Christ the Healer! God is faithful, and He wants you to be healed! And if you do not yet have a personal relationship with God through Christ, I am glad you are reading, because Jesus wants to heal you too — spiritually, mentally, emotionally, and physically. Thus, I hope that as you read along, you will come to the realization that you need Christ Jesus as your personal Lord and Savior, who desires to heal you so that you can be made "Whole" again.

Not Just For Those With Cancers

This book is not just written for those who are struggling with cancers, but for everyone struggling with any type of disease. **Even if you do not have any disease at this time, the lessons you will learn from this book will equip you to minister healing to yourself in the event that you are "attacked" with an illness, and to minister healing to others with confidence as you look upon the Lord Jesus — The Ultimate Healer.** This book will also enable you to gain a deeper understanding of the loving, compassionate and gracious God of the Bible.

A Teaching Handbook on Healing

Additionally, the content in this book goes beyond my testimony of being healed by the Lord from metastasis Colon cancer. This book is a practical handbook, with in-depth teaching on how to receive healing from the Lord of any disease and how to "walk" (i.e., live daily) in that healing. You will also learn practical insights on how to prevent diseases in the first place.

The Different Sections in this Book

For simplicity, I have divided this book into **4 major** sections. In Section 1, titled, **"The Journey to the Real Diagnosis"**, I discuss the painful journey of how I was diagnosed with metastasis Colon cancer. This section covers the initial few months of my story.

In Section 2, titled, **"The Fight For My Life"**, I started to discuss how I received the revelation from the Lord on how to begin my fight with cancer, and how I received my healing. This section covers about 4 to 5 months after the diagnosis of cancer. In Section

3, tilted, "**Waiting For the Visible Manifestation**", I discuss the lengthy and painful 5 to 6 years of waiting for the visible evidence of being healed.

Lastly, in Section 4, titled, "**You Can Be Healed Too**", I offer practical recommendations on how you, the reader, can receive your healing as well. Also in this section, I discuss some common barriers that prevent individuals from receiving their healing from God, and then I discuss ways that you can overcome these barriers and be healed. I then concluded this section by discussing some "do's and don'ts" with regards to ministering healing to others.

As you read through, I pray for God to reveal more of Himself to you as your Ultimate Healer. And I pray all these in the name of Jesus, Amen!

Sincerely,

Dr. Ruth Tanyi

September, 2018

PREFACE

Surely he took up our pain and bore our suffering, yet we considered him punished by God, stricken by him, and afflicted. But he was pierced for our transgressions, he was crushed for our iniquities; the punishment that brought us peace was on him, and by his wounds we are healed.

(Isaiah 53:4-5; New International Version, NIV).

The Lord Jesus Died for You to Receive Physical Healing Too!

As noted in Isaiah 53: 4-5 and many other Scriptures I will discuss in this book, Jesus Christ, The One Whom the above Scripture is teaching about, died not just for the forgiveness of sins, but also for physical healing in our bodies! I am quite aware that the topic of healing is very controversial in the body of Christ today, and I really do not understand why! I believe that any ardent student of the Word of God, who has invested some time to study the Scriptures in regards to healing, and is not biased, will come to the conclusion that when the Lord Jesus died on the cross over 2000 years ago, He died so that we, His followers, can receive physical healing in our bodies also.

Today, there are many Christians who believe that Isaiah 53:4-5 is not referring to physical healing. But, it is! Physical healing was also involved in the atonement (i.e., the death, burial and resurrection of Jesus Christ because of Mankind's Sinful Nature, etc) of Christ, and I will discuss more on this later in this preface section of this book. So, if you are upset with me right now because I believe that healing of our physical bodies was a part of the atonement of Christ, I ask that you be patient, read through this entire book before you quickly "shut" me out. About 2 years ago, I recall one Pastor who became extremely angry at me, and without even giving me the opportunity to educate him, he ignorantly called me a heretic (i.e., one who proclaims incorrect beliefs), because I said the Bible teaches that physical healing of our diseases was part of Christ's atonement. I hope you do not quickly "shut" me out like that one

Pastor did — He missed the opportunity to be educated in this area.

I am aware that the doctrine of healing is one of those doctrines that have raised countless of unanswered questions. None of us has the complete answer(s) to every single doctrine taught in the Bible. We are all learning and growing daily, although at different paces, and some individuals have a deeper revelation than others in regards to different biblical doctrines. Hence, it is relevant that we approach this topic of healing with humility, and even when we disagree, we should do so with grace and Christ-like love.

As Christians, we have to be honest and transparent about biblical doctrines we do not quite have a deeper spiritual revelation of, rather than quickly dismissing those who do. Spiritual pride is deadly, and in fact, God considers it a sin. Thus, honesty in seeking understanding in certain areas of biblical doctrines we are struggling with is necessary for our relationship with God, and with those He will put in our paths to assist. Therefore, I ask that you, the reader, humble yourself as unto the Lord and patiently read through this entire book before making any hasty decision(s) about the doctrine of healing.

I believe that if you keep an open heart, you will be able to learn from what I will share in this book about healing, then you can go and search the Scriptures for yourself and seek the Holy Spirit for further revelation; because, the revelation of healing can come primarily only from the Holy Spirit. **And as I will share with you using the Scriptures, it is always, I mean always God's will to heal, just like it is always, I mean always God's will for none to perish, but for all to have eternal life; although not everyone receives their physical healing in this life, for many known and unknown reasons** (more of this is discussed in this book).

Major Reasons Why Some Individuals Reject Healing as Part of Christ's Atonement

Every Christian accepts that the Lord Jesus died for the forgiveness of sins, but when it comes to healing, there is such division in the body of Christ! It is my opinion that, those who reject the notion that healing was part of the atonement are doing so for various reasons, such as, but not limited to the following:

I. Ignorance of this Truth due to wrong doctrine. The fact that someone might have a PhD in Christian theology does not mean that they have the spiritual revelation about every doctrine in the Bible, do not be deceived. I have heard some of the most respected and famous Pastors and Teachers in the body of Christ teach that healing of our physical bodies was/is not a part of Christ's atonement, and as such, it is not God's will to always heal — **this is scripturally incorrect**;

II. They choose to refuse the Truth because if they accept this Truth, then, they would have to "do something" about it, such as teach on healing and how to "walk" in "divine" healing, and they do not want to do so for multiple reasons;

III. They have prayed for someone, but the person died, and as such, they are discouraged, and are incorrectly believing that God chooses those to heal and those not to heal;

IV. They have not experienced healing in their own bodies, and as such, they are discouraged and have concluded that it is not always God's will to heal us;

V. They have taken situations from the Bible out of context and incorrectly concluded that it is not God's will to always heal;

VI. They have limited or no spiritual insight in the area of healing. I know many individuals who fit into this category. As an example, **some individuals may be excelling in an area such as finances; they may have much insight and spiritual revelation about giving and receiving from the Lord. But then, in another area such as receiving their healing, they may have limited or no spiritual insight — This has nothing to do with the Lord. Rather, each of us grows at different paces in our journey.**

To further illustrate, there are some Pastors/Ministers who may place more emphasis on say, the forgiveness of sins and salvation; thus, they will probably witness a lot of individuals accepting Christ as their Savior. Conversely, if they do not preach/teach on other relevant biblical doctrines such as healing or finances, then, guess what? These Ministers/Pastors will not witness as much deliverance from the Lord in the areas of healing or finances among their congregants, because faith comes by hearing the Word of God. Although it is God's will that we, as ministers preach/proclaim all of His Truths from the Bible, it does not always happen this way. Some Christian leaders do not have a deeper revelation of certain biblical doctrines, as such they do not proclaim/teach the full Counsel of God.

In my own life, as a result of fighting cancer, I quickly grew and received a deeper spiritual revelation in the area of healing. But, it was not until around 2012 that I started to gain much insight and spiritual revelation in the area of finances, as I studied the Scriptures in this area. Although it is God's will that we grow and mature in every area of life, it does not always happen this way because of our choices. Hence, so many people who love God and are excelling in other areas in their lives may not have the spiritual discernment with regards to receiving their healing— this does not make them a "bad person" or a "weak Christian"!

I do not say any of the above statements in arrogance, but in love, as one who has spent over 9 years of my life studying God's Word in regards to healing, applying principles of healing over my life, and overcoming, not just cancer, but a host of other diseases. I do not claim to have all of the answers (none of us do), but the "little" I know is working, and I have also taught others the biblical principles of healing, and I have seen them delivered from various diseases. Much more, I have prayed and stood in faith with others who were believing God for their healing, and God has worked through me to bring healing to many others suffering from various diseases. So I say these things with much compassion and love for those who have been taught incorrectly, and I hope you can learn from this book.

The above reasons why some people reject healing as part of Christ's atonement are just the major ones I have heard; I am certain there are several others. Nonetheless, very much like some individuals, before I was diagnosed with cancer, I firmly believed that it was not God's will to always heal. But as mentioned already, upon a very diligent study of the Scriptures, I came to the firm conclusion that it is always God's will to heal us, His beloved children, just like it is always God's will for people to be saved. Why do I say this? Because the healing Ministry of the Lord Jesus teaches us so (more on this in Section 2 of this book). Then, the Greek word **sozo**, which is often translated into the English language to mean "salvation", is also translated to mean "physical healing" from diseases; this has provided much clarity into the doctrine of healing as taught in the Bible.

The Greek Word Sozo

At times, when certain Biblical words were translated from the original Greek language into the English language, some of their meanings were lost or minimized during the translation process. This is because one Greek word has several meanings, which is why it is very critical to study the Bible out of different translations. A case in point is the original Greek word **sozo** which many contemporary English Bible Versions have translated to mean "saved". But, according to the Strong's Concordance, the original Greek word "**sozo**" (Strong's 4982), has many meanings, such as: (1) "to save", referring to "salvation" in Christ; (2) "deliverance from danger, suffering"; (3) to "preserve" from sickness; (4) to be "made whole"; (5) "deliverance from the bondage of sin"; (6) to "restore"; etc; etc.

So, in many cases in the New Testament when the word "saved" was used, the original Greek word was **sozo**, e.g., Matthew 8:25; Mark 13:20; Luke 23:35. Then, as an example, in Matthew 9:22, the same Greek word e.g. **sozo** is used in reference to physical healing: *"Jesus turned and saw her. "Take heart, daughter," he said, "your faith has healed* [**sozo**] *you"*. And the woman was healed [**sozo**] at that moment (emphasis author's). Thus, if you were to translate the word **sozo** into English to include the different meanings, the word **sozo** means: (1) to save; (2) to deliver from sin and demonic bondages and destruction; (3) to heal and make whole; (4) to forgive; (5) to restore; (6) to prevent from perishing; etc; etc. With the aforementioned explanation, here is another way of looking at Matthew 9: 22: **Jesus turned and saw her. "Take heart, daughter," he said, "your faith has 'sozo' you." And the woman was healed [sozo] at that moment.**

As another example, Romans 10:13, a very popular Scripture pertaining to our salvation in Christ (i.e., linked to Christ's atonement) reads: **For "whoever calls on the name of the Lord shall be saved"** (NKJV). Here is another way you can look at this popular Scripture, taking the Greek word **sozo** into consideration: *For* **"whoever calls on the name of the Lord shall be saved/physically healed/restored/ will not perish/ be forgiven, etc, etc."** With the above understanding of the original meaning of the word **sozo, it is my belief that it is always God's will to heal us, although not everyone receives physical healing in this life** for many reasons, just like not everyone will receive salvation, even though it is God's will for everyone to be saved!

It is my prayer that you will keep an "open heart" as you read my story, and hopefully, God will use my testimony to enable you to come to a firm conclusion that it is His will for you to be healed in every area of your life. And keep in mind that, God's will for us does not always happen automatically — we have a role to play — knowing and obeying the Truths in God's Word. This, in and of itself explains why some people do not receive their physical healing in this life.

Lastly, I want to emphasize that I have no problem, whatsoever, with anyone who disagrees with my Scriptural position on healing. I also have no problem with those who believe that we, as Ministers, should primarily focus on the Gospel Message of Christ, rather than "wasting" time on topics such as healing. **Well, I agree that the Gospel Message is the absolute Essential doctrine of the Christian faith, and it should always be of utmost importance. While healing is not an essential doctrine, it is <u>not an irrelevant issue to God.</u>** Hence, teaching the brethren how to receive their healing is something that pleases God, Who wants us, His children, to be healed spiritually, physically, emotionally, and mentally, as evident in the Ministry of the Lord Jesus.

In conclusion, I am aware that believing that it is God's will for you to be healed, especially when you may not be experiencing the physical healing at this moment, makes it very difficult to accept this biblical Truth. But take heart! I know how you feel! I have been there! And I can say, Yes indeed, God wants you to receive your healing, which He purchased for you with the perfect and precious blood of Jesus Christ on that Calvary's cross over 2000 years ago! So take heart! God wants to make you Whole, in Jesus name, Amen!

Sincerely,

Dr. Ruth Tanyi

September, 2018

ACKNOWLEDGMENTS

I give all the glory and thanks to God, Whose healing power through my Lord and Savior Jesus Christ and the empowering of the Holy Spirit, healed me! Thank You God, for Your unrelenting and unconditional love, grace, presence, and power in my life: yesterday, today and forevermore, in Jesus name! I will forever serve and worship You! You are awesome!

I especially thank all of the medical staff at Loma Linda Hospital Cancer Center for their dedicated care of me during my fight with metastasis Colon cancer. Even though they were doing their jobs, they did it with much care, compassion and warmth; it made a major difference. A special thank you to Dr. Wesley Fung, the surgeon who obeyed God and prayed for me to accept the emergency surgery I had ignorantly declined. Your obedience prevented me from dying of complications related to the complete abdominal obstruction I had experienced.

To all of my friends who stood by me during the surgical phase of my fight, and those who faithfully called the hospital and my home to check on me, I say thank you! Your love, care and presence really comforted me. A special thank you to Rev. Kitololo, J.; Rev. Dr. Ketcha, A. ; Rev. Dr. Itue, J., for their prayers while standing in the "gap" on my behalf during my extensive surgery and recovery period.

To my older sister, Elsie Metiege Tanyi, I say thank you. Your courage and display of bold faith fuelled me with hope and strength to fight. Your constant reminder to me during those "dark" and seemingly hopeless hours of my fight that, the Lord Jesus had already healed me, strengthened and emboldened me. A very special thank you to my brother, Gerald Tanyi, for his faithful financial support, love and prayers during my battle.

I thank my mother for her loving care of me during those debilitating and prolonged post surgical period when I was unable to care for myself. And to the rest of my family members who were "kept in the dark" about the cancer for about 4 years, I say thank you for understanding my reasons for initially keeping my diagnosis and prognosis a secret. Then, a special thank you to Ms. Felicia Akamande, for her diligence, tenacity and contribution throughout the editorial process of this book.

There are too many people to thank in the last 9 years. But most significantly, I again thank God for enabling others to be of assistance to me during my fight with cancer.

I thank You God, in Jesus name, AMEN!

DEDICATION

To you, the reader, who is battling cancer, right now. Be encouraged, because God is for you, regardless of how you feel. For as Christians, we walk by faith and not by how we feel (2 Corinthians 5:7). God's Holy Word/Scripture, which is The Only inspired, infallible and inerrant Word says He is for you, fighting this battle with you —every moment, step-by-step, every day! So do not give up! I pray for the Holy Spirit to use my testimony to speak to your heart, and to strengthen your faith and fight, and to reveal to you how much He desires to see you well! I pray all these in the name of the Lord Jesus Christ —our Savior, Healer, God and personal friend, Amen!

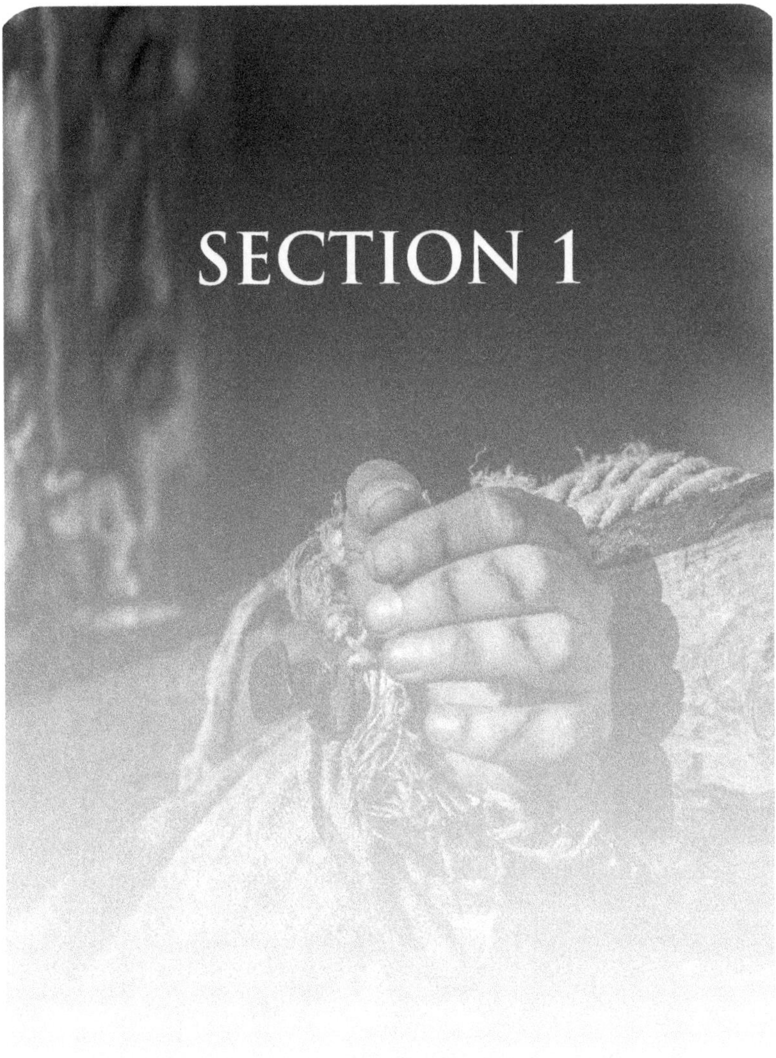

SECTION 1

THE JOURNEY TO THE REAL DIAGNOSIS!

CHAPTER 1

THE SUBTLE SYMPTOMS!

Now listen, you who say, "Today or tomorrow we will go to this or that city, spend a year there, carry on business and make money. Why, you do not even know what will happen tomorrow. What is your life? You are a mist that appears for a little while and then vanishes. Instead, you ought to say, "If it is the Lord's will, we will live and do this or that".

(James 4:13-15; New International Version, NIV).

I do not believe that most human beings get up in the morning with expectations of "bad things" happening to them. And as finite human beings, it is very easy for us to spend endless hours planning, down to the tiniest details, how we have imagined our day, week, month or even life to turn out! But, as the above Scripture out of the book of James is teaching, we never know what the future holds, in spite of how much time we spend praying, preparing and planning.

Although I knew this biblical principle taught in the book of James all along, it became a reality to me when one day, my life changed, and all of my diligent planning, and preparation for what I believed my future would be, was "at a balance" , and my entire life, in a way, came to a "stand still", with a 100% dependency and trusting on God's mercy and grace.

///

It would turn out to be the biggest battle of my life, an intimate "walk" with the Lord, and a deeper revelation of His unfathomable love, compassion, grace, presence and faithfulness!
///

It was a very beautiful Spring day in Southern California, in the first week of April of 2009, and I was in the Computer Laboratory at Loma Linda University preparing the final stages of my research project on preventing major depression using lifestyle practices. Then, while on the computer typing in the Computer Laboratory, for the first time ever, I started experiencing very mild on and off abdominal cramping, which I quickly attributed to the fact that while on vacation in Minnesota (MN) for a few weeks in March (still in 2009), I ate meat and chicken for the first time in over two years. Thus, I concluded that my "gut" was not used to animal products any longer, hence I was getting sick. But, for about 4 hours while on the computer analyzing my research data, the symptom persisted, on and off.

Prior to experiencing this subtle abdominal cramping, I had just returned from visiting some friends and family members who lived in the Minneapolis/St Paul area in MN. Before pursuing my degree at Loma Linda University, I had become a Family Medicine Nurse Practitioner (NP) in MN, where I worked for some time before relocating to California to further my education. So I had many friends and family members resident in MN.

It was the first time I had returned to Minneapolis/St Paul since I relocated from there to California in 2004 to attend Loma Linda University in pursuit of my doctorate degree in Preventive Care, popularly known as Lifestyle Medicine. My trip to Minneapolis/St Paul was awesome! I was away for about 16 days. It was a well-deserved break from 5 years of intense studies to become a doctor of Preventive Care/Lifestyle Medicine. It was the end of my educational pursuit, so I took that trip as a time to reconnect with friends and family before my upcoming graduation in June of 2009.

I Was Already a Vegetarian

Back in 2006, I officially became a Vegetarian, the Lacto-Ova-Pesto type Vegetarian, meaning, besides vegetables, I could eat Milk, Dairy products and Fish. I used the word "officially" because throughout my life, even before 2006, I had never enjoyed eating meat products or chicken, and there were times when I would easily not eat any meat or chicken for over a few months. My diet, I later found out while in school, was already Vegetarian, since on the average, I ate meat and chicken less than four times per month. But, while taking nutritional courses at school in preparation for my degree in Preventive Care, I learnt a lot about the benefits of a Vegetarian diet; thus, in 2006, I made it "official" to become a Vegetarian. Also, in 2006, I decided to eat only Organic foods, after much education about how foods are processed.

Becoming a Vegetarian was primarily for health benefits, and not for religious purposes. Thus, when I was visiting friends, family members, or was a guest at an event and no Vegetarian food was served, I would eat chicken, although this happened very rarely. In essence, I was flexible, and did not place myself under strict dietary bondage. Such was the case during my stay in Minneapolis/ St Paul while visiting friends and family. None of them served Vegetarian food, and because I did not want to offend anyone, I ate whatever food was served to me, which was mostly Omnivorous diet, including meat and chicken, although on a few occasions, I ate at a few Vegetarian restaurants in the area.

After that initial subtle abdominal cramping, I did not think much about it as I had attributed the symptom to my eating while on vacation. I left the Computer Laboratory that night without thinking much about the symptom. That night, I was able to sleep through the night without any abdominal discomfort; and upon awakening, I felt great and experienced no symptom whatsoever, so I proceeded with my day. About 1 week went by and I did not experience any abdominal cramping or any other symptom.

I had even forgotten about the incident at the Computer Laboratory; then suddenly, the abdominal cramping returned. This time however, the abdominal cramping was more severe, and I could hear my stomach "roaring", as if I was hungry, but I was not. It was weird! Also, the cramping was no longer on and off as before, this time it was persistent, and it caused an obvious discomfort that caught my attention. In spite of this increasing symptom of abdominal cramping, I did not think much of it because I was never sick. I was in perfect health, and during my last annual physical exam earlier in the same 2009, "everything" checked out as "perfect."

In Perfect Overall Health

Prior to this abdominal cramping, I was in perfect health. As mentioned earlier, I was already a Vegetarian. I was extremely physically active— I engaged in some form of aerobic exercise for about 60 to 75 minutes 6 days a week, plus I included light weight lifting at least twice weekly and a full body stretch daily. I was a "lean machine". Additionally, I took a Multivitamin, 1000 Mg of Vitamin C, Calcium 500 Mg plus Vitamin D 800 IU daily. I only took the vitamins to supplement my diet, being a Vegetarian. I did not, and still do not smoke cigarettes, drink alcohol, nor use any form of illicit drugs whatsoever. I had no prior medical health problems or issues, and I took no prescription medications. I only saw the doctor once a year for annual physicals; and in fact, because of my excellent laboratory results and physical examination, the doctor had asked that I should return to see him again in about 3 years because there was nothing wrong.

And as a Vegetarian, my daily diet was excellent and well balanced with rich sources of fruits and vegetables, plant-based proteins, healthy whole/brown carbohydrates, and healthier fats from Monounsaturated (i.e., avocado, nuts, etc) and Polyunsaturated (i.e., fish, etc) sources. I stayed well hydrated and had excellent sleeping habits. Although I was still a student of Preventive Care/Lifestyle Medicine, I put to practice everything I had learnt in school about lifestyle practices and preventing diseases.

Even before I graduated, I started producing Television programs about lifestyle practices and disease prevention, so as to educate others about the significant role of lifestyle practices, disease prevention, longevity and overall well-being. In fact, my first Television (TV) show, called Bad Sugar ®, which focused on Diabetes Prevention and lifestyle practices won an award for best documentary in its category. I was an "epitome" of excellent health!

I Was "Walking" with the Lord

Spiritually, I was "walking with the Lord" intimately at this time of my life. I was raised from a Christian home and my parents were devout Baptist Christians, and I had been involved in the church even as a child. When I relocated to the United States of America (USA) as a teenager, I continued with my Christian upbringing. Then, after many years of watching Reverend Billy Graham Telecast as a young adult, I had a deeper revelation of the Free Gift of salvation from God through Jesus Christ. As such, in 2006, I rededicated my life to the Lord again. I said again because I had done this a few years prior to 2006, but there was something different about this rededication in 2006.

So what was different about the 2006 rededication? In 2006, I made a vow to take my Christian "walk" (i.e., my daily lifestyle) seriously, and as such, I "officially" made some major changes in my life such as which friends to "hang out" with, what types of movies to watch, books to read, who to date, how to spend my time, etc, etc; and I became fully committed to my local church by serving God consistently as a volunteer.

Then, around 2007, I started sensing that God was calling me to become a Minister, and to obtain formal education in Bible Studies, but it would take several years later for me to accept this calling. So by the year 2009 when I started experiencing symptoms of abdominal cramping, which would later on be discovered to be late symptoms of metastasis Colon cancer, I was already "walking" intimately with the Lord daily and faithfully serving Him.

Emotionally I Felt Blessed

Emotionally, I was at a "great place" in my life by the year 2009. My career was excelling above and beyond my wildest dreams. I had produced several TV shows on lifestyle practices and disease prevention, which were being broadcast in various TV stations and networks across Southern California and worldwide. I was the recipient of several awards for my contribution in health and lifestyle practices to prevent diseases. I was a highly sought after public speaker at various events pertaining to lifestyle practices and disease prevention.

I had not even graduated with my doctorate degree, but I was already putting to practice everything I had learnt in school, and I was still working as a Nurse Practitioner part time, while completing my degree in Preventive Care/Lifestyle Medicine. Indeed I felt blessed! Academically, I had attained the goal for many professors desiring tenureship: I had published several review and research articles in highly acclaimed academic journals, advancing knowledge and making significant contributions academically.

So by the first week in April of 2009, just about 7 to 8 weeks before graduation, I thought I was "on top" of the world. Some family members had already made plans to travel from Cameroon, West Africa, where I am originally from, to California, to attend my graduation. Friends from other parts of the USA would be attending my graduation as well. Besides the excitement and all of the planning about the upcoming graduation, I was looking forward to beginning my private practice in Integrative Medicine. Nothing was going to stop me, so I thought, because I already had existing patients waiting, and looking forward to seeing me in my own clinic for lifestyle medical consult. I was very thankful to God, and for the first time in my life, I was finally, walking intimately with the Lord Jesus and hearing the voice of the Holy Spirit in the Word. I had peace with God, and I was walking in the peace of God! Life was perfect, so I thought!

But as the Bible teaches in James 4:13-15, "...**What is your life? You are a mist that appears for a little while and then vanishes...**" As noted in this Scripture, life is so fragile, and at times, it takes significant tragedies for us to realize that we do not

The Subtle Symptoms!

have Absolute control of certain circumstances. As that first week of April passed into the second, and then the third week, that subtle abdominal cramping started to reoccur, more frequently. Thus, I started to take notice, and I asked myself "How Can I Be Sick?" I would find out the hard way!

LESSONS LEARNED

- All of the physical things we do, such as, but not limited to eating healthier, engaging in regular physical activities, maintaining "excellent" emotional health, and even "walking" intimately with the Lord are significant in preventing diseases. But, all these things are not 100% guaranteed to prevent us from developing a disease as many people believe, because we live in a "fallen world" and "things" are not perfect in this life;

- There are many people who do all of the "right things" but they still die prematurely from the same diseases they have worked so hard to prevent through their lifestyle practices;

- We do not have Absolute control of all of the circumstances we will face in life. Absolute control belongs to God, Who is Sovereign.

CHAPTER 2

How Can I Be Sick?

Since no one knows the future, who can tell someone else what is to come?

(Ecclesiastes 8:7; New International Version, NIV).

With a history of "perfect health" and such grandeur plans I had envisioned for my future, I asked myself, "**How Can I Be Sick?**". But as the above Scripture in Ecclesiastes 8:7 is teaching, only God knew that all of my plans were about to be halted and be redirected. Nonetheless, by the second week of April 2009, the abdominal symptom was becoming annoying . Most Health Care Providers would agree that it is not unusual for patients to attribute their symptoms to the environment or other activities they had recently engaged in prior to them experiencing the symptoms. This is especially the case when the patient is generally very healthy, like I was.

By the third week of April 2009, the subtle abdominal cramping I had been experiencing had become a persistent, constant cramping, and I did not like it. Again, I attributed my symptoms to eating meat while in Minnesota (MN). But by the fourth week of April, it was obvious I had to do something because, "that" abdominal cramping was becoming unbearable, and I could not believe it. Thus I asked myself again and again, "How can I be sick?". I am in perfect health!

My Own Medical Investigation

Nevertheless, I knew I had to do something. So what did I do? I decided to "hit the medical text books," and to investigate all of the possible causes for my symptoms. At this point, going to see the doctor was not an option, besides, I did not get sick, right? The last time I suffered from any type of illness was in 2002 which was my fault, because I incorrectly fasted for 3 days without any food or liquids, then I went to work as a Nurse Practitioner and consulted with patients who were sick with the common cold, so I was infected. Thus, besides seeing the doctor for my annual physical examinations, I did not get sick. So I thought to myself "Why waste my time and go to the doctor's office and wait for hours to be seen?". So I decided to undertake my own medical investigation.

Thus, for about 1 week, I studied every medical symptom associated with abdominal cramping. In spite of my diligent research and study, I could not pinpoint why I was experiencing the abdominal cramping. As such, out of desperation, I decided that cleansing my Colon was the best thing to do in order to alleviate and/or "get rid" of the symptom, which I thought was from eating meat. To do this therefore, I decided I would give myself an enema to cleanse my Colon, then eat a Vegan diet for about 2 weeks, hoping that my "system" would be cleansed.

The Colon Cleansing Worked, So I thought!

Amazingly, after cleansing my Colon with enemas for a few days, the abdominal cramping subsided, and I said to myself, "I knew it, it was the meat!". I then proceeded with my cleansing and ate only Vegan foods for 2 weeks thereafter; it felt great! Interestingly, for about 2 to 3 weeks after the Colon cleansing, I had no symptom whatsoever. This was great because I took my mind off of my symptoms, and started preparing for my graduation party. Life was back to normal, I thought to myself! And my primary focus was on graduation, and all of the events and parties surrounding that season. It was going to be a "hectic" time.

God's Grace During The Graduation Season

It was now around the end of May 2009, graduation was less than 3 weeks away. I was very excited! I was expecting a lot of guests. My younger brother (now with the Lord), whom I had not seen in over 12 years had just received his Visa from the American Embassy in Cameroon, he would be attending my graduation; I was unbelievably excited about seeing him, although I was a little concerned I would not recognize him. He was barely a teenager when I relocated to the USA. My mother was also coming to my graduation, along with many other friends.

Then, I had been nominated and selected by the Faculty of Preventive Care/Lifestyle Medicine at Loma Linda University to receive the most prestigious award given to a graduating student for "Excellence in Preventive Care" for the graduating class of 2009, for outstanding community work and scholarship in advancing lifestyle practices and disease prevention. This was a major event for the department, and it was normally well attended by faculty, students, and family members, with great foods and refreshments. It was a "big deal!".

With the symptoms behind me, I quickly made plans for my graduation party. I placed my research project "on hold", since the University allowed the students extra time to finalize their research projects after graduation, that way they could focus on graduation plans. I took advantage of the extra time and focused on graduation. The week of graduation was super busy; again I experienced no symptoms. My brother and my mother arrived a few days before the graduation day. It was a blessing to see my brother again; and yes, I recognized him and our reunion was awesome! I was blessed by the moment, and I cried, and thanked God. My other guests and friends from out of state all arrived on time. It was a great time, with a lot of friends and family around, it was overwhelmingly amazing!

As I look back to that graduation season of 2009, I now believe that God's grace was upon me, as I was able to proceed with the busy graduation activities without being sick, even though, as I found out later, I had metastasis Colon cancer all over my body and I did not even know it. **It was as if God "placed the symptoms on hold," so that I could enjoy that graduation season with family and friends.**

A few days before graduation, I had a private graduation party with about 150 attendees. It was an awesome event with plenty of foods, laughing, dancing and memorable speeches by some faculty members I had invited, my classmates, and other guests. We enjoyed ourselves and danced our way into the night [until about Midnight]. Thereafter, my guests and I went to bed very late but joyful and grateful to God for the moment. We awoke the next day to attend the award ceremony in the afternoon. We were very tired but very excited and filled with extra adrenalin.

It was a blessing to receive the award for "Excellence in Preventive Care" in the presence of my family members, friends, other students, faculty members, and a few hundred attendees. **I felt highly honored by this award, as the chair of the department and the award giver all prophesied how, given my excellence in advancing Preventive Care/Lifestyle Medicine even as a student, they envision me making more of an impact globally upon my graduation.** The applause from the crowd was encouraging, and I said to myself, "This is just the beginning" , as I planned to teach on TV, radio, etc, about lifestyle practices and disease prevention. I had major plans, and faculty members and classmates believed in me as well.

It Was Graduation Time

Then, it was the day of my graduation — the actual day had arrived, and I would be receiving my diploma. It was a beautiful sunny day on June 19th 2009, and the weather was perfect. I was blessed to have a lot of friends and family who were all seated in the graduation auditorium, in one area, just waiting to "shout out" when my name was called to receive my diploma. It was a blessed time, with much love and support! Sure enough, the time came when my name was called, and I walked across that graduation stage with much confidence, hope and joy, as I heard some of my friends and family members shouting my name and screaming, "You did it!". "You did it!".

It was a proud moment for me. And as I shook the hand

of the President of the University, I reminded myself about that prophecy when I took the award in "Excellence in Preventive Care", and how my relocation from Minnesota to California was well worth it! I had done it! The evening after graduation day was quiet, as a few friends plus my family members gathered in my home to eat dinner and to reflect on the week.

As I reflected on graduation week, I thought to myself, "It is time for me to step out and fulfill that prophecy to take Preventive Care/Lifestyle Medicine to the world and change peoples' lives." However, there was a problem. Like Ecclesiastes 8:7 teaches, no one could have convinced me of what was about to unfold! God had a different plan for me!

It was now about the third week of June 2009, about 1 week after graduation. My brother had left for Washington DC, to visit my other family members there. All of my friends from out of town had left, but my mother was still with me, helping me to settle in after graduation and all of the activities; also, my other friends who lived locally were still around. It was time to return to work as a Nurse Practitioner part time, while finalizing my research project for the final approval by faculty before publication. I had graduated, but I still had a lot of school work to do.

That Subtle Abdominal Symptom Again!

Then, on one beautiful Tuesday morning in the last week of June 2009, while driving, I immediately noticed, "that same abdominal cramping" I felt that first week of April, remember? This time, the symptom came for about 5 to 10 minutes, persistently. Then, as quickly as it came, it left, and I thought to myself: "What was that?". At this point, I was beginning to realize that "something" was wrong, but I could not put my finger on it, and it was becoming very obvious that the abdominal cramping had nothing to do with eating meat while on vacation in Minnesota (MN). Then, for about a day or so thereafter, I had no symptom.

Shortly after graduation, I received a notification from the

University about my insurance health plan. Usually after graduation, the University would give students the option of either paying and keeping their health insurance plan for a few months thereafter, or opt out completely. Since I perceived my health as excellent, I did not want to pay the University for the health plan, I wanted to opt out. In fact, I had decided not to pay; but then, for a period of about a week or so thereafter, I experienced a relentless unrest in my spirit about my decision to opt out of the health plan. So finally, about a day or 2 before the University cancelled my insurance, I called and made the payment.

//

Boy! As I would later find out, that was God, the Holy Spirit, who spoke to my heart to pay that insurance premium in preparation for what was ahead of me! How awesome, that God will pre-warn us, if we would only listen and obey, whether or not we agree with Him!

//

Still not knowing what was wrong with me, I proceeded with my plan to finalize my research project while seeing patients part time as a Nurse Practitioner. But as Ecclesiastes 8:7 highlights, in spite of my excellent health, on and off subtle abdominal cramping, and seemingly lack of symptoms throughout the busy graduation season, I had no idea that I was a "dead woman walking!" Only the grace of God sustained me in the preceding weeks before July of 2009. But as you will soon find out, the subtle abdominal cramping started to "speak louder than I could ignore", and it was time for me to take action.

LESSONS LEARNED

- ➢ As children of God, He has Absolute control of even the tiniest details of our lives. As an example, it was because of God's grace and love, that I was able to enjoy that precious, yet busy season of graduation without "falling" sick, even though I had cancer all over my body, without knowing it.

CHAPTER 3

THE MISDIAGNOSIS!

There is a time for everything, and a season for every activity under the heavens.

(Ecclesiastes 3:1; New International Version, NIV).

God had sustained me during the very stressful weeks leading up to graduation. I had graduated and celebrated each moment with family and friends. Now, my body was "speaking" very loudly to me. It was time for me to act. In fact, I did not have a choice because I could not ignore the abdominal cramping any longer. One morning, a few days into the first week of July 2009, I awoke around 4 AM with that same persistent abdominal cramping; except this time, the symptom did not leave. It was a constant persistent pain, and I was essentially "guarding" my stomach. I quickly realized that I needed to do something. So finally, I called the doctor's office around 7:30AM for a same day appointment. I went in to see the doctor that afternoon.

My regular primary care doctor was not available, so I saw a Physician Assistant (PA). After I told him the history of the on and off subtle abdominal cramping, he examined me and concluded there was nothing abnormal in my physical exam, but he proceeded to order blood tests. After evaluating my medical history, he concluded I was probably suffering from acute Gastroenteritis (i.e., acute inflammation in the abdominal tract from a virus), and he sent me home with no medications, stating that after he received my blood test results, he would treat me if necessary. In the mean time, he advised me to treat my symptoms with over the counter remedies. Then, a few days later, I received a call from the PA stating that my blood test came back positive for Helicobacter Pylori (H.

Pylori), which is a bacteria that causes symptoms of gastritis, such as cramping, heart burn, and even ulcers.

His diagnosis was shocking to me, because he tested my blood for H. Pylori which was not a good test to investigate an acute H. Pylori infection in progress. I wondered how I could have contracted H. Pylori, because I had not been exposed to the bacteria. Nevertheless, I quickly concluded that I might have contracted the bacteria during my visit to Minnesota (MN). Boy! I was still attributing my symptoms to my trip to MN. Notwithstanding , I proceeded to start the treatment regimen which he had prescribed, even though I did not, and still do not like taking medications. But just a few days into the treatment, it was obvious that I was misdiagnosed, and H. Pylori was not the culprit to my abdominal symptoms.

It Was a Wrong Diagnosis

One beautiful morning, still around the first week of July 2009, after I had been diagnosed with H. Pylori infection, I noted bright red blood in my stool after using the bathroom. I did not know what to think of the blood, but I knew something major was wrong with me at this point. I revisited my medical textbooks to investigate all of the possible reasons for blood in the stool. Some of these include, but are not limited to diseases such as hemorrhoids, anal tears, rectal cancer, late stage Colon cancer, etc. I quickly concluded that none of these diagnoses fit into my medical history, so I was not worried, although I knew I would report the bloody stool to my primary doctor during my next visit with him.

The Pain Became Unbelievably Unbearable

Then, around 11AM on that same day I had noted blood in my stool, I was sitting in the living room area in my home with my mother and a friend eating an early lunch, and suddenly, I experienced a very sharp pain in my abdomen which caused me to be debilitated, and I immediately slumped over to the left side of my body. The

The Misdiagnosis!

pain was primarily focused on the left side of my abdomen. The pain was very severe. I could not continue eating, so I told my friend to take me back to the doctor's office, because I had been advised to return quickly if the symptoms persist.

So, without making an appointment, my friend drove me there, which was less than 2 miles away from my home. Luckily this time around, my Primary Care doctor was available, and after the nurse told him how miserable I appeared in the waiting area, I was brought into the examination room right away. After explaining the history of the subtle abdominal cramping to him, he examined all of my medical records and the recent blood tests, and decided he needed to repeat the blood tests. More blood tests were drawn on that day.

Much more, the doctor conducted a thorough physical examination on me, including a rectal examination for any source or cause of the bloody stool, but his examination was negative. He was shocked, he said, because he could not explain my symptoms. Nonetheless, he decided to order an abdominal X-ray study, and gave me a prescription for the pain. With the severe pain I was experiencing, he prescribed Norco, a moderately strong Opioid (a category of drugs used as pain killers), and advised me to present myself in the emergency room if the symptoms persist. He was very kind and compassionate, and apologized for his inability to ascertain a diagnosis for my symptoms. I left the doctor's office very confused and frustrated. One thing was certain though, the pain was beginning to be unbearable. But, I was very concerned about taking Norco, since I had never taken medications before, much more Opioids.

The Pain Became Debilitating

After leaving the doctor's office, my friend drove me immediately to the pharmacy to pick up the pain killer. As much as I was concerned about taking the medication, the pain was unbearable and I was barely walking. I was slumped over to the left side of my body, guarding my abdomen as I attempted to walk. Right there at the pharmacy, I took the first pill, hoping that I could return home and complete my lunch. We returned home rather quickly that afternoon, and my mother was very pleased that I saw my regular doctor, and hopefully, everything would be sorted out. Then, I sat down to complete my lunch. But the moment I placed the first bite of food in my mouth, **I experienced an indescribable, unbearable sharp pain that felt like someone had stuck me with a very sharp knife on the left side of my abdomen, then proceeded to twist the knife 180 degrees on the inside of my body.**

The pain was unbearable, and I screamed, crying very loudly and holding my stomach and chest. Just a few minutes thereafter, I was exhausted from the pain and I started to experience difficulty with breathing. My skin color became pale from the pain and screaming, I was later informed. My mother witnessed all of this agony, and she started screaming and crying too. She did not know what was wrong, but she knew something very bad was happening. At this point, my friend who was at the doctor's office with me, just less than a few hours prior to this incident, made a quick decision — Instead of calling 911 (he later told me he thought it might take longer to call 911 and wait, since I lived just a few blocks away from the emergency room), he immediately carried me into his vehicle, and rushed me to Loma Linda Medical Center Emergency Department. We were at the emergency room in less than 5 minutes.

I Demanded For an Answer

The moment we arrived at the emergency room, the nurses looked at me and immediately took me to the back room and started an Intravenous Line (IV), and they began treating the pain immediately. At the emergency room, a battery of blood tests were done, which all returned negative: the doctors were again mystified as to what the problem could be! Again, I explained the history, and after reviewing all of the blood tests done in the preceding weeks, they also concluded that it was some kind of viral Gastroenteritis. At this point, I knew they were wrong, so I refused their diagnosis. I insisted that the emergency room doctor should evaluate the

The Misdiagnosis!

abdominal X-rays ordered by my Primary Care doctor earlier on that same day, since my doctor did not get a chance to review the results with me.

If you know anything about Loma Linda University Medical Center, it is a teaching hospital, which means at any given point while there, you would be dealing with several resident physicians from different specialties, although you would be assigned to an attending physician. The emergency room resident physician was kind and he agreed to review my abdominal X-rays. **Upon his evaluation, he concluded that the X-rays showed "some kind of obstruction", and he wrote an order for me to talk to the surgical team on call.** I immediately refused, and requested for a Computerized Tomography (CT) Scan, normally referred to as a CT Scan.

A Computerized Tomography (CT) Scan utilizes a series of X-ray images of the internal organs taken from different angles, and then uses computer processing to create cross-sectional images of various parts of the body. During a CT Scan examination, a dye is injected into the vein (or given orally), which helps to better highlight blood vessels, body organs, and other structures within the body. CT Scan images provide more diagnostic and detailed information than plain X-rays do.

At this point, given my medical background as a Nurse Practitioner, I knew that an abdominal CT Scan would be a better diagnostic test for my condition, compared to just a plain abdominal X-ray. But the emergency room resident physician attending to me refused, stating that he did not want to expose me to unnecessary radiation. The physician added that they (meaning, the emergency room physician team) did not perceive the need for a CT Scan; but I insisted, and requested to speak to the attending physician on duty. Keep in mind that it was close to 10 to 11PM at this point, on the same day, and I had been in the emergency room since around 2PM or so [all of these events were happening within a 12-hour timeframe].

Persistent, Unrelenting Pain

During the process of advocating for a better diagnostic test and the back and forth dialogue with the various physicians, I was experiencing severe unbearable pain and I was constantly screaming. The pain was actually getting worse, even though they were doing their best to treat it. The pain was so severe, the emergency room staff got very concerned, and the doctor wrote an order for a very strong Opioid, Fentanyl, 25 to 100Mg Intravenously (IV) as needed, which was about every 1 or 2 hours. But, within just a few minutes of receiving the first dose, I experienced an adverse reaction from the drug, and I started hallucinating and saw "things crawling" on the wall, the ceiling and all over my body. The drug was immediately discontinued.

In spite of this unbearable pain during my emergency room encounter, I made certain to alert the emergency room staff that I had never taken prescription medications in my life; as such, I warned them to only give me the smallest dose possible, because my body was "naive" to medications. I was given a trial of IV Morphine, 1 to 5Mg about every 1 to 2 hours as needed; but again, I experienced intense vomiting and reacted negatively to it. After I was given Zofran, a very potent medication for nausea and vomiting, the Morphine was also discontinued. The pain persisted; it was constant, severe and unbelievably unbearable, as if "a sharp knife was being stirred inside my body". If you are a Health Care Practitioner, or a patient suffering from chronic pain, you are probably aware of the potency of Fentanyl and Morphine: they are on top of the list with regards to their potent ability as pain killers; yet, these drugs were not helping me. The pain was killing me before my time!

As a Nurse Practitioner, I had treated countless patients with various pain disorders, but the pain I experienced was "a type" I had never seen among my patients or heard of. **It felt as if my internal organs were being "stripped apart", yet I was alive to experience it**. I thought I was dying! Finally, I was given a trial of Dilaudid, the lowest dose, and although I started to vomit immediately, it

The Misdiagnosis!

helped with the pain. The nurses and doctors were very pleased that "something" was working! My emergency room presentation was a mystery to them. **They could not make the connection between my clinical symptoms and the pain I was experiencing; they kept apologizing for my suffering and their inability to identify the problem.**

Finally! The Initial Diagnosis!!

After about 1 hour or so of waiting for the response to my request for a CT Scan, the attending emergency room physician approved the order for a CT Scan study, and around Midnight, the nurse came into my room with a full glass of water with the dye for me to drink. At this point, I was in and out of drowsiness from the pain medication, but I quickly drank the solution because I knew that a CT Scan was my best hope in demanding for an answer.

About an hour after the CT Scan was completed, the attending emergency room physician, a very gentle, kind and pleasant gentleman came into my bedside, and kneeling by my bedside, as if apologizing for some wrong committed, whispered into my ears, **"Dr Tanyi, thank you, you saved your own life"**. I was not sure what he meant. So I asked him to explain. He looked at me with compassion and said, **"I am so glad you insisted on getting a CT Scan, because you have complete 100% abdominal obstruction [Intussusception], you need emergency surgery"**. He went on to explain how he had already contacted the surgical team, and a surgeon will be coming to talk to me very shortly. In response, I said: "NO"!

Complete Bowel Obstruction

Around 4AM or so, a young, arrogant, and insensitive surgical resident physician came to my bedside to explain the surgical procedure. Upon asking him what he thought could have caused this "intussusception" , he looked at me straight in the eye and without any compassion, he said, "You have cancer", just like that! When I heard those words, I mustered all the energy I could and sat up in my bed, and I looked at him straight in the eye and said, "Get out of my room, right now". "How dare you come in here and tell me this!" "No", I yelled, "You cannot diagnose abdominal cancer with just a CT Scan". He immediately left my room. I then called the nurse and requested to see the attending physician for the surgical team.

Then around 4:30AM or so, a very gentle, pleasant and kind gentleman, a surgeon (Dr. Wesley Fung), entered my room and sat down besides my bed. He apologized for the encounter with his colleague, and explained that I am correct, abdominal cancers cannot be diagnosed with just a CT Scan, further testing would be required. But he recommended that I should have the emergency surgery because, "I was essentially dying", with each day I delay the surgery. Again, I refused. This time, I said, "I need to pray about it first and hear from God before proceeding!"

//

Everything was happening so fast, I could not believe it! I was very confused and needed time to process everything. Imagine being in "perfect health" all of your life, then suddenly you are told you require emergency surgery, lest you might die within hours or a few days!

//

I believe this kind of news would be shocking to most people! By this time in the emergency room, my pain had been stabilized, and I started to wonder how I developed Intussusception.

Intussusception

Intussusception is a life threatening emergency condition, whereby the internal organs such as the intestines slide into an adjacent part of the intestines. Or, simply put, "the intestines twist around themselves", thus causing severe and debilitating pain, bowel obstruction, nausea, vomiting, requiring emergency surgery, lest

The Misdiagnosis!

death could ensue quickly from bowel perforation (i.e., tear), internal bleeding, etc. This condition is mostly common in children, but it is also seen in the adult population as a secondary reason for an underlying disease process, such as a "tumor"! There you go! First clue that there was something in my organs that led to this "intussusception", but it would be challenging for the doctors to figure out, since I was in excellent health.

Finally, after Dr. Fung realized I was not going to have the emergency surgery, he decided to admit me into the hospital under the primary care of the surgical department. By 7AM or so the next day, I was officially admitted at Loma Linda University Medical Center (LLUMC) hospital. During my emergency room encounter at the LLUMC, I had requested to talk with a Gastroenterology (GI) physician, because I wanted to understand why and how the obstruction occurred. Thus, shortly after I was admitted, an entire team of resident GI physicians (without their attending physician), came to my room. The GI team told me they were precisely unsure, but given my excellent overall health, it was probably a viral Gastroenteritis! Remember this diagnosis? "Not again," I said to myself! And I asked, "How could it be viral Gastroenteritis?" But, this time, the GI team believed that a viral Gastroenteritis probably led to the "intussusception" I was suffering from. The GI team concluded that I needed emergency surgery, and they insisted I should accept the plan of care from the surgical team.

Meanwhile at home, my mother would later tell me she could not sleep, and she called family members and friends to start praying. My friend who brought me to the emergency room had left around 3AM. But God was with me! He is awesome! And many times, He answers our prayers without us even asking. **Little did I know that God would use this particular surgeon, Dr Fung, to manifest His first miracle**. But as you will soon find out, the enemy, Satan, had a different plan for me, as the spirit of fear oppressed me, and I was in bondage, and I refused the surgery, even though I was dying!

LESSONS LEARNED

- God, in Hs foreknowledge knows exactly what we, His children, need even before we ask Him. And He orchestrates events in our lives to lead and guide us through the path He has preordained for us. Our role is to stay connected to the "Vine", Jesus Christ, trusting and obeying the promptings of the Holy Spirit;

- God specializes in revealing Himself in the midst of calamities, but we, His children, have to be discerning to perceive His presence through others;

- No matter how bad our circumstance might appear, God is always present, whether or not we believe it.

CHAPTER 4

THE SURGERY: THE FIRST MIRACLE!

God is our refuge and strength, an ever-present help in trouble. Therefore we will not fear, though the earth give way and the mountains fall into the heart of the sea, though its waters roar and foam and the mountains quake with their surging.

(Psalm 46:1-3; New International Version, NIV).

I am certain that some of you have experienced situations in your life when you were unable to pray for yourself, right? But as a child of God, we have the confidence that God is always with us, especially during those times when we are too sick, weak, confused, etc, and are unable to talk with Him directly. Like the Scripture teaches out of Psalm 46, I needed to remind myself of God's presence the moment I was admitted into the hospital, because the "spirit of fear" started to suppress me and clouded my judgment. I would later learn that this was a direct attack from the enemy, preventing me from receiving the emergency surgery.

A few hours after being admitted, I was given the surgical consent papers to sign, but I refused, and I requested two things (1) my Bible and (2) to speak to the Gastroenterologist (GI) attending physician. The surgical team could not believe I was still refusing surgery, in spite of the dire urgency to save my life. I told them plainly, "I need the GI attending physician to better explain to me how and why I got intussusception." Later on that day, the attending GI physician and his entire team of resident physicians came to my bedside and offered the same explanation, "Possibly viral gastroenteritis" and they brought all sorts of information for me to read about "intussusception." After much explanation why I should have the surgery, they left feeling frustrated because I still refused. At this point during my hospital stay, Family Medicine started to follow up with me as well on a daily basis, they too recommended the surgery, and of course, I refused.

By the next day in the hospital, I was beginning to get very, very sick and feeling miserable. I was vomiting on a regular basis, and the doctors were afraid that I was dying from complications of "intussusception." The surgical team had spoken to my mother and friend who took me to the hospital, and my mother had called my siblings. And in spite of everyone begging me to proceed with the surgery, I still refused. Instead, I mustered enough strength and called a few friends who were Pastors, and asked them to pray for me. As much as I could, I studied the Word of God, praying and hoping I would get clearance from God before accepting the surgery. My mother had also made some phone calls, and many God fearing people were praying for me to accept the surgery. **It is amazing how Satan can deceive us, children of God, to refuse help, under the guise of "waiting" on God!** I learnt this lesson the hard way!

The "Spirit of Fear" Kept me in Bondage

By the end of the second day of my hospital admission, the doctors were essentially frustrated and had become tired of begging me to have the surgery. Finally, Dr. Fung (the surgeon) asked me why I was still refusing. My explanation was very simple. I told him I did not believe anything was wrong with me, and I did not want to be used as a "Guinea Pig" for experimental surgery. I added that no one has convinced me about a precise diagnosis, so I did not trust them to operate on me. I went on to explain to him how as a Nurse Practitioner, I know of many patients who have undergone unnecessary medical procedures and surgeries, just because of financial benefits to the surgeon, and I refused to be in that category of patients.

As I look back today, I could not believe I said all those hurtful words to a surgeon! It is amazing what the spirit of fear would cause us to do! But, this physician was a "God Sent"! He listened to me attentively, and with compassion in his eyes, he explained that it was only an "exploratory surgery", because they

The Surgery: The First Miracle!

were uncertain why I had the "intussusception" in the first place. Then I insisted, "This is exactly why I needed to hear from God first, if I should have the surgery or not because it is an 'exploratory surgery', and you do not know!". I insisted, "If I do not hear from God, I will rather die than have the surgery!" I told him plainly, "I trust God, but not the surgeons!". He looked at me with compassion and said, "Okay"; then he left, telling me he would be back the next day.

While my explanation sounded "stupid" to the entire medical team, I was determined in my heart not to proceed until God spoke to me, one way or the other. I was so afraid, I could not explain it. The doctors had offered the best medical explanation for the surgery, God had sent people to explain everything to me, but I was so oppressed with fear; the devil was winning the battle at this point; I could not think logically. I was dying, yet expecting to experience an "epiphany" moment from God, after He had already spoken through over 2 dozen people for me to proceed with the surgery. I bet you, Satan was happy!

In my ignorance, I continued to study the Word of God daily and prayed as much as I could, waiting to hear from God. I now realize that I was not operating in Bible faith at all. I was waiting for the fear emotion to completely subside and/or disappear before acting in faith and accepting the surgery.

//

That was a lie from the enemy that, since I was experiencing fear, I should refuse the surgery until all my fears dissipate. On the other hand, true Bible faith is when you act in faith in spite of experiencing a fearful emotion.

//

But God saw my heart! He is compassionate and loving, and He was not going to allow Satan to completely deceive me unto death.

God Intervened!

By the morning of the third day of refusing the surgery, the GI and Family Medicine staff essentially gave up, and did not come around as much to beg me anymore. At this point, I was later told that medically speaking, it was just a matter of hours or days, and I would have experienced perforation throughout my intestines, internal hemorrhage and subsequent death. In fact, just within 48 hours of refusing the emergency surgery, my body was getting into compensatory mode: My body was giving up — I felt extremely weak, pale, and I was vomiting several times a day — my major organs were "shutting" down —I was dying!

I was on continuous oxygen at this point, and the pain was becoming unbearable again. Because of the constant vomiting, the pain medication was not taking its full effect. My hemoglobin level was also dropping to dangerous levels, I was getting weaker and paler with each passing hour. I was now bed-ridden and was too tired to even get out of bed. My mother came to visit me and she could not stand how I looked, she left crying and refused to come back because of fear I was dying. I later found out that I looked terrible, like a corpse, hooked up to all sorts of life sustaining machines!

By the morning of the third day of begging me to have the surgery, everyone, including my mother had given up — My mother resorted to trusting God. And the entire medical staff had completely given up the begging, except the surgeon, Dr. Fung, who remained patient, compassionate, and persistent. Then, one morning before noontime, Dr. Fung came into my room and asked me if I had decided to have the surgery, I said : "NO". He then took his business card and laid it on the table and told me that if I should change my mind, I should call him directly on his cell phone. **He then did something I never expected: He came closer to my bed, went on his knees, held my hands and prayed with me.**

I was in and out of consciousness, so I could not remember his exact words; *but I heard him pray something to the effect that*

The Surgery: The First Miracle!

God should open my heart so that I would accept the surgery in order to save my life. Thereafter, he got up, and while walking out, he reminded me to call him if I changed my mind. In spite of being very groggy, I knew God had spoken through Dr. Fung. Thus, before he could even leave the nursing station, I called out to the nurse to call the doctor back in my room. I announced to him, "I am ready for the surgery."

I Accepted the Surgery

The moment I announced I was ready for the surgery, you could have heard the commotion and "claps" from the nursing staff. It was as if someone had won a million dollar lottery! Everyone was elated!! The hospital staff immediately called my mother, who then called my friend who had taken me to the hospital. Within about 10 minutes of me making that decision, Dr. Fung and a few nurses from the surgical team brought all of the consent forms for me to sign. They also brought into my room a Colostomy bag, about 2 pints of blood, and other post "surgical gears" to show me, in anticipation of my post-operative care. The surgical team was certain I would be needing blood transfusion because of my dangerously low hemoglobin level.

For those of you unaware, a Colostomy is a surgical procedure whereby the surgeon removes part of the Colon, and the remaining part of the Colon is attached to the outside of the body, creating what is called a Stoma or a hole in the abdominal wall. A Colostomy bag is then attached to the stoma, and this bag is then used to collect feces. A Colostomy bag can be a temporary solution to enable the body to excrete waste (i.e., feces) while the Colon is resting following surgery, or it could be a permanent solution, depending on the extent of damage to the Colon.

Given that my surgery was very much delayed, Dr. Fung and his team were certain I would need a Colostomy bag. The surgical staff was assembling everything so fast I had to ask them to slow down. I later learnt that they wanted me to quickly sign all of the consents before I changed my mind against the surgery. The Anesthesiologist was also there. I advised him that I had never taken prescription drugs, so he should be very careful how much anesthesia he gives me during the surgery, he thanked me for the warning.

Immediately I signed the consent forms, the nurse started to explain all of the possible complications during and after surgery. I was shown the Colostomy bag, and was informed that I will be needing one after surgery because they were anticipating major complications and even damage to my entire Colon from delaying the surgery. I was asked to sign the consent for the Colostomy bag and for blood transfusion. **At that point, something happened supernaturally, which till today I am unable to explain, because at times it can be difficult to explain the supernatural with human words or language.**

Something Supernatural Happened!

The moment I was shown the Colostomy bag, pints of blood and other "surgical gears", it was as if there was a "shift in the spiritual realm", and all fear disappeared. I became numb, and I looked at the doctors and surgical team and I slammed my right hand, with so much force on the Colostomy bag, pints of blood and "surgical gear", and declared aloud and boldly in the hearing of everyone,

//

"In the name of Jesus Christ, I refuse to have a Colostomy bag after surgery. I refuse to have blood transfusion! My hemoglobin level will be fine. In the name of Jesus I have spoken, and it will be so".

//

The moment I said that, the surgical staff looked at me as if I was crazy. They could not believe the energy I had just mustered to say

The Surgery: The First Miracle!

all that! They looked at each other and in fear they asked, "So will you sign the consent for the Colostomy bag and blood then?". I said yes, and explained that I would sign the consents because it was part of the procedure, but "I won't be needing the Colostomy bag or blood transfusion", I clarified. They shook their heads in disbelief as I signed the consents.

God's Presence Through His Word

After signing the consents, I told them I needed to use the restroom and to pray. Thereafter, while still in the restroom, I went on my knees to pray, and I could not pray! It was as if I had suddenly lost all of my abilities to pray, and I could not remember the dozens of Scriptures I had memorized. **But as I struggled to mutter some words, it was as if the entire Psalm 23 flashed in front of my eyes. I suddenly remembered all of it verbatim! It was as if there was a visual image of Psalm 23 in my soul, right in front of me.** As I came out of the bathroom and was being placed into the gurney to be taken to surgery, I started to recite and to meditate on Psalm 23 aloud.

The surgical team was moving so fast! And my mother and friends did not have the opportunity to get to the hospital in time before I was rushed into surgery. As I was being rushed into surgery, it was as if I experienced a "mental block". I could not remember anything else except Psalm 23. And as I recited this Psalm aloud, I experienced an indescribable sense of boldness, peace, and confidence that God was with me, and all fear disappeared. Whoa! It was an amazing experience!

The Bible teaches that Jesus Christ was/is the living Word of God which supernaturally became a human being, like one of us (John 1: 1-14). Surely, as the Lord Jesus puts it Himself, the Word of God is life (John 6:63)! As such, we cannot separate God from His Word! The presence of God I experienced as I was being rushed into surgery was almost "tangible", causing the surgical staff to be shocked at how calm I was in spite of what had transpired in the preceding days.

I arrived in the preoperative area still reciting Psalm 23 aloud until I was taken into surgery early that afternoon. The Word of God is indeed the primary source of life and medicine to our souls (see Proverbs 3).

No amount of anti-anxiety drugs or tranquilizers could have comforted me like the Word of God did. As I focused on Psalm 23, it was as if God Himself took control of the situation and I experienced His supernatural presence, peace, and comfort.

Only God!

It was an extensive surgery which lasted about 7 hours or so; an exploratory open abdominal surgery (i.e., Laparotomy) with the removal of some of my Colon (i.e., Hemicolectomy). I do not know the details during surgery. But, I remember that I woke up around 11PM to a very excruciating, sharp piercing pain in my abdomen. As I awoke, I noticed a very pleasant nurse standing by my bedside, telling me I had surgery, and it was a success. Then, I quickly reached for my abdomen, and she was holding my hands, preventing me from touching the wound. I was not trying to touch the wound, but to feel if I had a Colostomy bag. I had all sorts of tubing attached to my body: the IV fluids, the Circulation Boots in my legs, the tubes attached to the pain pump, called PCA (meaning, Patient Controlled Anesthesia, whereby the patient could give him or herself pain killers at a preset dosage by the doctor).

So with all of the tubing, it was hard for me to reach my abdomen, and the nurse kept trying to gently push my hand down to the bed. **Finally, when she turned away from me, I mustered enough energy to touch my abdomen and noted that I had no Colostomy bag!** In the act of doing that, I set off the alarm to the PCA pump so she quickly turned around and gently told me to "take

The Surgery: The First Miracle!

it easy". I muffled a few words under my breath and said, "No Colostomy bag?", and she heard me and said, "Yes, your surgery was such a success, the surgical team called it a miracle!" I thanked God and went back to sleep, knowing that Dr. Fung will be coming the next day to explain more to me. Even though I was in and out of consciousness, I knew God had done it! Only God! **A major miracle that was even noticeable by the surgical team had just happened! Only God! Whoa!!**

LESSONS LEARNED

➢ Regardless of how we feel, we have the Word of God as our best and immediate source of help. But by faith, we have to choose to focus on God's Word in spite of how dire our circumstance might be;

➢ The Word of God works, 100%. You can depend on it! It never fails, and God has promised us that His Word, spoken in faith, will never return void, it will always produce results (Isaiah 55:11), in God's perfect time.

CHAPTER 5

THE REAL DIAGNOSIS!

The angel went to her and said, "Greetings, you who are highly favored! The Lord is with you."

(Luke 1:28; New International Version, NIV).

As children of God, true Christians are joint heirs with our Lord and Savior Christ Jesus, which means that all of the promises of God through Christ are a resounding Yes and Amen (2 Corinthians 1:20). Those promises include, but are not limited to His favor, protection, joy, peace, etc, etc, as we walk in obedience in accordance with God's decrees in the Bible. Even though in context, the angel Gabriel was speaking those precious words to Mary, the mother of our Lord Jesus (see Luke 1:28), as Christians, those encouraging and precious words apply to all of us today, as joint heirs with Christ.

God's Noticeable Favor

During my hospital stay, God's favor in my life was noticeable by the entire medical staff, and that Scripture, Luke 1:28, became the main Scripture that set the stage for my battle with cancer when I received the official diagnosis (I discuss more about this later in this chapter). The next morning after my surgery, I awoke and found myself in the Oncology unit, and I did not understand why I was there! It did not make sense, and no one was telling me anything. All of the surgical team came to check up on me, they were extremely kind, compassionate and pleasant.

The Anesthesiologist was the first one to see me. Again he thanked me for the advice and reassured me that he gave me the lowest dose of anesthesia during surgery. He commented that the surgery was a success! The resident physicians from the GI and Family Medicine team came as well, they were very pleased that the surgery went well. Then the lead physician for the surgical department, whom I had not met before, a very pleasant man came and introduced himself to me as well, congratulating me on how the surgery was a success. He told me he was the supervisor of Dr. Fung, and he was also in the surgery room during my operation.

It was a very busy morning, with multiple blood tests being done. The nurses, dietitian, physical therapist and social worker all visited me that morning, asking all sorts of questions in order to ascertain a speedy recovery. The love, kindness, gentleness and compassion I received from the entire medical staff was amazing: everyone was awesome! God's favor was over me, and I witnessed it through the entire medical staff.

I finally got to see my mother and friend who took me to the hospital; they had not seen me in a few days. Word had gone around my family and friends that my surgery was successful, and the phone calls and visits from friends started immediately, the morning after surgery. As I laid in my bed that morning, I wondered, "Where is Dr. Fung?". I had not seen him. Then, about 30 minutes after that thought crossed my mind, he came walking into my room, smiling and he hugged me.

Still Uncertain!

He pulled a chair by my bedside and explained how the surgery was a miracle! He proceeded to explain that over a third (i.e., over a 1/3) of my Colon was removed, and in spite of the delay to get me into surgery, my organs did not perforate, which was a miracle in and of itself. He then explained that with such a large size of my Colon removed, it was a miracle that I did not need a Colostomy bag, because most patients who have "that much Colon" removed always ended up with a Colostomy bag. Also, I did not require blood transfusion! I did not understand how! Only God! As he was saying all these, I thought to myself how I had declared, by faith, that I would not need the Colostomy bag nor the blood transfusion, and God answered that prayer!

He went on to explain that, based on the surgery, they could not ascertain the primary cause of the "intussusception", although during surgery he saw the twisting of my intestines. Nonetheless, a specimen of the tissue was collected and sent to Pathology for a biopsy (i.e., a detailed examination of a tissue from a bodily organ to examine it for a malignant disease), to rule out cancer, although cancer was the "last possible cause," he concluded. He reassured me that worst case scenario, it could be a benign (i.e., non cancerous) tumor that caused the "intussusception", "nothing to worry about", he said confidently! He advised that I would stay in the hospital for about 2 weeks, while waiting for the Pathology report which normally takes about 10 to 14 days.

A Miraculous Post-Surgical Recovery

My surgical site was very extensive, beginning from my pelvic area to the top of my abdomen, almost in-between my breasts. Because the surgeons did not know exactly what was wrong, my entire abdomen was cut open (exploratory abdominal surgery), in order for them to examine the organs throughout. As such, I ended up with a very huge abdominal incision, which placed me on high risk for complications such as infections, bowel obstruction, opening of the surgical incision, poor healing tissues, pain complications, etc, etc.

The surgical team had informed me that given the extent of my surgery, they would prefer that I go to a rehabilitation facility after the Pathology report was available. They wanted to keep a closer eye on me, because they were concerned about the surgical incision, and the fact that I would not be able to eat a regular meal for some time, depending on how my body recovers and on my ability to pass gas. Even after passing gas, my diet was to remain purely liquid for a few weeks, then it was to advance to a soft diet, and gradually to a regular meal. I was given specific instructions to avoid "roughage and high fiber foods" until my surgical site was healed.

The Initial Week After Surgery

The day after surgery was very busy, with lots of visitors and medical staff in and out of my room. On that second day following surgery, I started physical therapy, right away. The first physical therapy session was tough, as I was very dizzy and weak. I had to push the PCA pump as I walked. Boy! **The things we take for granted! It was hard to even walk 5 feet, but I was determined in my heart not to go to any rehabilitation facility.** I was believing God that I would leave the hospital and go directly home, but I had to fight through. I hated the fact that I could only eat liquids, but I had IV fluids running into my veins on a slow drip continuously.

By the third day after surgery, I was able to walk around the nursing station and even further without assistance. Thus, I personally asked the nurse to remove the compression boots from my legs as I did not need them. The compression therapeutic boots are electronic devices that are placed during and immediately after surgery to patients' legs, which inflate and deflate to stimulate and improve circulation in order to prevent blood clots.

By the fourth day, I was up and walking independently, and the nurses noted that apart from the first few hours immediately after surgery, I had not used the PCA pain machine at all. God had supernaturally preserved me from the pain complication the doctors had anticipated. I had no pain whatsoever apart from those first few hours right after surgery. The nurses and entire medical staff were concerned and shocked! They

The Real Diagnosis!

came and asked me several times if I really did not have pain! They could not believe how fast I was healing without any complications. My wound site looked healthier and healthier each day, and by the end of the fourth day after surgery, they disconnected all of the IVs, and the PCA machine from my body.

Abundance of Love

My room was always crowded with visitors. I had so many visitors on a daily basis that the medical staff asked me to request that my visitors not come as much, in order to allow me enough time to rest. I had flowers, cards, countless phone calls from friends and family across the world. A lot of my Pastor friends were constantly praying for me. My older sister who lived in Cameroon, West Africa, had gathered a prayer team for me at her local church where she served as a Minister; countless amounts of people were interceding on my behalf. Satan did not stand a chance; God's people were standing in the "gap", praying on my behalf! The outpouring of love was amazing. Even though I believed that I delayed the surgery due to fear, it appeared as if God preordained the perfect timing for the surgery, when some of my classmates, friends, and my mother who celebrated my graduation with me were still around to support me during this difficult time.

By the fifth day after surgery, the nurses and medical staff needed to make an appointment to meet me at my bedside, because I would leave my room every morning to walk around the hospital, then in the afternoon I would go downstairs to the hospital lobby and visit with friends; and in the evenings, I would go to the hospital chapel to study the Bible and pray. By the second week after surgery, I was already passing some amount of gas, and all of my post surgical blood tests were looking good.

Besides the surgical wound site, anyone who looked at me could not tell I had just had major surgery less than 2 weeks ago, because I was 100% independent and ready to go home, even though I was still on a clear liquid diet, and the biopsy result was still pending. **The surgical team was amazed at how quickly I was recovering, and all their plans to transition me into a rehabilitation facility was canceled.** One of the physicians in the surgical team commented on how people who normally have my type of surgery end up in a rehabilitation facility for about 4 to 6 weeks, but my speedy recovery was unique and unexpectedly rare. And I said to myself — "Only God!".

The Biopsy Report Is In!

Then, around the second week after surgery, between 2 to 3 PM on a hot and sunny day on the third week of July 2009, Dr. Fung came into my hospital room in a very inconspicuous manner. He appeared very, very sad. He pulled a chair and sat beside my bed, speechless; and he just stared at me for a few minutes but would not talk. I kept asking him, "What is the matter, what is the matter?" He just kept shaking his head to indicate, "Horrible news!". I then quickly realized it had to be the biopsy results. So I asked him, "Is the biopsy result in?". He responded by nodding his head to indicate, "Yes".

And I yelled at him, "Please talk! Is it cancer?", I asked: He nodded his head to respond, "Yes". Keep in mind that all the while in this dialogue, the doctor was in such shock, he was not verbally speaking, except by nodding his head in response to my questions. Then I paused for a few minutes before asking him, "How bad is the cancer?". **He then opened his mouth to speak, and stated, "Very bad!".** And I said, "What is very bad, please explain?". **"Metastasis Colon cancer (i.e., spread of the cancer to various body organs), very bad", he said! At that point, you could have heard a pin drop.** I looked at him for a few minutes, speechless, and he looked at me, speechless, and we both sat quietly for a few minutes.

The Real Diagnosis!

And the Prognosis Was Dire!

Thereafter, he went on to explain, very reluctantly, about the severity of the cancer, with several lymph nodes involvement already — very late stage 3, with suspicious spots noted in my liver and lungs seen on CT Scan. I later learnt there were even some concerns about possible early stage 4, and unsure how aggressive this particular type of cancer was. As such, more testing, such as entire body and bone Scans were ordered, but I would do the testing as an outpatient.

He explained that he had already referred me to the Oncology Department, and I should be expecting a call from them once I got home. In the mean time, he briefly explained my treatment options. He advised me that without medical treatment (i.e., Chemotherapy), according to cancer statistics, the chances of death within 1 to 2 years was about 85%. Even with treatment, statistics showed that the chances of surviving within 5 years was dire, maybe up to about 35% or so. Depending on the data source, some statistics even report a survival rate of about 10% to 15% within 5 years. He added that once I see the Oncologist, details would be explained. At the end of his brief explanation, he concluded that, "You can fight this, Dr Tanyi" and he then left for the day.

And My Response Was?

Shock! Shock! And shock! After Dr. Fung left my room, my entire body went into shock for almost 5 hours. I sat up in bed and starred at the wall and could not speak. The nurses came in and tried to talk with me, but I could not talk. Until today, I do not even recall what I was thinking, "my body and mind were numb". It was as if the entire world "stopped", but I was unsure why. I could not think of anything—much as I tried [everything was a blur]. I stayed in that shock mode until around 8:30PM when my friend who had taken me to the hospital walked into my room. When he saw me, he was afraid and immediately asked, "Has the biopsy result come in?". I nodded my head, and he asked, "So what is the result?". You could see fear written all over his face as he was waiting for my response. Then for the first time after about 5 hours of being in shock, I softly stated, "Let us get downstairs and talk".

The Initial Reaction Sets the Tone

We walked to the lobby of the hospital and sat down. He looked straight into my eyes and asked, "What is the diagnosis?" You could hear the fear in his voice as well. When I saw the fear in his eyes and heard it in his voice, **it was as if the spirit of boldness came over me and I looked at my friend straight in the eyes and stated: "I am highly favored and blessed, God is with me!"** . When I said that aloud, I could see the confusion in his eyes, but right away, I noticed that the fear I noted in his eyes was more of a confused look! I then proceeded to explain how God loves me and how He has favored me. Thereafter, I explained the diagnosis.

///

I simply explained to him that it was metastasis Colon cancer with a poor prognosis. But I added, "I am not afraid, and I do not believe the doctor's report, I will trust God and fight".

///

The interesting thing is that, on that day when I quoted that Scripture out of Luke 1:28, I did not quite know the exact Scriptural reference. It was months later when I looked up the exact address of that Scripture and noted that, that was the blessed greetings to Mary, our Lord's mother, from the angel Gabriel. Today, I now know that it was the Holy Spirit who brought that Scripture to my remembrance, enabling me to stand in boldness. As Christians, the Bible teaches that God has not given us a spirit of fear, but of love, a disciplined mind and boldness (2 Timothy 1:7).

My friend would later tell me that my courage and those first words that came out of my mouth encouraged him significantly. He also stated that my reaction was so out of the ordinary, he thought I was in denial. But I was not in denial. Those first few words that came out of my mouth reflected what was in my heart — God's Words [all the time spent studying the Word and praying while in the hospital was already paying off].

Our Lord, Savior and friend, Jesus Christ, teaches that in this present life, we will have trials and tribulations (i.e., hardships, pain, suffering, all sorts of evil things, etc), but he has reminded us that we should "take heart" (meaning, be encouraged, hopeful and stay focused on Him), because He has overcome the world. But unfortunately, some Godly Christians, somehow or the other, either forget or ignore to "run to Jesus" as the first source of help at that initial moment they are faced with "bad news". Not doing that is a sure recipe for losing the battle, I believe! Because, the primary key to overcoming any kind of disaster, hardship, trial or dire circumstance, etc , is your initial reaction to the loss or "bad report". If you "panic and lose heart", then you are in for a tremendously difficulty fight, because it would require more energy and momentum to shift your focus to that of an overcomer. But on the other hand, if you stay calm and focus on Christ, the Holy Spirit will enable you to stay focused and fight as a victor.

Additionally, If your initial reaction to "bad report" is fear, doubt, a "giving up attitude", and you verbalize fear-filled words, and express pity, etc, more than likely, you will set yourself up to lose the fight, in spite of God's willingness to help you: **You, not God, set the tone for your success.** God has given each of us a Free Will, and the Bible has several teachings on how we should live above our fears, overcome doubt, etc, so it is our choice how we choose to react to life's circumstances. God will always honor our choices, and He will not force His will upon us.

///

Conversely, if your initial reaction to "bad news" is that of resistance, boldness, while focusing on God, then more than likely, you will be approaching that battle with a "winners" attitude and perspective —this is God's will for the believer in Christ Jesus!

///

In my situation, those first words of faith that came out of my soul and through my mouth cemented my fate with cancer: "**It set the tone for a fight against premature death**". Amazingly, when I spoke out my faith with such boldness, the initial emotions of fear, discouragement, doubt, anger, uncertainty, that is normally expected following a dire diagnosis and prognosis like I had received, did not overwhelm me. Something on the inside of me (I now believe it was the Holy Spirit) told me "not to accept" the doctor's diagnosis and prognosis. My friend would later tell me that it came across as if I was in denial. But truthfully, I was not. I was supernaturally emboldened, and I was walking by faith , but my boldness and faith would be put to test in the upcoming weeks, months, and years.

LESSONS LEARNED

➢ Your first reaction to crisis will determine the outcome: whether you lose or win the battle;

➢ As Christians, God's favor is our portion! In spite of how dire our circumstances are, and even when we are among strangers, God is always with us, shinning His favor and blessings upon us through others, if we choose to perceive it;

➢ Christians are not exempt from the hardships in this present "fallen" world, but the Lord Jesus teaches that regardless of how dreadful our circumstances or problems might appear on the surface, we should always be encouraged and rejoice, because He has overcome the world. When it is all "said and done", all things will indeed work out for our good (John 16:33 ; Romans 8:28-29). Do you believe this?

CHAPTER 6

UNBELIEVABLY SHOCKING!

No temptation has overtaken you except what is common to mankind. And God is faithful; he will not let you be tempted beyond what you can bear. But when you are tempted, he will also provide a way out so that you can endure it.

(1 Corinthians 10:13; New International Version, NIV).

The above Scripture, First Corinthians 10:13 is one of my favorite Scriptures in the Bible, because it teaches and reminds us that no matter how severe the circumstance we might be experiencing is, many others have survived the same type of problems in the past, and God, in His faithfulness, will enable us to overcome. At times, Satan attempts to deceive us into thinking that our problems are very unique to the extent that, "no one" can understand — these are all lies that the enemy employs in order to keep us in bondage and isolate us from receiving Godly counsel and support. But, like the above Scripture teaches, *"No temptation has overtaken you except what is common to mankind"*.

With this Scripture in the forefront, I knew that my diagnosis and prognosis were "just another temptation" that my fellow brethren in Christ had experienced and are still experiencing, and God specializes in the impossibilities, but I did not know how to proceed. It was going to be an insurmountable mountain, and the milieu among the medical staff was that of "unbelief and shock"; people did not talk much!

In spite of the shock, I continued with my daily habit of spending time in God's presence by studying His Word, seeking Him, and in prayer. Nothing was making sense, but I had always enjoyed my Bible study and prayer time with God, so I figured that I would continue regardless of how I felt. Today, I believe that it was because I was in God's presence daily, that I was able to sustain that initial shock of the diagnosis and prognosis I had received.

Why The Unbelief?

I was an "outlier." An outlier can be described as any observation that is out of ordinary from all other justifiable observable evidence, as such it is considered either an "error", or an unknown. In other words, my clinical presentation and the diagnosis and prognosis did not "make sense". The diagnosis did not fit into the "pattern" of what is known, based on evidenced -based medicine (i.e., established medical research or data) of what to expect with Colon cancer.

Firstly, back in 2009, it was noted that the majority of Colon cancer was diagnosed in individuals over the age of 50; I was barely in my early 40s when I was diagnosed. **Secondly**, the majority of Colon cancers discovered in individuals over age 50 have been consistently linked to sedentary lifestyle practices, Omnivorous diet, and red meat consumption; I had been physically active ever since I was a teenager, and a Vegetarian for many years before the diagnosis. **Thirdly,** I did not experience the "typical" symptoms usually seen with late Colon cancer presentation. **Fourthly,** there was no family/genetic history of the disease or any other cancers whatsoever in my family. **Fifthly**, I had never experienced deficiencies in nutrients or vitamins, nor other nutritional deficiencies. **Sixthly**, my Carcinoembryonic Antigen (CEA) test, which is a blood test normally used in diagnosing and managing Colon cancer was negative. I was a mystery to them, and an exciting study for many of the resident physicians.

The entire surgical, GI, and Family Medicine staff, in addition to the nurses were shocked! They were at a loss for words for a few days after the Pathology report came in. It was a sad time for everybody. All of the doctors had been so supportive, encouraging me on how they believed it would be a benign tumor. They had expressed how they

Unbelievably Shocking!

were very pleased that I was no longer in pain, and my intestines did not perforate. They were excited for me, as they believed I would go home soon to pursue my dreams of opening my private practice in Preventive Care/Lifestyle Medicine. All of the medical staff knew I had barely graduated. So on several occasions, some of them would come into my room and joke with me about a "brand new" doctor spending her first few weeks in the hospital, and we would all laugh out loud! And they would often remind me how my hospital experience would make me a "better" doctor, as I would have more compassion for my patients. All of their words were very encouraging! Everyone was happy for me, I had survived the surgery! So the cancer diagnosis was confusing to all of us!

By this point, there were over a dozen resident physicians following my case from different departments. With the exception of the resident surgeon physician in the emergency unit whom I asked to leave my room when he mentioned cancer without any diagnostic evidence, none of the other physicians considered cancer as a possible diagnosis — I did not fit the profile for Colon cancer, much more Metastasis? So when the diagnosis was announced, no one could explain to me how and why!

An Abundant Harvest

After a day or so following the diagnosis and shock, everyone quickly accepted it, and the focus switched to words of encouragement from the staff. **The work of God in my life during this time was evident through the entire medical staff, as He used each person who treated me to speak words of kindness, encouragement and hope.** It was amazing how God was using the medical staff to "lift me up"; and while at the hospital, with so much love and compassion, I could not even process the loss of my health!

The Word of God teaches in Proverbs 18:14 that the spirit part of Man, meaning Mankind, sustains him or her in times of sickness; so true! And Christ Jesus added that the spirit is what gives life (John 6:63). Even though my physical body was very debilitated from the trauma of surgery and emotionally and mentally sick and in shock from the diagnosis and prognosis, my spirit man truly was what sustained me through my hospital stay, as I depended on God daily.

I still could not think the diagnosis through yet; I was still in shock, although I was able to move around. And for some reason, besides discussing the diagnosis with the friend who took me to the hospital, I had a reluctance about telling any other friend, family member, or even my mother while at the hospital, so I kept a "tight lip" about the diagnosis. I would later realize that this decision was wisdom from God .

Heavenly Harvest

The Bible teaches in Proverbs 11:25 that, *"The generous will prosper; those who refresh others will themselves be refreshed"* (New Living Translation), emphasis author's. I had planted abundant seeds in the lives of others, and boy!; I reaped a bountiful harvest! As a Nurse Practitioner, I treated my patients with love and compassion, as unto the Lord. I was faithful and consistent, treating each patient as a human being created in God's image. And, I had been very consistent and faithfully serving God wholeheartedly, volunteering at my local church. While I treated others as God would treat them, I never knew that I was planting heavenly "Seeds" that I would one day "reap" in this life. But the principle in Proverbs 11:25 came into fruition in my life, as I received an abundance of support from everyone who I came in contact with.

I had several visitors daily, and by the end of the second week after the surgery, I spent most of my time with visitors downstairs in the hospital lobby in order to prevent too much traffic in my room, and allow my hospital roommate some quiet time. The nurses had asked me to ask my visitors to "slow down the traffic", but I could not tell anyone who wanted to visit me not to come. So instead, I took my visitors downstairs in the hospital lobby and visited with them there.

Unbelievably Shocking!

I remember one day, Dr. Fung's assistant came to my room and informed me that given the uniqueness of my case, they would be presenting it to the "tumor board" at the Loma Linda University Medical Center hospital. I had never heard of any "tumor board", so he explained. The "tumor board" was a forum where experts in Oncology from the medical staff would meet to discuss and "brain storm" on some of the most challenging cases in Oncology, in order to come up with the best treatment plan for the patient moving forward. I was very impressed and glad to know that the "best in Oncology" at the hospital would be discussing my situation. It was very hopeful and encouraging. He asked me to relay to him again, all over, how my symptoms started.

After I explained everything to him, he looked at me and simply said, "Dr Tanyi, do not be discouraged, you can 'beat this cancer', don't give up, please fight, you can do it!" He added, "You made it through the surgery! You can't give up now!" His words were so encouraging, it energized me. I reassured him that I would fight. He shook my hand and left. The doctors and nurses were very encouraging, and focused on the fact that the surgery was a miracle. They verbalized over and over, how they were confident that "I could beat the cancer". They never failed to remind me that my experience will make me a better doctor.

It Was Time to Go Home

It had been about 2 weeks since I had the surgery, and I was recovering much better and faster from surgery than the medical staff had anticipated. All of my daily blood tests and other diagnostic testing following the surgery had been negative. I had been advanced into a soft diet. I was also passing gas frequently, and had had at least one bowel movement. I had determined in my heart that I would not go to a rehabilitation facility, and God had favored and blessed me with an uneventful recovery. The medical team agreed that there was no need for me to go to any rehabilitation facility. I had exceeded their expectation with an expeditious healing without complications. Thus, the "tumor board" agreed that I should be discharged home, and be referred to Oncology who would carry out more testing as necessary to ascertain the cause of the cancer. The "tumor board" agreed that my cancer case was an "outlier!".

    The day before my discharge was very busy. The social worker came to ascertain how much help I would need at home. She was very concerned about my ability to ambulate up and down the stairs at home. She suggested getting a hospital bed downstairs in my home for sometime; I had informed her that I lived in a two story home. When she recommended that, I considered it for a few seconds, but I quickly told her no, stating that the same God who brought me through the surgery would enable me to get up and down the stairs safely. I was well aware that her concern was very valid [I would have made the same recommendation for my patients], because I still had an open wound from my pelvic area all the way to almost in-between my breasts, and any strain or stress on the wound could have led to evisceration (i.e., the opening of a surgical incision and protruding of the internal organs), a potential complication after abdominal surgery. **But, I knew that going home was going to be the beginning of an insurmountable fight, so by faith I told her NO.**

    The dietitian, GI, Family Medicine and surgical staff came and discussed the necessary discharge plans and follow up care with me. Immediately after discharge, I was to follow up with Dr. Fung until the surgical incision was completely healed and no complications were observed. Thereafter, I would begin to follow-up with Oncology. I was advised that someone from Oncology would call me to initiate the first appointment, which would primarily focus on education: discussing the type of cancer I had, the diagnosis, prognosis and treatment options. That first meeting with the Oncologist was going to be the meeting to address all of my questions, I was looking forward to that call!

Fear Came Over Me

    The discharge date was set and I was excited to get home, into my own bed. Then, on the afternoon before my discharge date, a

Unbelievably Shocking!

"spirit of fear" started to come over me. All of a sudden, I was afraid to go home. I had so much support from the medical staff, I was afraid that at home, I would not have as much help, and my surgical wound was not completely healed. **All sorts of thoughts came to my mind, such as, "What if at night the wound opened?"; "What if at night I develop a fever?"; "What if I really can't get upstairs?"; "What if at home I stop passing gas and my bowels stop moving?";** etc; etc. I then explained my concerns to Dr. Fung's assistant, another physician who brought all of my follow-up discharge orders, but he was adamant and simply said: "NO, you are going home!".

After he said No to me, I realized I did not have a choice but to go home. And for the rest of that day after talking with him, I experienced an unexplained fear and anxiety. By evening time, I was tired of worrying and being afraid, then I reminded myself of what I had told the social worker that, "The same God who brought me through the surgery will enable me to get up and down the stairs safely". **I also reminded myself of God's Word in 1 Corinthians 10:13, that He is faithful, and I meditated on the fact that millions of my fellow Christians have been through the cancer journey and survived; I was not the first Christian with cancer and a poor diagnosis and prognosis, nor will I be the last!** With that assurance of God's presence, I awoke the next day and was ready to go home, and the fearful emotion went away.

LESSONS LEARNED

➢ There is no new temptation, problem or circumstance "under the Sun". Our problems may appear unique to us, but that is not true, as there are others, millions of others, who have encountered similar problems as ours, and God has been with them through it all. So do not allow Satan to deceive you that "no one knows your problem", that is not true;

➢ God has proven Himself, over and over in Scripture and throughout the creation of the earth as 100% faithful and consistent. You can trust Him! Depend on Him! He is the Only One who is 100% faithful;

➢ We reap whatever we sow, this is a biblical principle, a non-negotiable Law of God that you cannot avoid (Galatians 6:7-9). I often teach people that life is a "Seed", meaning that, our actions are either planting Godly or destructive "Seeds" that we will reap, in this life and in all eternity. When we choose to live lives that bring blessings to others through our speech and actions (i.e., planting Godly Seeds), God will be certain to align others in our paths that He will use to bless us as well. This Law of God applies to all areas of life, so take heed to this advice and be certain you are planting Godly seeds in the lives of others!

SECTION 2

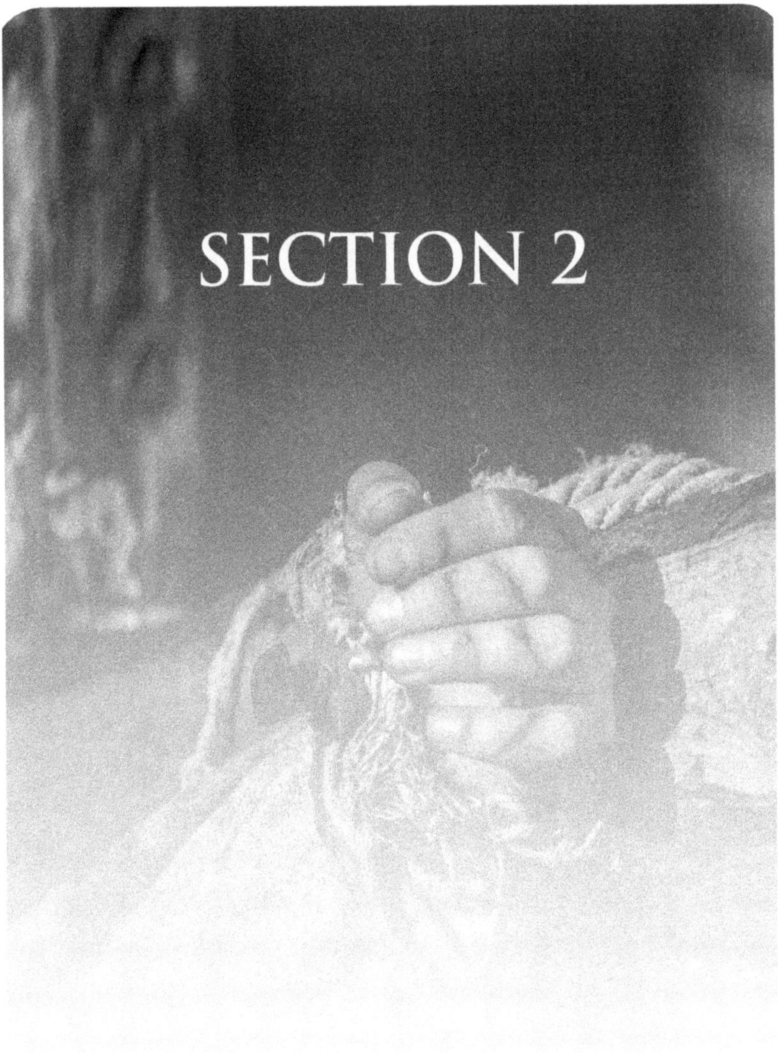

THE FIGHT FOR MY LIFE!

CHAPTER 7

WHAT JUST HAPPENED TO ME?

If you fail under pressure, your strength is too small.

(Proverbs 24:10; New Living Translation, NLT).

There is a popular saying that, *"talk is cheap but adversity reveals what is on the inside of a person":* I agree with this saying 100%. Another popular saying goes like this, *"circumstances do not cause an individual to become a bad or a good person; rather, it reveals who the person really is at heart";* so true, and again I agree 100%! While these two sayings are not directly from the Bible per se, the truths in them are consistent with biblical principles and teachings as noted in Proverbs 24:10. The above Scripture is from the New Living Translation version of the Bible, but I especially appreciate the way The Message Bible renders this Scripture, "**If you fall to pieces in a crisis, there wasn't much to you in the first place**" (Proverbs 24:10; MSG), (emphasis author's). Yes, "talk is cheap", and many individuals can talk but only a few can "walk the talk." For me, coming home from the hospital was going to be my initial test of that courage I had exuded while hospitalized. Was I going to "walk the talk," or start to quickly give up?

I had mixed emotions of joy and sadness on the day I was discharged from the hospital, because I had experienced so much love and support from the medical staff, it was somewhat scary to leave. Nonetheless, I realized that I had to face my "insurmountable mountain," alone with God, and the process would begin once I get home. After all of the discharge papers were signed and all of the outpatient appointments for more diagnostic tests and surgical follow-up care were scheduled, I simply thanked all of the staff and gently walked out of the hospital.

It had been a few weeks since I had been away. I was arriving home in the heat of Summer here in Southern California, around the third week of July 2009. The streets and the drive to my home appeared strange to me; it had been a while. I kept looking through the window with amazement. I thought to myself, "How interesting that I had driven through this same driveway many times and never noticed the trees!" This time however, I noticed everything. The diagnosis was already changing the way I appreciated the little things in life.

As I stepped out of the car in the parking lot of my home, this thought came to my mind, **"What Just happened to me?"**. **I asked myself, "Did the doctors misdiagnose me again?"; "Do I really have cancer?"; "Maybe this was another mistake?"; "How can this be?"**. **Suddenly, all of the emotions of fear, shock, and confusion, "set in" again.** I needed to mourn. And while at the hospital, I had had so much love and distraction, I really had not gone through the grieving process: "Is this what is happening to me now, all these emotions?", I asked myself. Meanwhile, I could see my mother outside the door of my home, laughing and thanking God, so I had to quickly act strong for her. Remember, I had not told her I was diagnosed with cancer yet. She was "all tears", crying with joy to see me.

Oh My! It Was Going to be Tough!

As I walked into my living room, I immediately glanced at the stairs leading to my bedrooms, fear came over me, wondering how I would make it up and down the stairs safely. As I walked into the living room area and attempted to sit down on the sofa, I realized it was going to be difficult as the sofa was too low. Right away, I regretted I had refused the offer for physical therapy to help me maneuver around my home. At that point, I knew I had to rely on all of my training as a Health Care Provider to function at home.

What Just Happened To Me?

While at the hospital, the toilets and showers had grab bars to enable the patient to easily change their body position, say, from a sitting to a standing position, without hurting themselves. But at home, I did not have this luxury!

Also, at the hospital, the bed had side railings, which enabled me to change my position in bed safely, and even the chairs by the hospital bedside had extra cushions which made it easier to get in and out of the chair. I had none of these supportive devices at home, yet I had strict post surgical restrictions not to bend, twist my body or drive for almost 2 months, or until I had clearance from Dr. Fung to do so. Within a few hours at home, I quickly realized I had to make a decision to either ask Dr. Fung to prescribe the supportive devices which I had refused in the first place because I was confidently trusting God, or "walk the talk" I had preached to the medical staff (i.e., telling them that God will enable me to function optimally at home). I quickly decided that I would trust God and not ask for supportive devices.

By not requesting for supportive devices, I am not implying that those who do so are not trusting God or are weak. For me, I did not want to depend on any device, knowing that it might slow down my rehabilitation process. I knew that if I attempted, as difficult as it was, to work through the process of performing my own activities of daily living (ADLs) without supportive devices while trusting God, my muscles and joints, which had been inactive for almost a month, would quickly begin to be strengthened, and the rehabilitation process would be much faster.

Oh Boy! The Stairs!

After a few hours lounging in the sofa, I decided I would overcome my fears of the stairs. So I decided to climb the two flights of stairs in my home which led into my bedroom. As I walked towards the bottom of the stairs, I paused for about several minutes and essentially "froze" in place; it was as if my mind gave up, I could not move. My mother and friend stood beside me and waited.

Then, I started to pray, asking God to enable me to get upstairs safely without help from my mother or friend. After I prayed, I still stayed there for another 5 minutes or so, "stupidly" telling myself I was waiting on God. But shortly thereafter, **I realized that actions must accompany true Bible faith; and I could stay in that position for however long I choose, but if I do not take that first step of faith and move, I would limit God's power.** With that thought, I took my first step, heading upstairs.

Rehabilitation At Home

It took me about 10 to 15 minutes to finally get to my bedroom. With each step, I paused to rest and to breathe, hanging onto the walls and the railings on the staircase. Later on, I was informed that during my hospitalization, I had experienced atelectasis (a partial collapse of the lungs) —which explained why I was still struggling with difficulty breathing with just walking upstairs. During this first attempt walking upstairs at home, I realized how significant my surgery was and how my body was traumatized —No wonder the doctors had recommended rehabilitation at a facility.

As I went up the stairs, I realized how weak my legs and joints were. I had no energy. It was difficult to even breathe. Several times I lost my balance, but I hung onto the steps, refusing help from my mother or friend. **I needed to overcome the fear of climbing the steps, and the only way "through the fear was for me to go through it", while trusting God.** The difficulty in breathing was the most frightening, because at the hospital I had passed physical therapy and the Incentive Spirometry (IS) test with flying colors, even though I was instructed to do the IS as many times as possible until I was fully recovered.

The Incentive Spirometry is a medical device that is used to help patients to improve their lung capacity and functioning after surgery. In using this device, the patient would inhale and exhale through a mouth piece attached to the device; doing this helps with breathing and circulation in order to prevent lung complications after surgery. Being that I had such extensive surgery, I used this device several times a day at the hospital which improved my breathing, and I had cut back on using it because I was doing so well. But at home, I realized that the extra effort to walk upstairs showed that my lungs were still very compromised following the surgery and the partial collapse of my lungs (i.e., atelectasis), thus I knew I had to quickly start using the IS again, several times a day.

After finally reaching my first goal of walking upstairs, I took a deep breath and realized that truly, nothing is impossible when we trust God. This might seem insignificant to some people, but just ask any patient who is disabled either temporarily or permanently, and I am certain he or she will tell you how, just making it to the bathroom alone is a major miracle to him or her! Once I sat down in my bed in the bedroom, I thanked God for helping me to overcome the battle with the stairs. I rested in my bed for about 10 minutes and decided it was time to fight the battle of getting down the stairs. Getting downstairs was just as difficult, but after about 10 minutes, I safely made it downstairs. I had just overcome my first battle! This was a major step that would set the stage for the upcoming 2 years, which would be the most intense years of my fight with cancer.

If you recall, I mentioned in preceding chapters how your first reaction to a crisis will more than likely determine the outcome. So I knew that this step of faith to trust God in my action would do one of two things (1) strengthen my faith in God for the remainder of my fight, but I had to take the first step to overcome my fear with the stairs; or (2) doubt God and rely on medical assistive devices and medicines. The only way around this was to put my words to the test, and trust God. So when I overcame my fear of the stairs, it painted an indelible picture in my soul, that God was with me, all the way through, even with the tinniest details. Many individuals know intellectually, that God is always present, but to know this experientially, is a whole different matter.

It is interesting how I had experienced the presence of God throughout my entire hospital stay and surgery, but it

appeared as if with every new challenge, I needed His assurance and presence even more. Although my faith in Him was being strengthened , I could not rely on His grace from the previous day, I needed His grace moment-by -moment, with each new battle. It truly is a step-by-step journey with the Lord, as we, His children, depend on Him daily. After my experience with the stairs, I was firmly assured and encouraged that, experientially, God was with me!

The Things We Take For Granted

While it may seem insignificant to some of you who have not experienced temporary or permanent loss of your ability to care for yourself; Boy! It is a very scary experience. Many people do not realize that it is a gift from God to get out of bed every morning and get into the shower, and to perform all of the basic activities of daily living such as grooming, etc, without requiring and depending on assistance. The initial 2 weeks being home from the hospital were incredibly difficult, and my faith and trust in God were put to the test. Like the Scripture in Proverbs 24:10 teaches, I needed to work through the pain and trust God, knowing quite well that if I gave up trying, and instead laid in bed all day while depending on others to perform my ADLs for me, it would be extremely difficult for me to walk with God in the remainder of my journey.

I was homebound for the first 2 weeks after the hospital discharge. Every morning, for almost 2 weeks, it would take me about 2 to 3 hours just to groom myself and walk downstairs to the living room area. **The first few weeks at home were also when I actually started to grieve and mourn about the loss of my "perfect health."** For over 3 weeks, I experienced intense sadness, depression, anxiety, fear, doubt, and I felt forsaken by God. It was surprising to me because it was obvious God had been with me throughout . So I was very confused when I started to experience all of the ungodly emotions I just described. I started to ask, "Why me?"; "What just happened to me?"

"Why Me?" "What Just Happened?"

For a period of about 3 to 4 weeks, I got up every morning and cried uncontrollably for hours. I had no appetite whatsoever. **The sadness and intense depression about the diagnosis and prognosis was overwhelming. I refused to see any visitors, and I would not answer my phone. I cried and asked God every day, several times per day, "Why Me?"; "What just happened to me?" ; "Do I really have cancer?" ; "Is this an error?"; "Am I really dying, God?"; "Did the doctors make a mistake?"; etc; etc.** I heard no response from God. I tried to continue with my regular routine of spending time in God's presence by studying the Word and praying, but I was unable to! I had no energy. I was distracted and grief stricken. I could not believe what was happening!

My mother started to notice that something was wrong with my demeanor. She would ask me every day, "Is there something you are hiding from me?". I would say, "Nothing, mum". I specifically did not want to tell my mother the diagnosis because knowing her, it would have "crumbled" her. I needed her to be strong for me, and at the right time, I would tell her. She knew I was withholding something, because I appeared withdrawn, sad and had no appetite. She spoke to my siblings here in the USA to talk with me, but I would not tell them the diagnosis and prognosis, yet!

By the third week of being home from the hospital, I was strong enough to go for walks around the block of my home. During my walks, I would cry, yell at God, **"This is not fair!", "Why are you allowing this?". I was very angry at God! I needed to "vent out my angry thoughts", and in my perspective, since I had done "everything" right to maintain a "perfect health", there was no other person to blame but God** —even though I knew in my heart He had nothing to do with the cancer. Nonetheless, I was just angry at God, because I concluded He could have prevented it. Well, today,

I strongly believe that God has given us the power and authority in the name of Jesus to prevent certain "bad things" from happening in our lives (more on this in Section 4 of this book)! One morning I said to God, "Why not diabetes, which runs in my family and I can easily reverse it, given my experience and expertise in this area?", "Why cancer, God?"; "Do I deserve this?" These outburst of anger, relentless questioning of God, sadness and crying went on for about 3 to 4 weeks, and it seemed as if God had shut His ears to my pleas.

Lies From Satan

Then one day, while I was weeping and lamenting, this thought came to my mind very clearly, *"Some Preventive Care doctor you are! Shame on you! You are a disgrace! You could not even prevent this cancer?"*. With that thought, I immediately started to experience shame and guilt. Keep in mind that before this diagnosis of cancer, I had TV shows on Preventive Lifestyle Practices, teaching people how to live a healthier lifestyle and prevent diseases, and the shows were still on TV at the time of this diagnosis. So when this thought came to my mind, it really made me to question whether or not I was qualified to teach anyone about preventive lifestyle remedies, because I considered myself as a failure, since I could not prevent myself from cancer. For about 2 hours after "that thought" came into my mind, I experienced intense shame and guilt. Then, as I was struggling with the emotion of shame and guilt, the Holy Spirit brought this Scripture out of Romans 8:1 to my remembrance, **"There is therefore now no condemnation to those who are in Christ Jesus, who do not walk according to the flesh, but according to the Spirit"** (NKJV), emphasis author's.

The moment Romans 8:1 came to mind, I immediately realized that, "that thought", which had led to much shame and guilt was directly from the devil. So I immediately yelled, "No, Satan, I refuse to allow you to condemn me!"; "I am proud of my accomplishments, and I will not be shamed!". The Bible teaches that the Word of God is life (John 6:63). So when I spoke life into my situation and refused to allow "death" to dwell in my soul, it was amazing how the guilt and shame I was experiencing left me, until this day! Boy! **The Word of God is truly The Only antidote against the lies and deception from the enemy. Once I realized that my "pity party", sadness, fear, anxiety, questioning of God had given Satan an inroad into my "thoughts", I immediately repented, and made a conscious decision to come in agreement with God that He is for me and not against me (Romans 8:31).**

Ungodly Emotions will Quench God's Presence and Power

While many people may not realize it, the ungodly, relentless emotions of fear, anxiety, worry, depression, will quench the power and presence of the Holy Spirit, because while experiencing these emotions, you will be unable to listen to that "still voice" of God. Satan knows this, thus he really likes it when we, as God's children, are consumed with our problems and are experiencing these emotions. **It is very okay to experience sadness and loss, but we should not allow these emotions to consume our thoughts in such a way that they prevent us from focusing on God, Who is the answer to our problems—** I had to learn this lesson the hard way.

After repenting for the relentless ungodly emotions, the crying reduced significantly. Although I was still mourning, this time however, I started asking God to heal me. It is interesting how it took almost a month for me to start asking God to heal me from the cancer; I cannot explain exactly why! **Perhaps because so much was happening, I needed to believe God for one thing at a time — first the surgery — then a speedy rehabilitation without going to a rehabilitation facility —then the battle with the stairs, and then performing my ADLs without assistance.** I suppose I was feeling a little stronger physically after about a month, thus it was the right time to start focusing on the "insurmountable giant": The cancer!

By the end of the fourth week at home, I started praying daily for God to heal me from the cancer. I was so confused. There were days that I could not even pray. <u>I did not know how to pray effectively for healing. I had never experienced this "giant" before.</u> So I did what I had heard many others do —

//

I prayed daily, "God, if it is your will, please heal me from cancer". I prayed like this daily for about 1 week. But, as I learnt later on, <u>this was an incorrect way to pray for healing, because this was a prayer of unbelief</u>—I did not know God's will in regards to healing. Thus in my ignorance, I was double minded, which was/is a major reason for unanswered prayers. Rather, the Bible teaches that we should know God's will, which is His Word, then pray specifically in accordance with His will — which will be a prayer of faith

//

(more on this in upcoming chapters). With each passing day, I perceived nothing from God, but I persisted in praying, although I was praying incorrectly! But God Who knows our hearts is loving, merciful, and compassionate; and the Holy Spirit will pray for us when we do not know how to pray (Romans 8:26).

Thus, one Monday morning, around the fifth week or so of being home from the hospital, I was grooming myself in my bathroom—I was beginning to feel a sense of connection with God again. The time I spent grooming had lessened significantly, I was getting stronger. It was a great day for me. The crying and sadness had significantly subsided. Then suddenly, as I picked up the comb to brush my hair, I heard from God! Finally, He spoke to my heart!

LESSONS LEARNED

- The ungodly emotions of fear, worry, anxiety, doubt, etc , will quench the presence of the Holy Spirit;

- Learning to be "still" in times of crisis, is the first step in discerning God's direction.

Recommended Resources For Further Studies: Available At: www.DrRuthTanyi.org

Available in a book and Audio CD Formats

Faith to Receive God's Promises: How to "Walk" in Biblical Faith and Allow the Blessings of God to Chase You. By Dr. Ruth Tanyi.

CHAPTER 8

And God Spoke!

Finally, be strong in the Lord and in his mighty power. Put on the full armor of God, so that you can take your stand against the devil's schemes. For our struggle is not against flesh and blood, but against the rulers, against the authorities, against the powers of this dark world and against the spiritual forces of evil in the heavenly realms.

(Ephesians 6:10-12; New International Version, NIV).

The Primary way God will speak to us is through His revealed Word or Scripture as found in the Bible. Hebrews 1:1-3 teaches that in the past, referring to the Old Testament era, God spoke through the prophets and in various other ways; but today, God has already spoken through Jesus Christ, Who was/ is the living Word that was made flesh (i.e., He became a human being with flesh and bones, just like one of us) and revealed God the Father to us (John 1:1-14). Plus, each true Christian is indwelt by the Holy Spirit, The Spirit of Truth, to illuminate Scripture to him or her (John 16:13). Additionally, God has proven Himself as consistent and orderly throughout the Scriptures. Under the inspiration of the Holy Spirit, the apostle Paul teaches us that the God of the Bible, Who is The Only God of the heavens and the earth is not the author of confusion (1 Corinthians 14:33).

With the above aforementioned knowledge, **it is relevant to know that when God speaks to our hearts, it will be absolutely consistent with His revealed Word in the Scripture. God will not reveal to our hearts information that is inconsistent with His Word. Rather, the Holy Spirit Who indwells us will quicken**

Scripture in our hearts, or illuminate Scripture thereby giving us more clarity about the Scripture, which will in turn enable us to apply it into our daily lives.

As I was attempting to brush my hair on that one Monday morning, around the fifth week or so of being home from the hospital, God spoke to my heart, and **I discerned a very audible impression of these words "spiritual warfare" — that was all I perceived! Nothing else, period!**

I Received a Sense of Direction

It is very difficult to describe the exact impression or quickening I received from the Lord. It was as if I heard those words out loud, or as if the words flashed in front of my eyes, but they did not. It was so clear and it almost felt like an "echo" in my heart, it shook me, causing me to pause. **The impression was so strong, I immediately stopped combing my hair. I paused for about 5 minutes, and froze in place. Then suddenly, I experienced a sense of indescribable peace, joy, relief, as I realized that God had just answered my prayer. I thought to myself, "God has spoken". He has given me a revelation on how to proceed. I screamed, "I have received a sense of direction".** Without finishing combing my hair, I headed downstairs to my living room dining table where my Bibles where, and I started looking up every Scripture on spiritual warfare.

I spent the entire morning and afternoon, almost 6 to 7 hours, studying all of the Scriptures about spiritual warfare from various Bible translations. I read, and studied the book of Ephesians in the New Testament over 5 times just on that one day, and I started to meditate (i.e., to ponder over and over on the truths over a prolonged period of time), on Ephesians chapter 6:10-20, the Full Amour of God during spiritual warfare. By the end of that day, although I still did not get a deeper revelation of spiritual warfare, I did not give up.

A Sense of Hope

Most importantly, I was beginning to discern hope and a sense of direction from God, so there was no turning back at that point. The Bible teaches that God will speak to our hearts in a "still voice" or in a "gentle whisper" (1 Kings 19:11-13; Psalm 46:10); no wonder, I could not discern His voice during the preceding weeks when I was caught up in all of the ungodly emotions that quenched His "still voice". Although, I now know that God was speaking to me throughout (because God always speaks to us), I was unable to discern His voice in my heart or through the Scriptures because of my "pity party". After that impression in my heart, I went to bed that night feeling especially reassured by the Scriptures.

I awoke the next morning and started studying and meditating on Scriptures pertaining to spiritual warfare again, except this time, I focused on Ephesians 6:10-20. I was determined and desperate to get specific directions from God on how to proceed. But the specific directions I desired would not come, because God had already outlined them in His Word — I was not mature enough in my "faith walk" back then to know this. So instead of acting on what the Lord had already revealed to me, I continued to ask Him for more revelation.

Guess what? I received no further quickening in my spirit from God about how to proceed with the information on "spiritual warfare" He had impressed in my heart — That was it, period! **Today, I now know that, this was because God was "waiting" on me to first act on the information He had revealed to me, rather than "waiting" around for more direction —this is consistent with Bible faith.** When operating in Bible faith, we, as Christians, have to take that first step of faith without much information to go by, then God will reveal the next step to us, because God guides us step-by step as we obey Him (see Genesis chapter 22; Exodus chapters 7-12; Hebrews chapter 11, etc).

Demonic Attacks

By noontime the next day, as I was still meditating on Scriptures on spiritual warfare, the Holy Spirit brought back to my remembrance certain incidents I had experienced in the preceding year, which were frightening enough for me to seek spiritual counseling. On several occasions about a year before the diagnosis of cancer, I experienced many " strange things".

As an example, I awoke one night with a sensation of "someone or something smothering me". During this experience, I could not breathe or scream and I felt paralyzed in the limbs. When I attempted to wake up , it felt as if there was a "heavy force" in my room, pushing me down; so I screamed, "In the name of Jesus, leave me alone!". Thereafter, the presence of that "heavy force" left me, and I awoke in the middle of the night, crying. The next day, I experienced intense stiffness and soreness in my neck area for a few hours . Initially, I thought I had experienced a bad dream, so I told no one what happened. But I started experiencing these types of "attacks" more often, several times per month.

On one particular day, I awoke to use the restroom in the middle of the night and suddenly I sensed a severe presence of "heaviness and oppression," a "feeling of doom" all over me. For a few minutes thereafter, I could not move, I felt paralyzed. Then, when I looked at the door, I saw what appeared to be a "figure" of a gentleman, standing there, and I screamed, "Jesus, help!" And immediately, the "vision" disappeared. Then on another incident, I saw a vision of a green serpent, over 6 feet long, entering my room, and I awoke, screaming, crying, and I prayed for hours until I was tired. Following this incident, I refused to sleep in that room for over 1 month. I shared these strange incidents with a few friends, and while everyone acknowledged that "something" was wrong, I did not take it seriously.

But, what led me to seek spiritual counseling was when I developed intense fear of sleeping at night, or being at my home alone especially at night. I knew that living in fear was not God's will for me, so I concluded I needed to take some kind of action. Hence, I sought spiritual counseling from a Pastor, who told me simply, "It is the devil. You are being attacked! These are demonic attacks you are experiencing." When he told me this, I was confused, and I asked him, "But why?". He simply responded, " I do not know why". Then he added, " You do not have to be afraid, just enforce your authority and power in the name of Jesus and you will be okay." He said it in a very nonchalant manner, but yet I could tell he was serious. And I said to him, "Just like that?", and he responded "Yep!". So I took his advice, and each night upon entering my home and before bed, I would pray aloud, speaking out loud and rebuking any demonic presence or attacks over my home and life. Even though I still experienced the fearful emotion, by faith, I made a deliberate effort to sleep at night. After a few months, I experienced no further attacks.

The Devil Can Still "Attack" For No Known Reason

About 6 months after I experienced the last "demonic attack", I was diagnosed with cancer. As I sat in my living room studying Ephesians 6:10-20, all of these incidents came to my remembrance. Then, it suddenly occurred to me that I was under another spiritual attack, except this time, it was cancer! **No wonder the doctors considered me an "outlier"; they could not pinpoint anything in my personal life that could have caused or contributed to the cancer. Furthermore, genetic testing by the Oncologist later concluded that there was no family history of cancer; and until today, the doctors who treated me are still baffled as to how cancer got into my body**: I remain a mystery to them!

Some of you may be thinking that the devil only attacks those who are practicing sin or those who are surrounded by the occult — this is true. However, the Bible teaches that there are times in the life of a believer when the devil will just "attack" the individual for no obvious reason(s), even though he or she would be "walking" in righteousness (1 Peter 5:8; Revelation 12:9-11; Matthew 4:1-11). In my situation, I could not discern anything in my life or immediate environment that could have "opened" the door for Satan to "attack me". So I concluded it was just a season in my journey with the Lord, and I moved on.

Also, a major deception by the enemy is to lead Godly Christians to believe that all of their sicknesses and/or diseases are related to physical or family/genetic causes. Yet, the Bible teaches that some sicknesses /diseases people are experiencing today are spiritual in origin — "demonic attacks", keeping people in bondage (see the Gospels), which explains why some Godly Christians are not being cured with modern medicine.

//

You cannot cure a disease and/or sickness that is spiritual in origin (i.e., a demonic attack), with a physical means, such as with medications— it will never work, period! Spiritual problems require a spiritual cure — Jesus Christ, just like it was in my situation.

//

However, spiritual discernment is required to ascertain if you are being attacked by the enemy.

A Righteous Anger

As I sat in my living room with my Bible wide open, I could not continue with studying, "things started to make sense". **I closed the Bible, and as I stood up, it was as if a flood of rage came over me, and I was extremely angry at the devil. I screamed, kicked the furniture, hit the wall and yelled, cursing the devil, all the while crying.** This went on for about 5 minutes, then I got tired from the screaming, and I paused for a little while to catch my breath!

Although there are several examples in the Bible pertaining to "righteous anger" towards the things of the enemy (Ephesians 4:26; Matthew 21:12-13), I had never experienced such "intense rage" at Satan like I displayed on that day. I was extremely hurt. It was personal, and I could not understand why I was being attacked. Again and again, I screamed. "Why me?", "Why me?". About an hour later, I decided that the yelling, angry fits and screaming would not help me; in fact, I was developing a headache, from being so angry. And for the rest of that day, I could not focus. The next day upon awakening, I decided that my anger fits towards the enemy would take me nowhere. Instead, I needed the Word of God. It was now about 5 to 6 weeks since I had been diagnosed with metastasis Colon cancer, and I had been keeping this secret from my family members. But after this revelation from the Lord, it was time for me to tell my older sister who was/is strong in the Lord and spirit filled.

I knew that among all of my family members, she would be the right person to share the diagnosis and prognosis, at least at that time. That same day, I called her; she lives overseas. As I was talking to her and crying uncontrollably, she listened attentively as I informed her of my "Goliath" (i.e., my cancer battle). She displayed such calmness, I was amazed! The diagnosis and prognosis did not cause her to even cringe for a second. **Then, in a very nonchalant manner, she simply said, with much confidence and boldness, "Don't be afraid, Jesus has already healed you". And I was thinking to myself, "Really?".**

The "Jesus Attitude"

My sister's attitude towards the dire diagnosis and prognosis immediately changed my perspective. Looking back, I now realize that she had what I call "**The Jesus attitude**", (a phraseology I learnt from one of my mentors, Andrew Wommack) because she was so calm, bold, confident and unfazed, in spite of how dire my circumstance was. I immediately started to wonder, "Isn't she listening to me?" "How come she's not concerned?" In fact, she was 100% concerned, but her attitude was not typical, hence I was confused.

But today, I know that her reaction to my diagnosis and prognosis was the best gift you can offer to anyone facing a dire circumstance: "**The Jesus attitude**". Her tone and attitude was like, "stop the crying and start focusing on Jesus". Boy! I got the message very fast. My sister's attitude caused me to pause, and to immediately re-evaluate my thinking processes, and I stopped the crying because I realized she was not "going there" with me.

I explained to her the revelation I had received from the Lord and the spiritual warfare studies I had been doing . She then recommended that I should contact the Andrew Wommack's Ministries and obtain some testimonial resources to quicken my faith. She specifically recommended a series called "Healing Journeys", which were DVD videos of individuals who had received healings from the Lord apart from medicine. She insisted that listening to the testimonies of others will strengthen my faith. She added that I should not reveal my diagnosis to any family members yet, because of the fear and anxiety that the "C" (C, meaning Cancer) word might invoke. She explicitly warned me, " This is not the time to be afraid or have any semblance of fear around you!".

She particularly advised me not to let my mother, who was still with me at that time, know about my situation. Her main concern was just like mine, that my mother would "breakdown," upon knowing of the prognosis; we wanted to protect her, at least at that time, until we received details from the Oncologist. This advice from my sister about not sharing my diagnosis and prognosis with others right away would prove to be the best Godly wisdom she gave me, as the Lord would confirm it later on (more on this later in this book).

This revelation from the Lord about "spiritual warfare" came at the perfect time, before I was scheduled to start outpatient treatment for the cancer. I was beginning to be reassured that God was truly on my side. Even though I had known this intellectually, this knowledge was becoming more of a personal knowing [experientially] in my heart. I was confident as I proceeded to meet the Oncologist!

LESSONS LEARNED

- Having the "**Jesus attitude**" during crisis will well position us to overcome, as we will be more dependent on Him, rather than ourselves;

- Satan still "attacks" believers today with all sorts of sicknesses and diseases, but we, as believers, have to be quick in discerning whether or not we are under a "demonic attack", and then act accordingly.

CHAPTER 9

THE SPIRIT OF "DEATH!"

O death, where is your victory? O death, where is your sting? For sin is the sting that results in death, and the law gives sin its power. But thank God! He gives us victory over sin and death through our Lord Jesus Christ.

(1 Corinthians 15:55-57; New Living Translation, NLT).

It was time for me to proceed with all of the outpatient testing such as the CT and full body Scans, Magnetic Resonance Imaging (normally called MRI, which utilizes powerful magnets, radio waves, and a computer to create detailed pictures of various parts of the body for analysis) etc, necessary before my first appointment with the Oncologist. The primary purpose for these extra diagnostic testing was to investigate further metastasis of the cancer. I did all of the testing as ordered.

Oh, That Spirit of "Death"!!

It was now around the early part of September 2009, and it was time for my first appointment with the Oncologist assigned to me by the "tumor board". This Oncologist was present at the "tumor board" meeting, so he was already very familiar with my situation. The primary goal for this first meeting was to explain more about the diagnosis and to discuss the treatment plan. I arrived at the Loma Linda Medical Hospital Oncology Center and I was shocked by what I witnessed. The spirit of death was all over the place. It was the most pitiful, saddening and "death filled" environment I had ever been to! In spite of the beautiful wall paintings with beautiful colors and scenery, and encouraging words plastered all over the walls of the cancer center, " you could smell death" all over the place.

Throughout this book, I will use the names Loma Linda Hospital Cancer Center and Oncology Center interchangeably.

While the medical staff was very upbeat, pleasant and loving, all of the patients in the waiting area appeared like "death". Many of them had no hair, they appeared sick, tired, depressed and hopeless, with most of them holding their heads downwards. I could not believe what I was seeing. Just walking into that environment was very depressing. In all of my years as a Nurse Practitioner, I had seen multiple patients die, and some patients had even died in my presence; but I had never seen anything like what I saw at the Cancer Center. It was especially sad because those patients in the waiting area were still alive, yet they appeared as if they were just waiting to die, and they had accepted it. Just like the Bible says, death is a sting! (1 Corinthians 15:55-57); that final enemy that the Lord Jesus had to conquer! Praise God for Jesus!

As I sat in the waiting area in that Oncology Center waiting for my name to be called, I kept thinking to myself, **"I cannot accept this; this is not God's plan for my life". For about 30 minutes while I sat in that waiting area before I was called to see the doctor, I started to experience feelings of sadness, and I had to fight those emotions from consuming me. Thus, I quickly opened my Bible and started studying, right away.** The scenery at the Oncology Center was an "eye opener" to me; thus I immediately knew that next time, I needed to be better prepared before going there.

After about 45 minutes of waiting, a middle aged, very pleasant and "bubbly" nurse called my name. She was very pleasant, full of energy, and as she took me into the examination room, she kept saying, " Welcome to the Oncology unit, you look really good, you have been assigned to the best Oncologist for your type of cancer." I was thinking to myself, " Did she really say welcome, to this death?". Nonetheless, given her bubbly personality, I chose to "cheer up" and smiled back at her, and thanked her. It is amazing how God works, because this nurse, " Rose", would become one of the most encouraging and positive nurses at this Oncology Center; she was a "God sent!". I would become so fond of her encouraging words that, when she left the Oncologist Center about a year later, I cried.

Shortly after the nurse took my vital signs (blood pressure, pulse, temperature, respiratory rate), the doctor walked in. He was a very soft spoken man, known around the Oncology Center as a man of "few words," yet highly respected by his colleagues and nurses for his excellence and expertise in treating Colon cancer. He spent a considerable amount of time with me, about 75 minutes on that first visit, explaining the disease, diagnosis , prognosis and treatment options. I took as much notes as possible. The outpatient testing I had done came back confirming it was metastasis Colon cancer as described by Dr. Fung, the surgeon (remember how he had explained all these to me, I hope you recall?). The Oncologist explained the survival rate with me, just as Dr. Fung had explained, and even talked about long-term cancer care for survivors.

The Oncologist's Plan

At the end of our meeting, he prescribed Chemotherapy to begin towards the end of September 2009, allowing enough time for me to recover from the surgery. It is interesting because the moment he said, "Chemotherapy", my mind went blank. I was very aware of the deadly effects of Chemotherapy; it was scary, but at this point I thought accepting the treatment was the best decision. Chemotherapy is a category of drugs used to treat various types of cancers. It works all over the body, attacking and killing cells, with hopes of killing the cancer cells and preventing them from multiplying and spreading.

The major problem with Chemotherapy is that it attacks other cells in the body as well, the good and the cancerous cells, hence causing horrible, and at times, unbearable and deadly side effects. The doctor further informed me how harsh the Chemotherapy treatment for Colon cancer was ; one of the lengthiest [about 6 months of treatment or even longer depending on the patient's ability to tolerate it], and harshest treatments compared to other types of cancers, because over 3 powerful Chemotherapy drugs would be used concurrently.

In addition, weekly shots and many other drugs would be used concurrently, the doctor said. He further added that Chemotherapy treatment for Colon cancer used to be about a 12-month treatment many years back, but with advancement in Cancer research, the length of the treatment had been reduced to about 6 months or so, if tolerated. He explained that most patients were unable to complete even 6 months of treatment; most of them either die or failed the treatment after just a few rounds of Chemotherapy. As he was explaining all these, I sat quietly and listened, speechless. I was in "good" health with no existing diseases before the Chemotherapy treatment plan, thus the Oncologist was hoping I would at least complete the minimal prescribed treatment. His plan sounded good to me, so I agreed.

Right before I left the Oncology Center, I signed the consents for the Chemotherapy, and he wrote the order for Intravenous placement of the Chemotherapy access site (a Porta-a- Cath Catheter) on my left upper arm. I left the Oncology Center with mixed emotions about the Chemotherapy. Yet, I reassured myself that I made the right decision. **But, as I would find out later on, the Chemotherapy treatment would lead to more health problems than I anticipated, and it would prolong my cancer fight, and push me to make a scary decision, " depend on God 100% without medications or trust medicine". I had to make a life changing decision!** (I discuss more on this later in this book).

Following that first encounter with the Oncologist, I quickly got home and called my older sister overseas and informed her of the details of the meeting. She was in agreement with me to receive the Chemotherapy. About a week or so later, the Chemotherapy access site was placed, I was scheduled to begin Chemotherapy shortly. It was now sometime around the third week of September 2009, and my mother was preparing to travel overseas. It was a perfect coincidence because I was scheduled to begin Chemotherapy towards the end of September 2009, and my mother would have traveled overseas by this time. My sister and I were very pleased because, again, it was not the right time to let our mother know of my situation.

While the number of visitors who came to my home started to slow down by August, a few friends continued to visit. Besides the friend who took me to the hospital, who had agreed not to mention anything to my mother about the cancer, my sister and I also decided it would be best not to tell any of my other friends, primarily because, we were concerned they might tell my mother by accident.

The Oncologist had warned me I would need a lot of help while undergoing Chemotherapy; it was going to be more difficult and challenging than the battle with surgery, he had advised. But at that point in the journey, God had already spoken to my heart as previously described, so I had a sense of direction, "spiritual warfare". Thus, in spite of the Oncologist's genuine concern, I was not worried, at all. Plus, my friend who took me to the hospital, who had been involved since day 1 of my battle was going to be around to assist me.

The Chemotherapy: "A Death Sentence"

The Oncologist had given me a "slew" of information about the different Chemotherapies I would be receiving, the side effects, and the necessary follow-up care. It was going to be a lengthy treatment, if I survived it. While Chemotherapy has helped countless of individuals, it has also led to the demise of countless others. The treatment plan he described to me was like a "death sentence". No wonder many people did not survive it. In my opinion, the pain and suffering from Chemotherapy is worse than the cancer itself, in many cases.

The Chemotherapy regimen for me comprised of a weekly visit to the Cancer Center at Loma Linda University Hospital for about 7 to 8 hours, blood test analysis and evaluation, physical examination by the Oncologist, and then the Chemotherapy IV infusion for about 3 to 4 hours with over 3 Chemotherapy drugs concurrently. After the infusion at the Cancer Center, I would return home with another Chemotherapy infusion bag which would run continuously for about 72 hours. Thereafter, a nurse from the Cancer Center was to visit me at my home to disconnect the continuous infusion. Then, I would have about a day or two of rest; thereafter, I was to return to the Cancer Center to receive more shots, several days in a row. This treatment was brutal, and in my case, worse than the cancer itself.

Recall how I had mentioned earlier that Colon cancer is known to have one of the most "brutal" Chemotherapy regimen compared to others. And unfortunately, as already described, Cancer statistics showed, at least back in 2009, that in spite of this treatment regimen, the prognosis for Colon cancer was very dire for anyone with late stage 3 or stage 4 Colon cancer (I hope you recall this statistics?). With such dire prognosis, accepting Chemotherapy treatment was very discouraging, at least for me!

Submitting to Doctor's Orders

Some weeks before Chemotherapy started, my surgical site was still healing with no evidence of infection, the surgical stitches were already removed. I felt so great, and I accelerated my diet to a regular diet, ignoring the strict post surgical warning to avoid roughage and high fiber foods until the internal and external wounds were healed. As a result, I developed an ileus, which is a lack of movement in the "gut", and a subsequent build-up of food. This was because my Colon was not healed enough to handle a regular diet and high fiber foods. It was a very miserable condition, which caused me to experience prolonged vomiting and dehydration, and I was readmitted in the hospital again for a few days. While at the hospital, I realized that if I wanted to receive my healing from God, one thing I must do is to submit to doctor's orders. This is such an important lesson that, it can be easily missed by many Godly Christians who are believing God for their healing.

The Spirit of "Death!"

God is humble! And the Bible teaches extensively about submitting to authority (see Romans chapter 13) . Even our Lord Jesus had to submit to the will of God the Father (see Philippians chapter 2; see the Gospels). As such, if we, as Christians, want God's favor and blessings in our lives, it is relevant that we obey Him and submit to the leadership and authority of those above us. **Even when we acknowledge that God is our Healer, we should not exert a deviant attitude towards doctors, whom God can use to bring about the healing.** This is crucial because a defiant attitude could prevent the manifestation of the healing.

I returned home from the hospital and determined I would adhere to strict doctor's orders, and to "take it easy" with my nutrition. I did not realize it would take over 2 years for me to begin to eat like I used to before surgery (meaning high fiber and lots of roughage foods). Even before the end of September 2009, my mother left the USA and traveled overseas. The "traffic" in my home environment was "slowing down", fewer visitors were coming at this point. Besides, everyone believed I was healing expeditiously from surgery, and the worst was over, friends assumed; but, they did not know that "the biggest battle was just about to begin — the actual fight for my life" —The Cancer!

I Refused to Read the Cancer Information

As Christians, every trial, tribulation or hardship we encounter in this life will present an opportunity for our faith to be strengthened, if we choose to take advantage of the opportunity and allow the Holy Spirit to help us. Dealing with cancer presented the opportunity for me to choose: life or death—I came into agreement with God and chose life (Deuteronomy 30:15-20), even though it was going to be an insurmountable mountain (i.e., the fight for my life).

Upon awakening one morning, about 1 week before I began Chemotherapy, I was meditating on the revelation I had received from the Lord on "spiritual warfare," and I said to myself, "I cannot allow all these information about cancer and Chemotherapy into my soul". Just looking at the pages of cancer information given to me caused me to feel sick in my stomach. The Lord had given me a sense of direction, and even though I had invested some time studying on spiritual warfare, there was still a lot to learn. By this point, I had already listened to the various testimonies of healing from Andrew Wommack's Ministries , in addition to his other teachings on healing, over and over. However, I still needed to receive the revelation for myself that Jesus Christ was my Ultimate Healer! **Hence, I had a decision to make, either to (1) study all of the medical information I received from the Oncologist about my diagnosis, prognosis, Chemotherapy and all its side effects, in addition to calling the support line from the American Cancer Association; or (2) focus on Jesus as my Ultimate Healer, and read about Him, instead.**

//

With much fear, uncertainty and limited knowledge, I said to myself, "I can't let Jesus down." With this thought, I decided to totally ignore the information package given to me from the Oncologist — I did not even open it.

//

This decision would turn out to be one of the best decisions I made in fighting this cancer. While my decision not to read the cancer information might have appeared as non compliant with the doctor's plan; it was not, because, while I still expressed humility and respect to the medical staff who followed me, I chose instead to saturate my mind with God's Word, and not with medical facts. This turned out to be the initial step of receiving my healing from the Lord.

//

With my decision not to read any Cancer facts, I also did not call people to find out about their cancers. And, I did not go to the internet to read more on Colon cancer. I

decided that I was going to only allow God's Word about healing to saturate my soul, because Only God's Word has proven to be 100% reliable and Truthful— I was determined to be single minded

//

(i.e., focusing on God's Word only), which was essential for me to receive my healing, because the Bible teaches us that a double minded person cannot receive anything from the Lord (James 1:7-8). **Hence, I decided that the best way to stay single minded was to eliminate all other knowledge about cancer and healing, and just focus on God, period!** I figured that, Cancer facts and all other related information would engender fear; thus, I refused to read-up on the disease in order not to saturate my soul with fear.

In spite of the blessings we have today from medicine, I chose God's medicine, His Word, over medicine — It was the best decision I made. Even today, I carry on with this practice, as I have trained myself to believe God's Word more than medicine, even though I practice medicine.

Now proceed to the next cheaper to learn how I started the process of saturating my mind with God's Word instead of cancer information.

LESSONS LEARNED

- ➤ It is necessary that at the onset of crisis, we immediately saturate our minds with the solutions of our problems, (i.e., God's Word), rather than with all sorts of other information;

- ➤ If we choose to saturate our minds with all kinds of facts and knowledge about our problems, and then, turn to God as a last resort, we will encounter significant difficulty in overcoming the problem. This is because we would have to first "get rid of" all contrary information to God's Word that we would have allowed in our minds.

CHAPTER 10

"I CAN'T LET JESUS DOWN!" THE HEALING MINISTRY OF JESUS (PART A)

Therefore, since we are surrounded by such a great cloud of witnesses, let us throw off everything that hinders and the sin that so easily entangles. And let us run with perseverance the race marked out for us, fixing our eyes on Jesus, the pioneer and perfecter of faith. For the joy set before him he endured the cross, scorning its shame, and sat down at the right hand of the throne of God.

(Hebrews 12:1-2; New International Version , NIV).

I have heard many Christians misinterpret Hebrews 12:1-2 to imply that there is a "physical cloud" in the heavenly realm where our loved ones who have died are gathered to intercede for those who are still alive today. This interpretation is of course, very incorrect. If you study the above Scripture in context, beginning with Hebrews chapter 11, which is considered the "Hall of Faith" in the Bible, you will notice that Hebrews 12:1-2 is a continuation of the teaching on Bible faith, heroes of the faith, who excelled as they "walked" by faith and trusted God. Thus, Hebrews 12:1-2 is teaching that the lives of those great heroes of the faith, as listed in Hebrews 11, serve as " a great cloud of witnesses" for us to emulate today in our "walk" (i.e., Christian lifestyle) with the Lord.

How Can I Let Jesus Down?

As a result of the teachings out of Hebrews chapter 11 and 12:1-2, **I knew that in order for me to receive my healing from cancer, I needed to work on my faith journey, completely focusing on Jesus — The Author and Finisher of my faith. Besides, after receiving the revelation on "spiritual warfare" from the Lord, I kept telling myself, " I can't let Jesus down".** I felt a sense of responsibility to "do something" with the revelation and direction the Lord had impressed in my heart. And I thought to myself, "How can I let the Lord down, when He had been loving , compassionate and gracious enough to reveal to me how to fight?" With this thought, I was determined I was going to fight till death! There was no turning back! My older sister later told me that, that statement I made, "I can't let Jesus down," was very hopeful and encouraging to her.

I was determined to fight cancer! I concluded that if I were to die, I would die fighting, period! I was not going to allow Satan to steal from me! But, there was a problem—I had heard so many conflicting information about God and healing; it was confusing. I had seen so many Godly Christians die of diseases. I had heard countless stories of people who fasted and prayed, and believed God all the way, yet, they died. **Today, I now know that a lot of what I heard about healing before I was "attacked" with cancer was unscriptural.**

Let us briefly examine some of these erroneous beliefs about healing; then, using the healing ministry of Jesus, I will later discuss why these beliefs are unscriptural.

Some Erroneous Beliefs About Healing

Some Christians Erroneously Believe that:

1. *God can heal, but He is not healing people today like He did during the "era of the Apostles", as recorded in the book of Acts;*

Of course this is FALSE! God is immutable in His core essence. In the same way He healed people during the apostolic era as described in the book of Acts and throughout the Bible, His healing power is still available to heal people today, but many people are not receiving it (see Matthew 13:58), for many reasons. I will be discussing some of these reasons in the next chapter;

2. *God chooses those to heal, and those not to heal;*

    This too is FALSE! God is no respecter of persons (Romans 2:11; Acts 10:34). We receive from God in accordance with how we believe, and the Lord Jesus teaches us that "**According to your faith let it be to you**" (Matthew 9:29; NKJV). This is not implying that if you have "weak faith," you cannot be healed: NO. Rather, the biblical principle is that, our faith in receiving God's promises is what positions us to see the physical manifestation of His promises. In other words, your faith positions you to access God's healing power, nothing else, period! (I discuss more on this in Section 4 of this book).

    So, if you do not believe (meaning, you do not have the faith to receive God's promises), then, as much as you love God and you pray to Him, you will not be able to receive from Him directly (Hebrews 11:6). I know there are many people who are now screaming, "I believe!", "I believe!". Well, while that might be true, have you examined other hindrances to your faith, such as, but not limited to, unforgiveness, unbelief, sin, etc, etc? (more on this in Section 4 of this book).

3. *God is punishing some people today with sicknesses and diseases;*

    This line of thinking in my view is purely demonic! The Bible teaches that Christ Jesus took upon our sins, sicknesses and diseases, etc, on His sinless body, in order that we should be delivered from these things (Isaiah 53: 3-5). Since this is the case, why would God turn around and punish His children with sicknesses and diseases? We do not serve a God of confusion, but of order and peace: God is 100% consistent in everything He does (1 Corinthians 14:33). Moreover, it is completely out of God's character and nature to promise that He has already healed you, then turn around and punish you with a disease —Only Satan can deceive people to believe such a lie about our loving and compassionate God. If you really knew The God of the true Christian Bible, you would never even consider such a lie! Are you getting the point? This line of thinking does not make any logical sense!

4. *God uses sicknesses and diseases to mold and shape people.*

Again, **another lie from Satan,** because God has already told us that His Word, is the primary way He uses to mold and shape us to walk in righteousness (2 Timothy 3:16). **Often times, people do not pause to evaluate their thinking processes, or why they believe in what they believe? They just believe because others tell them so, or because their church or some man or woman of God says so. Some Christians have not even taken the time to study the doctrine of healing in the Bible for themselves; yet, they are quick to believe the lies from Satan and then turn around and blame God, especially if they do not see the manifestation of physical healing in their bodies. This is wrong, and unfair to God, Who is on your side!**

For me, in those few months dealing with a dire diagnosis and prognosis, I needed to get all these conflicting beliefs about healing straight, " once and for all." **As such, I concluded that I would not ask anyone about healing or read any books on healing until I received the revelation from the Bible for myself.** I reasoned that once I received the revelation, I would not be swayed by anyone's opinion. Most importantly, I reasoned that since the Lord Jesus was/is God Himself, The Giver of life and the Ultimate Healer, studying His healing ministry and nothing else, was sufficient for me!

It was about 1 week before I began Chemotherapy. I was desperate! I needed answers, very quickly! So I figured, what better place to begin, than to hear from the "horse's mouth", Jesus Christ Himself. Hence, I decided I would embark on a thorough study and research of the healing ministry of Jesus Christ until I received the revelation from the Holy Spirit about healing of my physical body.

The Healing Ministry of Jesus

Since I could not work, I had a lot of time to spare; thus I decided to put that time into excellent use — studying the healing ministry of Jesus. It became like an obsession. My study time involved about 8 to 10 hours a day, just studying the Gospels, over and over again, looking up words in the original languages (Greek and Hebrew), and doing cross references with other healing Scriptures. Typically, after studying for about 4 to 5 hours in the morning, I would take a break for about 1 hour to meditate on what I had just learnt. Then, in the afternoon, I would study again for another 4 to 5 hours. I was so disciplined, I approached my study time like a regular job, and I only watched about 30 minutes of Christian Television and news briefs daily, nothing else. This intense studying went on for several months.

I needed answers to **4 major** questions. I concluded that once I received the answers to my questions, I would be healed. Here were the questions:

Answers to 4 Questions that Changed My Life!

1. Was healing a part of the atonement when Christ Jesus died on the Cross over 2000 years ago?
2. How did different people receive their healing from Jesus?

3. Did Jesus choose those to heal and those not to heal?

4. Why were some people not healed by Jesus?

Question #1

Was Physical Healing a Part of the Atonement when Christ Jesus Died on the Cross over 2000 Years Ago?

Unfortunately, there are many Christians today who have refused that physical healing was/is a part of the atonement of Christ. The answer to this question was the most crucial for me, because if Christ died on that Cross for my physical healing as well, then, it meant that healing of my physical body was just as important to God, as my salvation.

And The Answer Was?

To begin my study of this question, I began with Isaiah 53:3-5, a very popular prophetic Scripture written by the Old Testament prophet Isaiah, about 700 years before the birth of Christ, prophesying the kind of suffering and pain the Messiah (Jesus Christ) would endure. Under the inspiration of the Holy Spirit, Isaiah wrote:

He was despised and rejected by mankind, a man of suffering, and familiar with pain. Like one from whom people hide their faces he was despised, and we held him in low esteem. Surely he took up our pain and bore our suffering yet we considered him punished by God, stricken by him, and afflicted. But he was pierced for our transgressions, he was crushed for our iniquities; the punishment that brought us peace was on him, and by his wounds we are healed.

(Isaiah 53:3-5), emphasis author's.

The above Scripture teaches how the Messiah (i.e., Christ Jesus) would suffer in our place, and how He would take our pain, suffering and all of our punishment upon His physical body, which would in turn bring about our (those who believe in Him) salvation, deliverance and healing. A casual reading of Isaiah 53:3-5 might cause a person to say, " but wait a minute, there is no mention of physical healing in these verses." Yes, this is true, physical healing is not specifically mentioned, which is one reason I believe some people have denied that this Scripture is pertaining to physical healing of our bodies. Others are even saying that this Scriptural verses pertain to the deliverance of the Nation of Israel; others believe it pertains to spiritual healing only, and not physical healings —these are all incorrect interpretations! You know why? Because the Bible itself tells us!

What I really like about the Bible is that it offers the best commentary about itself. Here is the commentary in the New Testament, from Matthew 8:16-17, referring to Christ Jesus fulfilling the Prophecy in Isaiah 53:3-5. As you read below, take note that under the inspiration of the Holy Spirit, the apostle Matthew clarified that, Isaiah 53:3-5 pertains to the healing of our physical bodies as well. Here is how Matthew penned it:

That evening many demon-possessed people were brought to Jesus. He cast out the evil spirits with a simple command, and he healed all the sick. This fulfilled the word of the Lord through the prophet Isaiah, who said, ***"He took our sicknesses and removed our diseases."***

(Matthew 8: 16-17, NLT), emphasis author's.

With the clarification from the apostle Matthew under the inspiration of the Holy Spirit, it became obvious to me that healings of our physical bodies, was/is a part of Christ's atonement on the Cross. This was awesome news for me! Hallelujah!

Then, here is another awesome news! The apostle Peter added clarity to the notion that the Lord Jesus died on the cross for our physical body by penning it down in the **past tense (i.e., it has already happened)**. Under the inspiration of the Holy Spirit, the apostle wrote:

*"He himself bore our sins" in his body on the cross, so that we might die to sins and live for righteousness; "by his wounds you **have been healed**"* [**past tense**] (1 Peter 2:24), emphasis author's.

The Greek Word Sozo

As I was studying and researching the healing ministry of the Lord Jesus, I came across the Greek word **sozo** (Strong's 4982), so I decided to do a word study. This word is significant because it pertains to our salvation in Christ, and the same word has other significant meanings, such as, but not limited to, healing of our physical bodies, etc. Therefore, in many cases when the word **sozo** is used to pertain to our salvation, it is also implying physical healings, deliverance from suffering, etc, if you were to consider all of the different meanings of this word. Space limitation in this book prevents me from delving much into this topic, which requires an entire book of its own, but I want to talk about this briefly here, because it is paramount to you receiving your healing. Given the brief upcoming discussion, I recommend that you go back and reread the **Preface Section of this book**, where I discussed more on the word **sozo**.

Indeed, He Died For Your Physical Healing Too!

Briefly, one of the meanings of the word **sozo** in the English language means to be "saved", referring to salvation in Christ, which is absolutely correct. But, to my amazement, I learnt that this word **sozo**, which our contemporary English Bible versions have translated into the English language as "saved" (e.g., Matthew 1:21; Acts 2:47; Ephesians 2:5, etc), has several other meanings which are significant to the atonement of Christ and our relationship with Him. For example, the word **sozo** is also translated into the English language to pertain to deliverance or healing from danger and/or sufferings (e.g., Matthew 8:25; John 12:27; 2 Timothy 4:18).

As discussed in the **Preface Section** in this book (please refer there for details), my word study of the Greek word **sozo** also revealed that this word has another significant meaning — "to be healed" from physical diseases. Hence, as I dug further into my word study and meditated on all of its meanings, it became obvious to me that, indeed, healing of my physical body was 100% involved in Christ's atonement on the Cross. **This settled the matter for me 100%, and I was firmly convinced that when the Lord Jesus died on the Cross, He not only died for my sins, He also died so that I could be delivered from pain, troubles, hardships, and physical healings, if I choose to believe and receive it.**

Receiving Your Healing is a Choice

Choosing to accept and receive the healing of Christ is a choice, just like everything else with God, because He has given us a Free Will. As much as Jesus' death and resurrection has paved the way for "whosoever" to believe and accept this Free Gift of salvation and enter into a relationship with God; unfortunately, many people reject Him, and send themselves to hell. Likewise, many people reject and/or refuse to receive healing from the Lord, and thus die prematurely.

Also, as much as it is God's will for everyone to receive salvation (2 Peter 3:9), it does not always happen, because people choose to reject God. **Likewise, because physical healing was/is part of Christ's atonement, it is also God's will for everyone to receive physical healing, although it does not always happen, again, because some people refuse to be healed for various reasons (to be discussed in the next chapter), and/or there are internal and external barriers preventing them from receiving their healing** (more on this in Section 4 of this book).

<u>Some of you may already be upset at me for making such a comment that, it is always God's will to heal</u>. Please, I ask that you keep an open mind and be patient, read through this entire book, and I believe that by the time you get to the last chapter, you will have enough Scriptural information to make a meaningful and complete evaluation for yourself. The Bible teaches that God's children perish due to a lack of knowledge (Hosea 4:6) so please, be open, and do not perish because of ignorance.

Refusing to be Healed

Some of you may be shocked to hear that some people would refuse to receive healing and endure pain and suffering. Well, unfortunately, it happens every day, and in the Gospels, many people refused to receive healing from Jesus (see Matthew 13:56-58). In my own ministry, I have ministered to several people who on the surface, appeared as if they wanted to be healed, but upon further counseling, it became obvious that they did not want to receive healing from their diseases. For some of them, they had believed a lie, and Satan had deceived them to believe that they did not deserve to be healed because they were (1) a "bad person"; (2) their sinful lifestyles brought about the disease, and even though God had forgiven them, they refused to forgive themselves, as such, they erroneously believed that they deserved the suffering they were experiencing; (3) the disease was because they never sought God for a relationship all of their life, etc; etc; **which are ALL lies from Satan!**

Unfortunately, in spite of the considerable amounts of time I spent ministering to some of them, they refused to believe they were worthy to receive their healing from God, very sad!

///

God is always willing to forgive, heal, and to restore us, His children; but we must be willing to take that first step of faith to initiate that restoration, and then God will honor our decision.

///

It was sad, and of course, at least 2 of the people I am referring to died within 3 months, in spite of my prayers and counseling, because they had a Free Will, and God will always honor our decisions — whether bad or good, although His will is for us to always choose life and prosper (Deuteronomy 30:19).

Most importantly, with the biblical knowledge I received while studying and researching physical healing and the atonement of Christ, it became apparent that accepting this had to come through a spiritual revelation from the Holy Spirit. I was getting there! While I was 100% convinced in just the first week into my research that Jesus' precious blood had purchased my physical healing as well as my sins, and delivered me from the Kingdom of darkness belonging to Satan, I still needed to allow that Truth about the physical healing part to become my reality— it would prove to be more difficult than I had ever imagined.

Proceed now to the next chapter for the answers to the other three life changing questions; after which, I will teach you how I allowed this Truth (physical healing being a part of Christ's atonement) to become my reality, which then positioned me to receive my healing!

LESSONS LEARNED

➢ As Christians, the physical healing of our bodies was/is a part of the Lord's atonement on Calvary's cross when He died for us over 2000 years ago;

➢ Receiving physical healing from the Lord is a choice, just like receiving salvation is a choice;

➢ Satan has, and continues to deceive many Godly Christians that, healing was not a part of Christ's atonement on the cross; this deception has led many of them to ignorantly succumb to diseases in their bodies and die prematurely.

~~~~~~~~~~~~~~~~~~~~~~~~~~~~~~~~~~~~~

Recommended Resources For Further Studies:

Available At: www.DrRuthTanyi.org

All by Dr Ruth Tanyi.

1. *The Heart of True Christianity: The Gospel Message of Jesus Christ: Answers to 10 Major Questions Pertaining to Your Salvation in Christ Jesus.* **A 5-Set Audio CD Teaching.**

2. *Are You Moving Forward with Jesus? How to Excel In Your Identity in Christ.* ***Also available in Audio CD.**

3. *Who is the Real Jesus? Answers to 25 of the Toughest Questions About the Real Jesus: Simple & Straight forward to the point answers that will change your life!*

CHAPTER 11

"I CAN'T LET JESUS DOWN!" THE HEALING MINISTRY OF JESUS (PART B)

For we live by faith, not by sight.

(2 Corinthians 5:7; New International Version, NIV).

The Christian lifestyle is a faith journey, as we make a deliberate effort to focus on Christ Jesus daily, and grow in our faith and relationship with God. Second Corinthians 5:7 is a very popular, to the point Scripture; and in my view, it encompasses the totality of the Christian pilgrimage here on earth —"we walk by faith!" I really appreciate the way the New Living Translation (NLT) version of the Bible renders this Scripture, "**For we live by believing and not by seeing.**" Much more, the Bible admonishes us that without faith it is impossible to please God or receive anything from Him (Hebrews 11:6); thus, faith is the primary channel by which we can receive **All** of God's promises available to us by grace.

It was about a week or so before I started Chemotherapy; and as I investigated further into the ministry of the Lord Jesus, I was certain that studying and understanding how different people received their healing from the Lord would be the primary way I would strengthen my faith and position myself to receive my own healing. With that thought, I began my research to the answer to my second question.

Question #2

How Did Different People Receive their Healing From Jesus?

The answer(s) to this second question was significant, as I knew it would provide the impetus for my faith "walk," and offer some clarity on how I would receive my healing. This was significant to me because knowing that Jesus also died for the physical healing of my diseases was what I called, "head knowledge"; but, the answer(s) to question 2 was the "application" of that "head knowledge." **And usually, transitioning "head knowledge" into a physical reality and living it out is where "the rubber meets the road"; and unfortunately, it is at this point when many people easily "give up!"** But, as I said before, " I Can't Let Jesus Down!" So giving up was not an option for me!

And the Answer Was?

To my amazement, as I studied the ministry of the Lord Jesus in the 4 Gospels, the answer(s) to this question was very apparent, simple and straight forward, just like everything else with the Lord — it was obvious that the primary way individuals received their healing from the Lord was by faith, period! Nothing else was required — they expressed different levels of faith, such as weak, bold/active, passive faith.

Regardless of how these individuals expressed their faith, I identified **5 major qualities** about them, qualities that I believed were necessary for me to transfer/transition that "head knowledge" I had received about healing into my physical reality and expect results. But before I talk about the 5 qualities I noted, I want to briefly talk about true Bible faith, which is the only channel by which we can receive anything from God.

What is True Bible Faith?

Before I describe what true Bible faith looks like, here is how the Bible defines faith, *Now faith is confidence in what we hope for and assurance about what we do not see* (Hebrews 11:1), (emphasis author's).

//

As seen in the definition, Bible faith requires that you <u>first believe</u> that you will receive "something" from the Lord, without actually seeing "that something" first.

//

In other words, true Bible faith is simply believing and receiving God's promises which are already available to us in His Word. By His grace, God has already made available to us thousands of promises, but it is our choice to believe in them. When walking in Bible faith, you would believe God's promises first in your heart without seeing any physical evidence (2 Corinthians 5:7; Hebrews 11:6) then, you would act on what you believe (i.e., take some kind of corresponding action), in order to complete your faith. Corresponding action is required because the Bible teaches that faith without action is useless (James 2:14-26).

To illustrate, if you are believing God for financial breakthroughs, you will first believe in your heart that God has already made the provision for you to receive that breakthrough. Thereafter, without first seeing the physical results, you would, as an example, give financially into His work and/or step out in faith and look for a job (which would be the corresponding action), regardless of how you feel (2 Corinthians 5:7), and then you would "rest" and trust God's timing with the outcome. As another example, if you are believing God for physical healing in your body, you would pray for other sick people, etc, even though you might be sick yourself; again, because we live by faith regardless of our circumstances or how we feel (2 Corinthians 5:7).

Bible faith is not a "blind faith"; rather, it is a faith that has been proven by the death and resurrection of Jesus Christ. Hence, because of the Absolute Truth about Jesus Christ and His Ministry, we can be emboldened by the Holy Spirit to live and act in faith daily and receive all of God's promises. Space limitation in this book prevents me from talking more on this very essential topic of Bible faith. But, for those of you interested in learning and growing more in this area, I recommend that you order my book titled: **Faith to Receive God's Promises: How to Walk in Biblical Faith and Allow the Blessings of God to Chase You.**

Let us now examine the **5 major qualities** I observed among those who received their healing from the Lord —qualities that I believed positioned them to appropriate their healing, and would help me as well.

The 5 Qualities I Observed

Those who received their healing from the Lord:

1. Believed that Jesus was the **primary source** of their healing, and thus were single-minded, and expressed a 100% unwavering confidence in Jesus as their Healer;

2. Expressed **no fear whatsoever**; they trusted Jesus with the outcome and they were positive and expectant;

3. **Did not care about the opinions of others,** as such, they were unashamed to depend on Jesus 100% as they called out to Him publicly;

4. **Sought after Jesus wholeheartedly,** in desperation; and wanted to be healed;

5. **Used "their mouth" as a weapon,** that is to say, they spoke out their faith and verbalized their desire to be healed, and concurrently acted on their faith (e.g., see Matthew chapters 8; 9:1-8; 9:18-33; 15:21-28; 17: 14-18; Mark 2:1-5; 5:25-34; Luke 5:17-26; 7: 1-10; John 9:1-7, etc).

While the above qualities may seem insignificant to some people, you would be amazed how these are some of the major barriers that prevent countless of people from receiving their healing today. And, do not be deceived, **displaying the above qualities is extremely difficult and impossible to do without help from the Holy Spirit, especially when you are facing a death sentence like I was, and you are bombarded with all kinds of potential medical remedies with promising cures! It was, and is still very difficult to do!**

As I studied and meditated on the answer(s) to question 2, I figured that since Christ Jesus is the same yesterday, today and forevermore (Hebrews 13:8), all I needed to do was to grow in my faith and exhibit similar qualities as those mentioned above, in order to align myself with God's will —receiving my healing.

With the answers to question 2 settled in my heart, **I moved on to question 3, which, in my opinion, is shrouded with the most falsehood, confusion and misrepresentation with** regards to healing among the brethren in the body of Christ (i.e., all true followers of Jesus Christ globally, regardless of geographical location or denominational preference).

Below is the third question, and what I found.

Question #3

Did Jesus Choose Those to Heal and Those Not to Heal?

While the answers to all of my questions were equally significant in receiving my healing, the answer to question 3 was by far the most significant. This was crucial because it would make a major difference whether or not I approached my healing from a single-minded position, wholeheartedly dependent upon the Lord, or from a position of uncertainty, double mindedness and doubt if I was among the ones that God "wanted" to heal!

This double-minded position of uncertainty in and of itself implied and still implies no faith, because God has already told us that a double minded person will receive nothing from

Him (James 1:6-8); hence, the answer to question 3 was going to be a " game changer" for me. While this may seem obvious, you would be amazed that many people who believe that God chooses whom to heal and those not to heal do not consider James 1:6-8. In one breath, they would say "they are trusting God to heal them", then in another breath they would say, "they are unaware if it is God's will to heal them" — this is a very confusing position to be in, and God is not the author of confusion (1 Corinthians 14:33), all confusion is from the devil or from ourselves!

And the Answer Was?

The Bible admonishes us to know the will of God, and pray the will of God in our lives in order to see Godly results (Ephesians 5:15-17; 1 John 5:14-15). **Thus for me, I needed to know that it was God's will to always heal, that way I would pray in accordance with His will and expect His results.** With my curiosity and desperation to search for answers, I delved into my study of our Lord's ministry, and I was amazed to learn that the Lord Jesus healed everyone who came to Him —He never turned anyone away! This was very encouraging to me, and it caused me to wonder, "Why then did some people not receive their healing?". I provide the answer to this question very shortly in this chapter.

But for now, I want to briefly discuss **two powerful examples** of healing in the ministry of the Lord, that led me to conclude that the Lord did not choose those to heal and those not to heal. Then, later in this chapter, I will discuss other noted Truths about our Lord's healing ministry that affirmed and validated my answer and conclusion to question 3. Below are the two examples.

Example # 1: The Woman with the Issue of Blood

This is a very powerful story, which the synoptic Gospels: Matthew, Mark, and Luke reported about (see Matthew 9:20–22; Mark 5:25–34; Luke 8:43–48). Here is a brief background about this story. This woman had an abnormal bleeding disorder. Today

"I Can't Let Jesus Down!": The Healing Ministry of Jesus (Part B)

in medicine, we would diagnose her with Metrorrhagia, commonly known as abnormal uterine bleeding. And, in accordance with the Mosaic Laws (i.e., the Old Testament Laws God gave to Moses for the Israelites to adhere to), this woman was prohibited from coming out to public places because she was considered unclean, and anything or anyone she touches would also be considered unclean as well (see Leviticus chapter 15). With her disorder, the woman had sought help from all of the physicians of her day, had spent all of her money, but to no avail, then the Bible tells us that:

*She had heard about Jesus, so she came up behind him through the crowd and touched his robe. For she thought to herself, "If I can just touch his robe, I will be healed." Immediately the bleeding stopped, and she could feel in her body that she had been healed of her terrible condition. Jesus realized at once that healing power had gone out from him, so he turned around in the crowd and asked, "**Who touched my robe?**" His disciples said to him, "Look at this crowd pressing around you. How can you ask, 'Who touched me?'" **But he kept on looking around to see who had done it.** Then the frightened woman, trembling at the realization of what had happened to her, came and fell to her knees in front of him and told him what she had done. And he said to her, "**Daughter, your faith has made you well. Go in peace. Your suffering is over**"* (Mark 5:27–34, NLT), emphasis author's.

There is a lot we can learn about the Lord in this story: let us take a closer look. Before I briefly expound on this story and explain why this example explicitly teaches that Jesus did not, and still does not choose those to heal and those not to heal, let me set the stage by making a few statements about the Lord, which is relevant and essential for your understanding of the answer to question 3.

Most significantly, **it is relevant for you to understand that as Christians, we serve one God in three unique/distinct persons: God the Father, God the Son (referring to Jesus Christ), and God the Holy Spirit, equal in essence, power and divinity, yet distinct in their roles.** This teaching is called the teaching or doctrine of the Trinity. Although the word Trinity is not found in the Bible, the teaching is evident across the entire Bible, from the book of Genesis to the book of Revelation (e.g., Genesis 1:26-28; 2 Corinthians 13:14; Matthew 28:19, etc).

With this knowledge, here are a few comments about our Lord Jesus, that will help you to better understand the answer to this question. And for those of you interested in better understanding the ministry of the Lord Jesus, I recommend that you obtain my book titled: **Who Is the Real Jesus? Answers to 25 of the Toughest Questions About the Real Jesus: Simple and Straight Forward to the Point Answers that will Change Your Life**!

Below are a few comments about Christ Jesus:

A Few Comments About the Lord Jesus Christ

- The Lord Jesus was 100% man, meaning a human being like one of us (e.g., Matthew 25:31), and He was/is also 100% God in His essence —Jesus Himself made this claim (e.g., John 14:9), that He was/is God, and He backed it up with 100% eye witness corroborated evidence such as , but not limited to, the forgiveness of sins, raising the dead, etc;

- While on this earth as a human being, the Lord Jesus was filled with the Holy Spirit (see Luke 4:1-2), and operated in all of the gifts of the Holy Spirit (see 1 Corinthians 12:8–10; Romans 12:6–8; 1 Peter 4:11);

- As a human being, the Lord Jesus, by His own choice, walked in perfect obedience in accordance with the will of God the Father (see Hebrews 10:9);

- While functioning as a human being, the Lord Jesus chose to be 100% submissive to the will of God the Father (see Philippians 2: 1-11);

- In His nature as a human being, the Lord Jesus chose to limit His knowledge of all things, that is to say, His omniscience

"I Can't Let Jesus Down!": The Healing Ministry of Jesus (Part B)

(i.e., ability to fully operate in His All knowing ability as God) (Matthew 24:36).

With the above brief statements about the dual nature of the Lord Jesus, let us now revisit Mark 5:27-34 (NLT), beginning with verse 27, in order to answer question 3.

Practical Lessons From the Woman with the Issue of Blood

The woman with the issue of blood, "....***had heard about Jesus,*** *so she came up behind him through the crowd and touched his robe. For* ***she thought [that is to say, contemplated, meditated] to herself, "If I can just touch his robe, I will be healed."*** *Immediately the bleeding stopped, and she could feel in her body that she had been healed of her terrible condition. Jesus realized at once that healing power had gone out from him, so he turned around in the crowd and asked, "Who touched my robe?",* (emphasis author's).

In this Scripture, take note that this lady: **(1) had heard about the healings of the Lord** Jesus, and she had meditated on it until her faith was strengthened; as such, she believed in her heart and thought to herself that Jesus would heal her too; then **(2) she spoke aloud her faith,** that is to say, she verbalized what she believed would happen when she acted on her belief; she stated, "*If I can just touch his robe, I will be healed"* (v.28); and **(3)** once **she boldly acted on what she believed** (*most specifically, she reached out in faith and touched the clothing of the Lord in spite of the fact that she could have been stoned to death for coming to the public openly while considered unclean*), she experienced an immediate result — the physical healing manifested.

Most importantly, take note of the Lord's response to this woman, He said, *"****Who touched my robe?****"* This question by the Lord is the absolute key to unlocking the answer to question 3. You may wonder why? Remember how I discussed earlier that the Lord Jesus was 100% a human being and 100% God in one person? But yet as a human being, He was filled with the Holy Spirit and operated in all of the gifts of the Holy Spirit. And, by His own choice, He limited His ability to fully operate in His omniscience (i.e., His all knowing nature as God)? I hope you recall?

Here is the deal: When the Lord asked the question, *"Who touched my robe?",* He was operating as a human being with limited knowledge, by His own choice, which meant He had no prior knowledge of this woman's "spiritual achievements" or standing with God, before she touched His garment. The Lord honestly did not know who touched Him, period! And the Scriptures even confirmed this by saying, " *But he [Jesus] kept on looking around to see who had done it* "(v. 32). The Lord Jesus was a perfect and sinless man with no deceit in Him (1 Peter 2:22); and as such, He was 100% honest — He really did not know who had touched Him from the crowd.

The Lord knew that someone in the crowd had displayed bold/active faith and had touched Him, to the extent that, "..**healing power had gone out from him...**" (v. 30), but He had no idea who the person was. However, the moment "virtue" (i.e., healing power) flew out of Him, the Lord operated in the gifts of the Spirit and discerned the woman's strong/active faith, and acknowledged that her faith had healed her.

Practical Lessons of Healing

This woman displayed such an amazingly bold and active faith that she received her healing from the Lord, purely because of her faith, before the Lord even questioned her. **This story debunks all of the wrong notions that many people have about healing, such as the fact that a person has to**:

1. Fast and pray for extended periods of time before he or she could be healed;

2. Be "super religious" [whatever that means], before he or she could be healed;

3. Be a Christian for some time and perform all sorts of good works, before he or she could be healed;

4. Give his or her tithes and offerings faithfully to his or her local church before he or she could be healed;

5. Gather a group of prayer warriors to "bombard heaven" with their prayers, before he or she could be healed, and most mistakenly;

6. God chooses those to heal and those not to heal for reasons that only God knows, etc; etc; which are all wrong and considered "works of self- righteousness", which are offensive to God (see the books of Romans; Galatians 2:16). **You cannot receive your healing or anything else from God based on your self-righteous works or actions — you will only receive and experience the physical manifestation of your healing from God and His other blessings through faith in Christ Jesus because of His grace, period!**

This woman with the issue of blood highlights the absolute Truth that God does not gauge us spiritually before we can receive our healing.

//

No, we receive by faith because of God's grace and our relationship with Christ Jesus, and the empowerment from the Holy Spirit, that is it! — No addition or subtraction, period! So the answer to question three is: NO—God does not choose those to heal and those not to heal because of our spiritual barometer, or for some other reason(s) that only He knows.

//

Human beings bless and reward us based on our actions, but God blesses us because of His love, compassion, grace, mercy, primarily because of our inherited standing/position with Jesus Christ, and in accordance with our faith in Him (Matthew 9:29; Ephesians 3:20-22), Halleluiah!

With the revelation I received from this woman's story, I was so encouraged and strengthened, because since God is impartial, I was confident that I would be healed likewise, just like the woman with the issue of blood, but I had to learn how to receive it!

Let us now examine the second example to showcase that Jesus did not and does not choose those to heal and those not to heal.

Example # 2: The Faith of the Canaanite [Gentile] Woman

This is another powerful story recorded in the Gospels of Mark and Matthew, which exemplified that Christ Jesus healed people without discrimination. As a brief introduction, in this story, a Canaanite woman (i.e., a Gentile woman) approached the Lord Jesus, begging for Him to heal her sick daughter. Keep in mind that this woman, who was a Gentile (today in the 21st century, we would say she was a pagan, or an unbeliever), did not believe in the true living God of Israel, the God of Abraham, Isaac or Jacob, and as such had no covenant (i.e., a mutual agreement between two parties; in this case, between the Jews and God) relationship with the only true living God. Also, take note that this woman's story happened before the Gentiles entered into a covenant relationship with God through Christ (see Acts chapter 10).

Under the inspiration of the Holy Spirit, below is how the apostle Matthew recorded the story:

A Canaanite woman from that vicinity came to him, crying out, "Lord, Son of David, have mercy on me! My daughter is demon-possessed and suffering terribly." Jesus did not answer a word. So his disciples came to him and urged him, "Send her away, for she keeps crying out after us." He answered, "I was sent only to the lost *sheep of Israel." The woman came and knelt before him. "Lord, help me!" she said. He replied, "It is not right to take the children's bread and toss it to the dogs." "Yes it is, Lord," she said. "Even the dogs eat the crumbs that fall from their master's table." Then Jesus said to her, **"Woman, you have great faith! Your request is granted."** And her daughter was healed at that moment* (vv. 15:21-28; NLT), emphasis author's.

And the Answer Was?

As you can clearly see from the above story, the woman unashamedly and boldly pursued the Lord. Initially, the Lord acknowledged that she did not have a covenant relationship with God. Here is how the Lord responded, **"I was sent only to the lost sheep of Israel"** (v. 24). The woman did not give up, but rather, she displayed an unwavering faith in reaching out to the Lord, Who again responded, **"It is not right to take the children's bread and toss it to the dogs"(v. 26).** But, as she relentlessly displayed bold and active faith, the Lord acknowledged her faith and healed her daughter. Take note that the word "dogs" in this context does not have a derogatory connotation as some Bible critics have claimed. If you were to study this passage of Scripture within its proper context and cultural consideration, it will become obvious that the use of the word "dogs" by the Lord is referring to what we will consider today as a "house pet" (and there is nothing derogatory about having house pets, right?).

This is a powerful story about how the Lord did not judge her (i.e., an unbeliever) because she was not a Jew. Rather, **He healed her daughter purely based on her unwavering faith in Him**. Also, take note that the Lord engaged in this dialogue (see Matthew 15:21-28) with the Gentile woman so as to highlight and teach on the fact that she, being a non-Jew, had expressed more faith than the Jews who were supposedly expecting the Messiah. Again in this story, just like the story with the woman with the issue of blood, this Gentile woman was bold, verbalized her faith, unashamedly pursued the Lord for the healing of her daughter, and the Lord responded to her positively and healed her daughter without telling her she had to first become a Jew, or fast, give her tithes, and/or pray for hours on end, etc.

Practical Lessons of Healing

This story also debunks the myth and incorrect notion going around the body of Christ that only Christians, and especially those Christians who are "holier than thou", are easily positioned to be healed by the Lord. **In fact, I have heard of multiple stories where pagans have attended a Christian meeting, church or healing service for the first time, heard about the healing power of the Lord, believed it, and then received their healing, and thereafter, accepted Christ as their personal Lord and Savior.** <u>In these examples, it was easier for the unbelievers to receive their healing because they had not been indoctrinated by all of the erroneous Man-made beliefs pertaining to healing, such as the notion that they had to pray for days on end, perform good works, attend church regularly, etc. etc. before they could be healed.</u> The unbelievers simply expressed an innocent child-like faith, and they received their healing, just like the Canaanite woman did. **Friend, as you are learning, it is all about faith in the Ultimate Healer: Jesus Christ, and not about your self-righteous works! Are you learning this lesson?**

After receiving the answer(s) to question 3, I was determined and convinced in my heart that I would receive my healing likewise. Thus, at this point in my investigation of the Lord's healing ministry, I refused to entertain any other contrary opinion such as the fact that the Lord discriminately chooses those to heal and those not to heal.

Before I provide the answer to the last question I had, I want to highlight other significant Truths about the Lord's healing ministry that validated my conclusion that He did not, and does not choose those to heal and those not to heal.

Other Truths About the Lord's Healing Ministry

As you will find out, these Truths are also consistent with the nature of God the Father. Below are the Truths:

❖ Throughout His ministry, the Lord **consistently displayed a willingness to heal everyone**, and He willingly healed all those who sought for His help (e.g., Matthew 8:1-4; 8:5-9; 15:29-31; Mark 1:28-34; 3: 1-6; Luke 4: 38-39; John 9: 1-41, etc);

❖ In His desire and willingness to heal people, at times, the **Lord activated their faith**, by asking them questions (e.g., Matthew 9:27-28; Mark 1: 40-43; 8:22-26; 10:46-52, etc);

❖ The **Lord never refused to heal anyone**; rather, some people refused to receive healing from Him (e.g., Luke 4:14-30; Mark 6:3-6, etc);

❖ The Lord **did not tell anyone they were not spiritually mature enough** to be healed; rather, He was moved with love and compassion and healed all those who came to Him (e.g., Matthew 9:36);

❖ The Lord **did not heal anyone against their wish or will**. All those who received healing from Him sought after Him directly or a close acquaintance of the diseased person sought for the Lord. Even in a few examples when it appeared as if the individuals did not approach the Lord directly to request for their healing, they expressed their intent and desire to be healed as they displayed their faith in action (i.e., acted out their faith), when they willingly agreed and complied with the Lord's instructions, which enabled them to release their faith and receive their healing (e.g., Matthew 12: 9-14; John 5:1-18).

Since Jesus is the same yesterday, today and forevermore, it means that He is still willing to heal all those who come to Him in faith, today! **He does not discriminate! God is no respecter of persons, that is to say, He shows no favoritism — in the same way He healed people over 2000 years ago, He is doing the same today (Acts 10:34). Our faith is what positions us to receive God's healing through Christ, nothing else! Which means, anyone has the potential to be healed, as we believe!** <u>**It is not up to God; rather, it is how we receive from Him, that propels the manifestation of our healing**</u> (Matthew 9:29).

With the above revealed Truths about the Lord's healing ministry, it was time for me to move on to my investigation of the last question. Below is the question, and the very simple, and straight forward answer from our Lord Jesus Himself.

Question # 4

Why were Some People Not Healed by Jesus?

My interest in this last question was primarily so that I would avoid the same mistake as those who did not receive their healing from the Lord. The simple and straight forward answer to this question is found in Matthew 13:54-60. Below is the Scripture:

He returned to Nazareth, his hometown. When he taught there in the synagogue, everyone was amazed and said, "Where does he get this wisdom and the power to do miracles?" Then they scoffed, "He's just the carpenter's son, and we know Mary, his mother, and his brothers—James, Joseph, Simon, and Judas. All his sisters live right here among us. Where did he learn all these things?" And they were deeply offended and refused to believe in him. Then Jesus told them, "A prophet is honored everywhere except in his own hometown and among his own family." ***And so he did only a few miracles there because of their unbelief*** (Matthew 13:54-60; NLT), (emphasis author's).

And the Answer Was?

Right away, the above Scriptural text tells the story why some people refused to be healed by the Lord. **Firstly,** some people were too familiar with the Lord, and as such refused to view Him as the Messiah, God's Only begotten Son, with the ability to heal them. There is a popular saying that goes like this, **"familiarity breeds contempt"** (meaning, when you are too familiar with someone, there is a human tendency to not acknowledge their worth); this was exactly what happened with the Lord. Because of the peoples' familiarity with Him and His family, they refused to view Him in any other way, except as, **"...the carpenter's son, and we know Mary, his mother, ... Where did he learn all these things?"**(Matthew 13:55-56). Thus, by their own choice, some people could not be healed by Him.

Secondly, as a result of their familiarity with the Lord, they were deeply offended and refused to believe in Him (v. 57). **Because the people rejected the Lord's ministry, their unbelief, which was their choice, made it impossible for them to be healed by Him.** *Here is the bottom line* — unbelief is the primary reason why people did not, and are still not receiving their healing from the Lord Jesus today. While some of you may be screaming right now, "I believe!, I believe!, I do not disagree", **it is important however, to take note that your definition of unbelief may not be consistent with what the Bible describes as unbelief, which may be hindering the manifestation of God's promises in your life** (I discuss more of this in Section 4 of this book).

The Many Facets of Unbelief

In brief, unbelief has many facets. As an example, those who do not believe that Jesus Christ is the Messiah, Savior of the world, outrightly harbor unbelief in their hearts, and they will not receive anything from Him, period! This is simple to understand, and I am certain you agree with me on this one, right? However, for the Christian, whose faith is in the Lord Jesus, because he or she is genuinely saved, unbelief can manifest in many ways, such as, but not limited to: (1) chronic fear; (2) focusing more on the doctor's diagnosis or prognosis than on the promises in God's Word; (3) chronically worrying about the diagnosis/prognosis; (4) meditating on the disease and its outcome versus meditating on the solutions in God's Word; etc; etc, which are all things that will definitely prevent God's healing power to flow through you (more on this in Section 4 of this book).

So, with the straight forward answer to the last question in my investigation of the Lord's healing ministry, I was absolutely confident, that I had gained enough "head knowledge" to avoid the confusion regarding the false teachings and information circulating in the body of Christ about healing. By this point, it was a few days before I was scheduled to receive my first dose of Chemotherapy; and while it was scary, I had made great progress, and my anxiety level was significantly reduced — I was armed with biblical knowledge about my healing, and all confusion from conflicting opinions had stopped!

Once all of the confusion stopped, it was time for me to put into practice all of the "head knowledge" I had acquired. **And, I was very aware that somehow or the other, I was not going to receive my healing until I put into practice everything I had learnt, because the Bible is 100% clear and consistent that, only those who practice the Word of God receives God's blessings** (Luke 6:46-49; James 1:22-25). With the above thought, I asked myself, " How do I begin to practice what I have just learnt from the Lord's ministry?" There was only one answer — to work on my faith — this would turn out to be more difficult than I had ever imagined.

Let us now turn to the next chapter where I begin to explain how I started the process of positioning myself, **first by changing my thinking processes, in order to receive my healing**. Then in chapters 13 and 14, I will explain how reducing unbelief in my environment and practicing meditation positioned me in accordance with God's Word to receive my healing.

LESSONS LEARNED

- Acting in true Bible faith was the common denominator among those who received their healing from the Lord during His earthly ministry, this is still the same today;

- During His earthly ministry, the Lord Jesus healed everyone who came to Him to be healed;

- During the Lord's earthly ministry, those who received healing from Him sought after Him wholeheartedly, this is still the case today;

- Unbelief was, and is still the primary reason that many people did not and are still not receiving their healing from the Lord today.

Recommended Resources For Further Studies:

Available At: www.DrRuthTanyi.org

*Books by Dr Ruth Tanyi.

1. Are You Moving Forward with Jesus? How to Excel In Your Identity in Christ. **Also available on Audio CD.**

2. Who is the Real Jesus? Answers to 25 of the Toughest Questions About the Real Jesus: Simple & Straight forward to the point answers that will change your life!

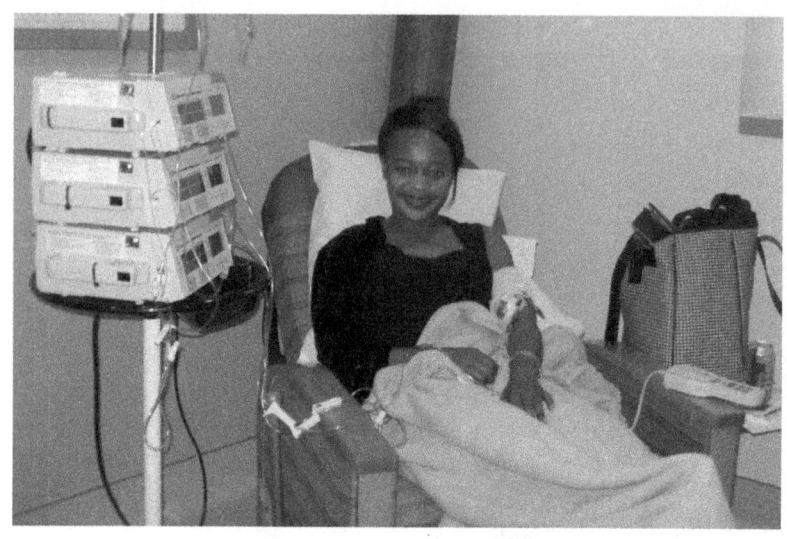

*At Loma Linda Medical Center (Cancer Infusion Unit):
First chemotherapy infusion*

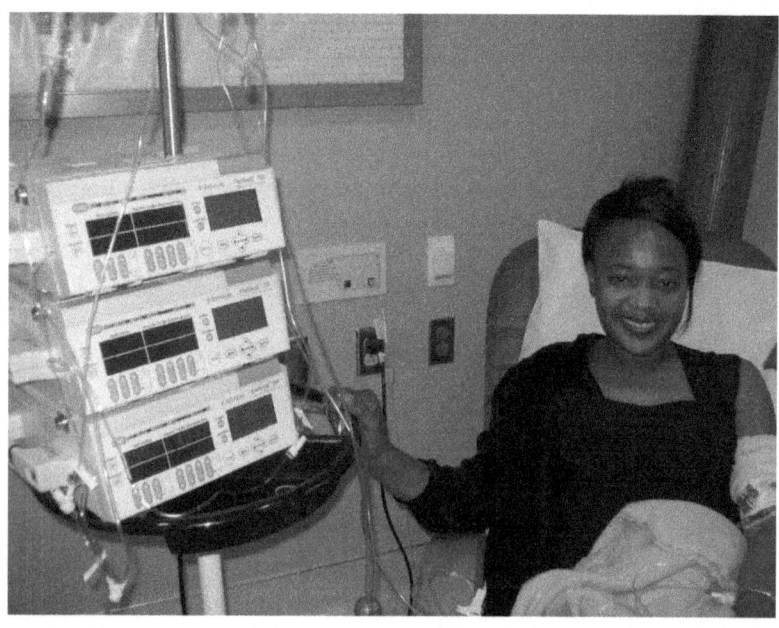

*At Loma Linda Medical Center (Cancer Infusion Unit):
First chemotherapy infusion*

CHAPTER 12

RECEIVING MY HEALING: CHANGING MY THINKING PROCESSES

Don't copy the behavior and customs of this world, but let God transform you into a new person by changing the way you think. Then you will learn to know God's will for you, which is good and pleasing and perfect.

(Romans 12:2; New Living Translation, NLT).

As a previous journalist, I had employed all of my journalistic skills in investigating the healing ministry of the Lord Jesus. That intense investigation took slightly over a week; now it was time to put into practice what I had learnt, and Romans 12:2 was the "game changer" for me. As I meditated (pondered, contemplated, focused) on this Scripture, especially this first part, ***Don't copy the behavior and customs of this world, but let God transform you into a new person by changing the way you think,*** it became obvious that the initial step in receiving my healing was to change my thinking processes about healing overall, period! In my situation, I concluded that if I could change my thinking pattern, then part two of Romans 12:2, which reads, **Then you will *learn to know God's will for you, which is good and pleasing and perfect,*** will manifest effortlessly; and for me, that perfect will was the manifestation of my healing.

This may sound surprising to some of you, because I had acquired all of the "head knowledge" that the Lord died on the Cross for the healing of my diseases as well, right? Boy! Let me warn you —Knowing something in your head is one thing, but allowing that information or knowledge to get deep into your soul is a whole different matter, and for me, it was a major struggle. This was primarily because as a Nurse Practitioner back then, I had been indoctrinated with all of the medical ways of treating all sorts of cancers. I knew all of the medical facts in my soul —that was what I did for a living — I knew medicine, very well! However, I knew that I needed to change my thinking process 100%, in order to align myself with God's perfect will for me —receiving my healing!

It Was Up to Me, Not God

Since faith is the primary channel by which we can receive anything from the Lord, including the physical healing of diseases, I was determined to strengthen my faith, " in a hurry". And during the study of the Lord's ministry, I had learnt a lot about true Bible faith, thus I refused to pray like the father of the boy with Epileptic Seizure who cried out to the Lord Jesus, ..."*I do believe; help me overcome my unbelief!" (Mark 9:24)*, (emphasis author's).

While there is nothing wrong with crying out to the Lord in this manner, for me, it was inappropriate to do so because God had already revealed to me, through His Word, during the process of studying the Lord's ministry, how to strengthen my faith. In addition, the Bible teaches that, "... *to whom much is given, from him much will be required...*" (Luke 12:48, NKJV). Hence, I knew that crying out to the Lord to strengthen my faith would not be a prayer of faith; rather, I had to practice what He had already revealed to me, thereby strengthening my faith. Knowing this, I believed that the primary way to strengthen my faith was to put Romans 12:2 into practice in my life, "renewing of my mind", that way, I could position myself with God's perfect will for me — receiving my healing.

Learning to Receive My Healing

Keep in mind that I said, "receiving" my healing! I was not praying for God to heal me, because I had "head knowledge" and believed that He had already healed me, and my job was to receive it, period!

//

To receive my healing therefore, I needed to work on myself, my faith! God has already done His part, but it was up to me to minimize unbelief, purify my faith by strengthening it, thereby positioning myself to easily receive my healing

//

(more on this a little later in this chapter).

This is very significant because if you approach your prayer from a position of "begging God" to heal you, then, that would be considered a prayer of unbelief, which will hinder your ability to receive the healing, because He has already healed you on the Cross, remember? On the other hand, if you approach your prayer from a position of faith, believing that God has already healed you, and you just have to grow in your faith and believe this in your heart and minimize your unbelief (more on this on the next chapter), then you will be well positioned to receive that healing! Please take note of this difference — it is powerful, and for some people, this is all you need to receive your healing. So do not "beg" God to heal you, He has already healed you! I discuss more about this in Section 4 of this book.

Know that, Romans 12:2 is teaching that in order for us, God's children, to know His perfect and pleasing will for us, we would have to allow His Word to change us from the inside out. That word, transform, in Romans 12:2, translated by the translators of our contemporary English Bible came from the original Greek language word "***metamorphoo***" (Strong's 3339), which implies a complete 180 degree change into another form, such as when water is totally transformed into ice.

In the case of God's children therefore, it means that we have to allow God's Word to saturate our souls (meaning, our thinking processes) to the extent that it changes us from the inside out; that is to say, it changes our deepest thoughts, so that, that change would be reflected and/or evident in our daily actions and lives—such as the healing of our physical bodies.

While I was contemplating on how I had to change my thinking, it was already time to begin Chemotherapy. After that initial experience I had when I first stepped into the Cancer Center (meaning, that "spirit of death", remember?), I was determined to be better prepared this time. And as I thought about receiving Chemotherapy for the first time, I was paralyzed with fear. To prepare therefore, I decided I had to overcome that "spirit of fear", which was not from God. Thus, the night before that first treatment, I spent the entire evening, about 4 to 5 hours, studying Scriptures on fear, then I decided to meditate on Psalm 91 and Isaiah 41:9-10.

Overcoming the Fear of Chemotherapy

Upon awakening in the morning of that first Chemotherapy treatment, my fear was slowly, but surely dissipating. Nonetheless, I had written all of Psalm 91 and Isaiah 41:9-10 on a 4 by 4 card, placed it in my Bible, and I was armed and ready to face Chemotherapy. The Oncologist had warned me that I should not drive myself to the Cancer Center, as I would not be able to drive myself home after completing the treatment. So my friend who had been with me all along drove me to the Cancer Center.

Throughout the drive to the Cancer Center, I continued to meditate on Psalm 91 and Isaiah 41:9-10, while engaging my sense of imagination and wonder — I closed my eyes and imagined myself in the presence of God, surrounded by His protective angels, guarding me, and protecting me from any harm. I verbalized out loud 2 Timothy 1:7, except that I personalized it, by saying, " **God has not given [me] a spirit of fear, but of love and a sound mind"**, and I would add, *"so [I] refuse to be afraid."* I quoted 2 Timothy 1:7 over and over, as we were driving. When we arrived at the Cancer Center, I was amazed how instead of fear and a feeling of dread like the first time, I actually experienced compassion for the other patients there. And I thought to myself, " Whoa! God is with me."

While waiting for my name to be called, I focused on meditating on Scriptures written on the 4 by 4 cards; and interestingly, I started wondering how I could minister to the other patients there; this thought came to my mind as a surprise, and yet it was liberating! The biggest hurdle in overcoming cancer is to initially overcome the fear associated with the disease and the Chemotherapy treatment. **So as the Lord was delivering me from this fear, He started placing it in my heart to begin the process of giving healing to others, as a way of receiving my own healing; this is a powerful principle about receiving your healing (more on this in Section 4 of this book).**

Courage While Facing Chemotherapy

After a little while in the waiting room at the Cancer Center, it was my turn to see the doctor. Blood work was done, and everything checked out normal. After the Oncologist's examination, I was taken into the infusion center, hooked up to multiple tubes, given multiple drugs intravenously, and then the infusion of the Chemotherapy drugs started. **Before the infusion started, I looked at all of the cancer drugs in my room, over 3 of them, and I laid my hands on them and said out loud, " You, Chemotherapy drugs, I am not afraid of you, you have no power over me; you will not cause any permanent damage over my body, in Jesus name, Amen."**

Speaking to Inanimate Objects

While this (talking to an inanimate object) may sound strange to some of you, the Lord Jesus did the same thing when He spoke to the fig tree, and it [the tree] obeyed Him and dried up the next day (Mark 11:12-25). Much more, God says His Word, spoken in faith will not return void, it will accomplish the desired purpose (Isaiah 55:11). So, I was determined to release my faith with my words, and to declare and agree with God that Chemotherapy had no authority over me, a child of God.

There was a TV in my infusion room, but I told the nurses I wanted it turned off, and throughout the infusion process, I studied the Bible; again, the healing ministry of Jesus, and I would pause occasionally and meditate on the Scriptures on fear. **Right away at that first treatment encounter, the nurses observed my courage, and noted that I had the most "upbeat and encouraging attitude" among all of the cancer patients in the Center, and from that day onwards, the majority of them requested me as their patient for future infusion treatment days.** That infusion, which lasted about 3 to 4 hours, was uneventful, to my amazement. Thereafter, the tubes were disconnected, and the 72 hour Chemotherapy infusion bag was hooked to my infusion site, and I was discharged to go home, and reminded that a nurse would make a home visit to discontinue the bag after the 72 hours.

My friend picked me up and when I arrived home, I was extremely thankful to the Lord for the uneventful experience. I said to myself ," This isn't bad at all, I can handle this", but as I would find out later on, I was 100% wrong about Chemotherapy. I went to bed that night with the 72 hour Chemotherapy infusion bag on me, and I awoke in the morning and began to feel a slight tingling in my lips, and I knew right away it was a side effect from the Chemotherapy. Nonetheless, I proceeded with my task of working on strengthening my faith. With that thought, I put aside the Scriptures on fear and I revisited Romans 12:2, knowing quite well that the Key to receiving my healing was in renewing my mind.

Transforming My Thinking

As discussed earlier, Romans 12:2 teaches that in order to live out God's perfect will in this life, we will begin by (1) not behaving and acting like the unbelievers do; but, rather, we should (2) transform our lives by "renewing" (**making new, restarting again, beginning again,** etc) **our minds (thinking processes, attitudes, personality) to be in agreement with God's Word. Some of you may wonder, how do you renew your mind? Well, you do so simply with the Word of God; that is to say, you allow the Word of God to change your thinking processes; and the best and only way to do so is by meditating on God's Word, until it changes you from the inside out** (more on this in chapter 14). There are no short cuts to this, friend! This is the Only way!

God's Kind of Change Starts From Within

Take note that, the Bible admonishes us to simply "renew" our minds; implying that, we already have a Philosophy about life (meaning, our view of life), before we became Christians. But as soon as we enter into a relationship with God through Christ, we have to start the process of renewing or restarting to change our views of life to be consistent with God's Word, in order to start receiving His blessings in our lives. This process of renewing our minds is the key to enjoying that blessed life that Christ Jesus died for us to enjoy in this present life.

God created us in His image as tripartite beings, consisting of a mind, a body, and a spirit, bound together as one unit (1 Thessalonians 5:23). At the time of salvation when we accept Jesus Christ as our Lord and Savior, our spirits are instantly regenerated (i.e., given a new life; born again); but our souls (i.e., our minds, personalities, attitudes, wills, etc) are unchanged, and of course, our physical bodies, remain the same. The Bible teaches that the spirit gives life to the soul and physical body, and the Lord Jesus further explained that life is in the spirit; and His Words (i.e., the Word of God) are what gives life to the soul and body (John 6:63).

As Christians, we have life (i.e., God's peace, joy, healing power, etc) in our born again spirits, but in order for that life to transfer from our spirits, then into our souls, and subsequently to our physical bodies, the Bible says we must change our minds or souls (i.e., our thinking processes, attitude, will), using God's Word, which is the Only source of life to the soul and body. If we allow God's Word to change our view in life, then the life in God's Word will reflect in our souls (such as more joy, peace, contentment, etc), which will in turn reflect in our physical bodies (e.g., a healthier immune system, ability for the body to heal itself, ability to overcome sicknesses and diseases, etc, etc).

God's Truth is Superior

As I meditated on Romans 12:2, I decided that somehow or another, I needed to allow the Word of God to saturate my mind/soul to the extent that it would cleanse me from all of the medical facts and incorrect information I had been exposed to as a Nurse Practitioner, and from talking with other Christians about their erroneous perspectives on healing. **Some of you may think that I am minimizing medical information: absolutely Not! Friend, there are many truths in life, such as medical truths (with a small t), purely based on facts, and at times, not even observable facts because medical science cannot measure human beings in a "test tube," such as in a research laboratory.**

So medical truth is purely based on statistics and extrapolated data from animal studies with some general applications to human beings, which I admit, have some benefits, and have helped countless individuals. However,

//

God's Truth (with capital T, meaning, The Truth), which is The Absolute Truth, surpasses all different types of pseudo truths out there today, and forevermore. So it is up to you to decide if you want to focus on God's Truth, or the other truths (with a small t).

//

Receiving My Healing: Changing My Thinking Processes

The Truths found in God's Word are superior, peaceful, pure, enduring and more consistent and reliable than medical truths or other so-called truths, period! And since God has proven Himself as consistent and faithful throughout the history of the earth, I decided that I would be safer with God's Truths, than with medical science.

To this end, I came up with a plan to initially heal and cleanse my soul from all of the incorrect information (so called truths) I had been exposed to about healing. To do this therefore, I chose to only use God's Word to purify or cleanse all of the "false information" about healing from my soul. The Bible clearly teaches that the Word of God sanctifies (i.e., cleanses, purifies our soul) (John 17:17); hence, I was determined that I would only allow God's Word to "detoxify" my soul from all of the "garbage" I had accumulated there over dozens of years.

There is a popular saying that goes like this, "**garbage in, and garbage out!**". I agree with this statement 100%, because whatever you allow into your soul is what will come out of you (i.e., from your speech and through your actions). In my case, I knew that in order to change my perspective and be healed, I had to first change my thinking patterns/processes to be consistent with God's Word, which would in turn reflect in my daily habits and lifestyle. Proceed now to the next chapter to learn how I began the process of detoxifying all of the "garbage" out of my soul, that way only The Truth —God's Truths would dominate my thoughts.

LESSONS LEARNED

- There are many pseudo-truths in existence today. But Only the Truths found in God's Word are authentic and will yield Godly and lasting results in our lives;

- The primary way to allow God's Absolute Truths to change us from the inside out is through the process of meditation;

- God's healing power is always available, but we must learn how to receive it, rather than begging God to heal us when He had already done so.

Recommended Resources For Further Studies:

Available At: www.DrRuthTanyi.org

Holy Spirit-Led Healthy Emotions: The Fruit of the Spirit and Your Health. **A 2-Set audio CD teaching.**

CHAPTER 13

RECEIVING MY HEALING: REDUCING UNBELIEF

How can you believe since you accept glory from one another but do not seek the glory that comes from the only God?

(John 5:44; New International Version, NIV).

As already discussed throughout this book, unbelief is the primary reason why several Godly Christians do not receive their healing from the Lord today, and in the past. As noted in the Scripture above (John 5:44), elevating the opinions of others is a major source of unbelief that will hinder us from receiving our healing or anything else from the Lord. In my case, I was dealing with a "death sentence", and I had to take drastic measures to deal with the problem of unbelief round and about me in order to receive my healing. To do this therefore, it was essential that I detoxify my immediate environment.

Detoxifying My Immediate Environment

This cleansing of my soul/mind was mandatory, if I needed to renew my mind, strengthen my faith and receive my healing, because God has already told us that when our souls are prospering, then we will likewise enjoy good health and prosperity in every other area of our lives (3 John 2). To undertake this endeavor therefore, I had to:

1. Detoxify my immediate environment;
2. Separate myself from the unbelief round and about me;
3. Meditate on God's Word until its life engenders healing of my soul and physical body.

I believed with all of my heart that if I accomplished the three activities listed above, I would be able to (1) change my thinking and depend on God 100% rather than medicine; (2) strengthen my faith quickly; and (3) correctly position myself in the spiritual realm to easily receive my healing. Let us now take a closer look at how I approached the first two activities in this chapter. Then in the next chapter, I will discuss the last activity: meditating on God's Word.

My primary mission for detoxifying my environment was to limit and/or eliminate unbelief from my immediate surroundings, which might impede my progress at renewing (i.e., changing) my mind. Even though I had described what unbelief looks like Scripturally, I believe this is a good place to further clarify what I mean by unbelief, again, from a biblical perspective.

Some Examples of What Unbelief Looks Like

In its very simplistic description, unbelief is any manner of speech, thinking, or action that is contrary to the ways of God as taught or described in the Bible. For example, since the Bible teaches that Christ Jesus died for the physical healing of diseases as well, if you refuse to believe this, even in ignorance, it is unbelief, which will prevent you from receiving God's healing, promises, or other blessings in this area of your life.

Other often ignored actions that are contrary to God's teaching, such as living in chronic fear, anxiety, worry, doubt, etc, are all forms of unbelief, because you do not trust that God is with you. Additionally, elevating the opinions of others more than God's Word is unbelief, because you do not trust God. As another example, not giving financially into God's work because of fear is unbelief, because you do not trust God with your money, etc, etc. Although the list of things that are considered unbelief is endless, I am sure you get the point.

Faith and Unbelief Can Coexist

Most importantly, unbelief does not mean that a person does not have faith in God; rather, it means that the person's unbelief is polluting his or her faith, which will prevent the flow of God's miracles, blessings or provisions from manifesting. While most Christians probably believe in God's healing power, their unbelief, such as chronic doubt, anxiety, fear, etc, can negate their ability to fully operate in true Bible faith and receive their healing.

Most unfortunately, unbelief can engender double-mindedness, which is a major "faith killer", and will definitely prevent you from receiving anything from the Lord (James 1:5-8). People can hide their unbelief from others very well, but not from God, Who knows the heart (1 Samuel 16:7). But there is always hope! And the only remedy to deal with unbelief is to "get rid of it", period, using God's Truths in His Word!

In my situation, because I only wanted God's Truths in my soul, I considered everything else as false and "garbage!" Therefore, to begin the process of detoxification, I had to examine my immediate environment — friends, relatives, and other associates, in order to evaluate their thinking processes and beliefs about receiving healing from the Lord, so as to eliminate unbelief in my immediate surroundings. This was most significant because I was not going to fellowship (at least during the first few years of my battle with cancer), with anyone, Christian or non-Christian alike, whose thinking pattern was contrary to what I had learnt about healing — I was not going to allow their unbelieving thoughts any entrance into my soul whatsoever — I was done with that!

While some of you may think that my decision was extreme, it was not, because unbelief, as already stated, is the primary barrier to preventing the physical manifestation of any miracle from the Lord, and I was not going to allow that!

Below are other reasons why I had to cleanse my immediate surrounding, so as to easily renew my mind, strengthen my faith, and receive my healing:

Major Reasons For Detoxifying My Environment

1. I wanted **to create a faith filled milieu,** whereby the Spirit of the Lord could flow unhindered, and the only way to do that was to completely "get rid of" all unbelief to the best of my ability;

2. I wanted an environment whereby **I could only hear the voice of God** and no one else's voice; thus, I needed to reduce the "noise" from my surrounding;

3. I was determined to **cleanse all of the incorrect information** about cancer out of my soul, so as to begin the process of renewing my mind and allowing God's Truths to take root in my heart. Plus, the Bible teaches that bad company corrupts good manners (1 Corinthians 15:33); as such, I was not going to allow any false or incorrect information about healing from friends, relatives, etc, to penetrate my soul;

4. The Scripture teaches that **we should guard our souls** (i.e., minds) with all diligence (Proverbs 4:23), because out of it comes issues of life. So to me, one of the ways of doing this was to **limit the type of information I allowed into my soul**;

5. **It was critical that I knew my friends and even family members who purposefully held incorrect and/or contrary views about healing, because I did not want Satan to work through them, to get into my soul. You have to keep in mind that when Satan cannot get to you directly, he will work through friends, family members, and other close**

associates, etc, to get to you (Matthew 16:23); I knew this, so I was not going to allow that;

6. **I did not want the emotion of "pity" from anyone.** I wanted to surround myself with "faith filled" Christians, and not those who were not matured in trusting God. I serve a God of compassion, and not "pity". Pity, has an element of shame, disappointment, doubt, etc, associated with it, and is a major "faith killer"; thus I wanted nothing to do with such ungodly emotions whatsoever, so as to prevent Satan inroad into my soul. I wanted the joy of the Lord around me, not "pity!" It was a spiritual warfare, and Satan was not going to win the battle, period!;

7. **I did not want anyone to "feel sorry for me";** I hated that attitude, and I still do today, because it engenders depression, which is not from God. Feelings of depression is another "faith killer", and I was not going to tolerate that! As Christians, we have, in our born again spirits, the joy, peace, love, etc, of the Lord, (Galatians 5: 22-23), which are all emotions that engender hope, and releases God's healing power into our physical bodies, so I did not, and I still do not believe in going around and feeling "sorry" for people. It is okay to have Godly compassion towards others, which can lead us to support them, but not an ungodly attitude of "feeling sorry" for them;

8. Most importantly, I did not want to defend God's Word or my position to anyone, that was not the right time to do so. Since the people I knew had contrary views about healing, I concluded that getting into lengthy discussions and debates about healing was not best for my soul at that time; I needed to get well, in a hurry, then later on, I would teach others, I figured.

I evaluated my friends and relatives by simply asking them a few questions about their views on healing. And upon my evaluation, it was discouraging, as I noted earlier, that with the exception of my older sister and the friend who had been with me from day one, everyone else around me believed that God could heal, but not all of the time.

Some of them even verbalized that God chooses those to heal and those not to heal. Sadly, some of my friends and relatives were grossly ignorant, and stated they did not even know what the Bible said about healing. Unfortunately, ignorance, as mentioned before, is a major source of unbelief that Satan preys on. With these findings, I decided I had to completely separate myself from these friends and relatives, for some time, in order to avoid any temptation to say something.

Separating Myself to Minimize Unbelief

After my investigation and findings of my immediate environment, I was so troubled. I started to talk to the Lord about it in prayer, because I was concerned about not telling those who had been there for me during the surgical stage of my journey. The Oncologist had warned me that I would need more help undergoing Chemotherapy than I did after the surgery. Although I knew that telling my friends and family members about the cancer and Chemotherapy meant that I would ensure their help, I was torn; because at the same time, I knew that sharing my diagnosis and prognosis with them would engender unbelief, and possibly open the door for their reaction such as fear, doubt, confusion etc, etc to negatively affect me. I had struggled with those emotions, and I felt as if the Lord had been slowly but surely delivering me from them, so I did not want to go back and taste my vomit (Proverbs 26:11).

But one day, as I was meditating on the healing ministry of the Lord, the Holy Spirit brought to my remembrance some instances when the Lord had to seek seclusion (i.e., separated Himself from others) multiple times in His ministry before He performed certain miracles. **Even though the Lord Jesus had 12 disciples, there were some instances when He only called three of them: James,**

Receiving My Healing: Reducing Unbelief

Peter and John along with Him, right before He performed certain miracles, such as during the Transfiguration (see Matthew 17); raising the synagogue ruler, Jairus' daughter from the dead (see Mark 5: 21-43), etc.

Even though the Scripture does not tell us, it was obvious, especially in the case about raising Jairus' daughter from the dead, that the Lord simply drove all of the people and their unbelief out of His immediate environment before He raised the little girl from the dead. Then, the apostle Peter did the same thing, when he sought seclusion (i.e., drove people out of his immediate environment), before he raised Dorcas from the dead (Acts 9:36-42), again, to get rid of the unbelief. Even the Old Testament Saint, Elijah, sought seclusion (i.e., getting rid of unbelief) when he raised the widow of Zarephath's son from the dead (see 1 Kings 17:17-24).

With the above examples from the Scriptures, I had the peace of God, a confirmation that it would be okay to separate myself from my immediate environment which was "toxic with unbelief". I also decided it would be best not to share my diagnosis and prognosis with other friends who were not even in my immediate environment, just to be consistent with my decision to separate myself (later on I informed one of my brothers and a girl friend in Minnesota; this girl friend did not know the details).

Also, remember how I had mentioned earlier that my older sister had informed me not to share my diagnosis and prognosis with my mother, family members, and other friends, I hope you recall?. Well, after I perceived that confirmation of peace from the Lord about separating myself in order to decrease peoples' unbelief around me, it turned out that my older sister's initial advice to me not to share the cancer diagnosis with anyone was the best advice I received; because God confirmed it with His peace. Also, separating myself from others was the best decision because it provided an environment with less confusion, stress, worry and care; and most importantly, it fostered my ability to be single minded in meditating on God's Word and saturating His Truths in my soul.

To separate myself from others and reduce their effect of unbelief on me, below are the things I did in the initial 24 months of fighting cancer. I carried out some of these practices for up to about 4 years thereafter:

How I Reduced Unbelief in My Environment

- ❖ Besides my older sister, my friend who had been with me from the beginning, my medical staff [later on I informed a brother and a girl friend in MN], others, including people from my church did not know what my diagnosis and prognosis were (this went on for about 4 years). Friends and family members only knew I had recovered from surgery and moved on. It did not matter how compassionate someone was, I did not share my health status with them, period!;

- ❖ For about 15 months, I wore clothing that disguised the IV tubing and its markings in my body;

- ❖ I did not allow visitors in my home for about 9 months, because my living room area was a "little" Cancer Unit (that was where the Oncology nurse came weekly to disconnect the Chemotherapy infusion and cared for my IV sites;

- ❖ I significantly limited the amount of time I spent talking with certain people over the phone — I mostly texted those who contacted me, which was very infrequently. I did not want to give anyone the opportunity to ask me questions about my health, which might have led into the temptation of me talking;

- ❖ For a period of about 12 months, I engaged in no social activity whatsoever;

- ❖ For about 9 to 10 months, I limited myself to only watching about 10 minutes of TV news a few days a week, and about 30 to 60 minutes of Christian TV daily;

- ❖ I could not work in the initial 8 to 9 months; thereafter, I was able to work about 1 day a week for about a year, then by the second year, I was able to return to work gradually. Thus, I put that extra time into excellent use, spending about 8 to 10 hours a day for a period of about 11-12 months, studying the Word of God, focusing on healing, the art of meditating on God's Word, and how to overcome unbelief. During the initial few months, my primary goal was learning to overcome unbelief, because I had faith, but my faith was "poisoned" with all sorts of unbelief.

It Was Do or Die!

While the above actions may seem too extreme for some of you, to me, I believed it was not God's will for me to die of cancer; thus, I took extreme measures to deal with unbelief. Also, this was the fastest and best option for me to strengthen my faith and receive my healing. There is a popular saying that goes like this, you "do or die" while trying to accomplish a goal!

///

For me, it was truly a "do or a die", because I was either going to die while fighting with my last breath, or I was going to survive cancer, it was non-negotiable!

///

This is not implying that you have to take similar measures before you could receive your healing: No! However, there are times when extreme measures have to be taken, in order to overcome unbelief, detoxify our souls and prepare ourselves to receive God's blessings. This is the same principle behind fasting and prayer, whereby you would deny yourself of food and/or drinks for a set period of time, in order to draw closer to God so as to become more sensitive to His voice, and experience the visible manifestation of whatever you are seeking Him for. Even though God is always present, we are often bombarded with all sorts of internal stimuli (i.e., from our souls) and externally from our environment that often quench His "still voice"; thus, extreme measures (such as during fasting and prayer) might be necessary in order to aggressively reduce stimuli (noise) from our surroundings, that way we would be wholeheartedly focused on God.

Even the medical field understands this principle of taking extreme measures in order to minimize contamination and expedite healing. As an example, in the hospital, there are some instances whereby a patient might be very sick; as such, he or she is placed on what is called "reverse isolation" (i.e., separating the patient from health care workers and others who might contaminate the patient) for a period of time, in order to foster expeditious healing and recovery.

I Never Felt Alone

Most importantly, undertaking extreme measures as I did does not imply that you are alone —God was with me, and He is still with me, always. And, I wholeheartedly believed, and still believe that, me and the Lord Jesus were sufficient; plus, He had already spoken to the hearts of my older sister and friend, thus the 3 of us entered into a prayer of agreement for my healing — that was sufficient! This prayer of agreement was a 100% consecrated process, because we were all in agreement with the Word of God that I was already healed, and the manifestation will be evident soon. <u>This was, and is significant because in a prayer of agreement, all parties involved must be in one accord with God's Word, lest it would not work</u>. If one person in the prayer chain is not in agreement with the Word of God in whatever you are believing God for, then that person will be the weak link that will nullify the prayer.

But in my case, I was 100% at peace because all 3 of us were in one accord in seeking the Lord, thus I needed no one else! Besides, as I spent more time in the Word with God, I was so comforted, I did not even miss being around people at all — The Holy Spirit is truly our Comforter, if we allow Him to comfort us! (John 14:26). It is important for me to say that often times, **people erroneously believe**

that they have to come in agreement with a lot of people before God will answer their prayer: this is wrong! You and Jesus are enough, and He can send other like-minded believers in your path, if that is necessary. But you, and a few, or even hundreds of people who are not in one accord with God's Word is useless, I am sorry to say this! And unfortunately, this is what happens with many people who do not understand the concept behind a prayer of agreement.

With the process of separating myself from unbelief well delineated, it was then time for me to actually begin the process of harnessing the "art of meditation" without distractions, thereby strengthening my faith and allowing God's healing power to manifest in my physical body. Turn now to the next chapter to find out how I did this.

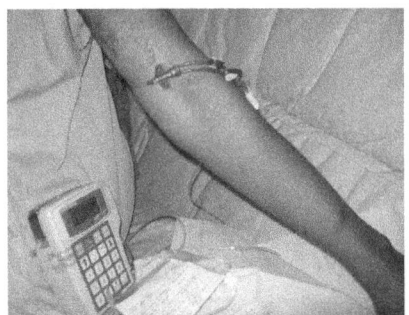

72 hours continuous home infusion chemotherapy bag

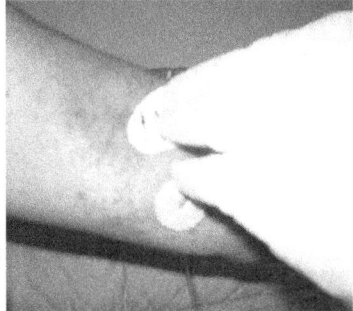

Markings and scaring on the skin from chemotherapy infusion site

LESSONS LEARNED

- ➢ The Truths in God's Word are superior to all other truths;

- ➢ Every Christian has faith to receive his or her healing, but one major problem preventing the manifestation of the healing is unbelief, which unfortunately, many individuals choose to ignore;

- ➢ Reducing unbelief in your immediate environment is the initial step in receiving your healing;

Recommended Resources For Further Studies:

Available At: www.DrRuthTanyi.org

How to Overcome Doubt and Receive God's Promises.
10 Life-Changing Lessons Learnt from Overcoming Metastasis Colon Cancer: **A 2-Set Audio CD teaching.** By Dr Ruth Tanyi.

CHAPTER 14

Receiving My Healing: Strengthening My Faith Through Meditation

So then faith comes by hearing, and hearing by the word of God.

(Romans 10:17; New King James Version, NKJV).

When it comes to healing of physical diseases, the Bible teaches about various methodologies for the impartation and release of God's healing power; although faith (specifically, a prayer of faith) is the Only channel by which God's healing power can be activated. And faith, has to be present from both parties involved — the sick person, and from the minister or individual doing the praying or ministering. So where does this faith come from, you may wonder? As noted in Romans 10:17 cited above, faith to receive our healing or any other promise from God comes from studying and meditating on the Word of God. Before I discuss how I strengthened my faith using God's Word and subsequently received my healing, I want to briefly talk about some of the different ways by which God's healing power can be released, as described in the Bible.

Releasing God's Healing Power

There are various methodologies described in the Bible by which God's healing power can be activated and released. Some of these methodologies include: **(1)** laying on of hands, a practice that even our Lord Jesus carried out (e.g., see Matthew 8:3, 14-15; 9: 28-29; 9:18; Mark 7:32; 8:22-23; Acts 28:8); **(2)** praying and anointing the sick person with oil (e.g., see James 5:14-15)**; (3)** healing power flowing through clothing (e.g., see Acts 19:11-12); **(4)** healing power present via individual's shadow (e.g., Acts 5:15); **(5)** healing power being present in the Lord's meeting (e.g., see Luke 5:17); **(6)** healing power flowing through the spoken Word, that is, the Word of God (e.g., Matthew 8:13; 9:2; 15:28; Mark 10:51-52; John 5: 1-9; Psalm 107:20; Proverbs 3:5-8; Proverbs 4:20-22); etc.

While each of the above methodologies are equally effective when carried out in faith, it has been my experience thus far that, the laying on of hands and the anointing of the sick with oil are the most popular methodologies in the body of Christ, today.

Power in the Word of God

In my situation however, after the decision to separate myself from every kind of perceivable unbelief and entering an agreement with my older sister, friend, and the Lord, I chose to focus on the Ministry of the Word —healing through the Word of God. The Word of God is powerful, and it is the most accessible tool we, as Christians, have today. Over 2000 years ago during the Ministry of the Lord and the apostles, individuals did not have the Word of God in their possession as we have been blessed to easily have today. Plus, we have the Holy Spirit indwelling us (those who are true Christians), to illuminate Scriptures to us, if we so desire (John 16:13). So in my opinion, the Word of God is the fastest and most convenient way for any of us to receive our healing today.

But unfortunately, many people often bypass the Word of God and get into a frenzy in search of a healing Minister to lay hands on them, all the while losing valuable time they could have invested in the Ministry of the Word. The Bible teaches that we cannot separate God from His Word: The Word of God is God, and God is His Word! The Word of God is eternal (it has always existed); it is the Only Absolute Truth!; It is alive, active, and flawless (Proverbs 30:5; Hebrews 4:12; Psalm 119:89).

We are also told how the Lord Jesus was/is the living Word of God which was supernaturally joined with humanity (i.e., during the incarnation), and became flesh and bones (i.e., a human being), like one of us (John 1: 1-14). During the Old Testament era, God spoke through the prophets, but today, He has already spoken through His Son: Christ Jesus (Hebrews 1:1-2); and He has sent His Spirit to indwell us, and to reveal all His truths to us (Ephesians 1:13; John 16:13). **Thus, the primary way God will speak to us today is through His revealed Word, period!**

Meditation Releases the Life and Medicine in God's Word

There is power and life in the Word of God when spoken aloud in faith. Additionally, the Word of God is the most potent medicine to our souls and entire bodies (John 6:63; Proverbs 4:20-22). But to release the life and medicine in God's Word, one thing is essential— meditation. Simplistically put, to the Christian, meditation is defined as " a *quiet contemplation of spiritual truths*" (Strong's Concordance). Then, according to Vine's Complete Expository Dictionary of Old and New Testament Words, meditation also means, "*to attend to, practice*,... to ponder, *imagine,*" etc.

Meditation Requires Contemplation, Imagination, and Patience

As you can see from the above descriptions of the word meditation, it requires contemplation, pondering, giving attention to (i.e., thinking over and over again) on the Truths found in the Word of God. The word "practice," as used by Vine's to describe meditation adds clarity to the word, implying a repeated action (i.e., to practice); in this case, "repeating" or thinking about the Word of God over and over and over, over a prolonged period of time. Then, there is the word, "imagine", used to describe meditation as well, which implies utilizing our sense of imagination (i.e., to visualize in our hearts) what God is teaching us in His Word.

//

Thus, in the practice of meditation as Christians therefore, we would first study God's Word to get an understanding of what He is telling us. Thereafter, we would ponder (i.e., contemplate, think about His Truths), over and over, and over and over, again, until our spiritual eyes are enlightened (i.e., open) to receive the spiritual Truth(s) in the Scripture(s).

//

In the process of meditating, we can even engage our senses; meaning, put ourselves in the scene of the story or Scripture(s) we are contemplating about, that way we could experience similar types of emotions the individual(s) in the Scriptural scene experienced — this alone can plant indelible seeds in your soul about the Truths in the Scriptural text you are studying.

Keep in mind that for the Christian, meditation is not the same thing as Transcendental Meditation (TM), popularly practiced by various Eastern Religions such as Buddhism, etc, which involves emptying of the mind. On the contrary, when we, as Christians, meditate, we do not want to empty our minds. Rather, we would want to purposefully allow God's Word into our minds/souls, then focus on it, and think about it over and over again, until the power and life in God's Word transcends from our spirits, then into our souls, and that transformation will subsequently radiate into our physical bodies, and it will be perceived with our senses.

As much as studying the Word of God is crucial, the Bible teaches that the practice of meditation is what releases the life and power in God's Word, which in turn leads to success and prosperity in our lives (Joshua 1:8). Below are other benefits of meditating on God's Word. It leads to:

1. Better understanding of God's Word;

2. Acquisition of Godly (higher) knowledge;

3. Acquisition of Godly revelation, Truths and/or insights;

4. Easier application of God's Truths, which in turn yields Godly results.

During the practice of meditation, as you ponder on God's Word and ask the Holy Spirit for revelation, He will begin to reveal Godly truths to you about whatever Scripture(s) you are pondering about. And as God's Truths are revealed to you over a prolonged period of time, they will take root in your soul and begin to transform your thinking, and subsequently your actions, and Godly results will be a byproduct of the change in your soul. Friend, do you see why meditation is powerful? Hopefully you do! In fact, the Bible admonishes us to meditate on the Word daily (e.g., Joshua 1:8; Psalm 119-148; 1 Timothy 4:15).

A Complete Dedication to the Ministry of the Word

Being that I had chosen to use the Word of God (Ministry of the Word) to renew my mind in order to receive my healing, I needed to invest some time in the practice of meditation. For those of you unaware, in its simplistic description, the Ministry of the Word means using and/or applying (i.e. practicing) the Word of God as the sole means of ministry. **Keep in mind that the Word of God should be the underpinning in everything we, as Christians do for the Lord, anyway.** But by using the Word of God as my means of healing, it meant I focused on it more than any other methodology to receive my healing.

Before I proceed in this section, I want to explain the **4 major reasons** that led me to decide on the Ministry of the Word as the best option for my healing:

Why the Ministry of the Word?

1. **God has already proven Himself throughout history as 100% consistent and faithful**. As mentioned earlier, you cannot separate God from His Word. knowing the Word

of God is equal to knowing the nature of God! And God's Word never fails, if practiced in faith and correctly; thus I was confident I could count on it 100%;

2. **I needed lasting results**, rather than a "quick fix." I was quite aware that fighting cancer was going to be a long battle, and only God's Word was/is dependable 100%. I wanted to be "rooted" in God's Word to the extent that I had no fear or threats from any disease ever "attacking" my body again. In essence, I wanted to learn how to "walk in divine health", and not just to be healed of cancer;

3. Additionally, **I did not want to rely or depend on any Pastor or Minister** to pray for me; I wanted to learn how to lay hands on myself and receive my healing. God's will is for us to mature and learn how to receive His blessings directly from Him through Christ, rather than waiting and depending on others; thus I wanted to be "grounded" on how to rely on God, rather than on people;

4. **Most importantly, the Word of God was/is accessible.** I did not have to worry about calling for a Pastor/Minister for help — I had God's Word in the Bible readily available. **I am not implying that there is anything wrong with asking Pastors/Ministers to pray for you: absolutely Not.** However, I wanted to depend on God and nobody else.

I Saturated Myself with the Word of God

As explained in previous chapters, faith is the primary, and only channel by which we can receive God's promises. And God has already told us that we can strengthen our faith by hearing, reading, or meditating on His Word (Romans 10:17). Thus, I wholeheartedly believed that with the decision to saturate myself with the Word of God through the practice of meditation, I would absolutely strengthen my faith and receive my healing, effortlessly.

Being a very disciplined person, I came up with a schedule to meditate on God's Word, and I approached it as a "full time job". Since I could not work, I implemented a very rigorous schedule — about 8 to 10 hours a day of studying and meditating, and I was committed to doing this until the life in God's Word is released into my soul and strengthened my faith. Below was how I approached my study and meditation time:

My Study and Meditation Schedule

- **I went back and started to reread the healing ministry of Jesus.** For about 3 hours every day, over a period of about 3 to 4 months, I restudied the 4 Gospels. I started with the Gospel of Matthew, then to Mark, and to Luke and John. This time however, I focused on specific stories of individuals who displayed bold and active faith in receiving their healing from the Lord, such as **(1)** the woman with the issue of blood (Matthew 9:20–22; Mark 5:25–34; Luke 8:43–48); **(2)** the story about the faith of the Centurion (Matthew 8:5-13); and **(3)** the story about the faith of the Gentile woman (Matthew 15:21-28; Mark 7:24-30). After about 3 hours of studying these stories, I would close my Bible and then for about another 1 hour or so, I would meditate on these individuals' stories.

- As an example, **I would close my eyes, visualize and mentally imagined myself** in the **place of the woman with the issue of blood.** I would ponder on her courage — how she stepped out in faith to the public arena in pursuit of Jesus in spite of the Mosaic Law that prohibited her from doing so. This woman was fearless, and it was a "do or die" decision for her. She risked being stoned to death; yes, she was desperate! I would meditate on how in spite of the crowds of people attempting to get to the Lord, this lady went on her knees and crawled, just so she could touch the edges of the Lord's garment, with a firm belief that once she did so, she would be healed.

This woman's story was the most significant to me, because she had everything going against her, yet, she did not care — she just believed and acted on her faith. As I meditated on her story for months, I constantly engaged my sense of imagination, and I imagined myself in her "shoes". I thought to myself, " **Just like this lady, I have everything going against me"; thus, I visualized myself, on my knees, crawling and touching the Lord's clothing, while believing and expecting that in the same way virtue flew from Him and healed her, virtue would likewise flow from the Lord and I would receive my healing.** I meditated on this scenario over, and over and over, daily, for about 3 to 4 months, and I continued doing so for several years thereafter, although the intensity and frequency decreased.

- I also placed myself in the place of the Centurion, and I would verbalize something like this, "Lord, your Word had already healed me, I receive it, thank you God, in Jesus name".

- Then, just like the Gentile (Canaanite) woman, I would say something to this effect, "God, I do not deserve to be healed, but I come in the name of Jesus, my Lord and Savior, so I am receiving my healing, right now, thank you God."

After my morning routine of meditating on the healing stories in the Gospels, I would spend another 4 hours in the evening on studying all of the other healing Scriptures in the Bible, in context, (meaning, studying a few chapter and verse before and after each healing Scripture, plus studying each healing Scripture in light of all the other healing Scriptures in the Bible). After studying the hundreds of Scriptures pertaining to healing, I selected 15 of my favorite ones, wrote them on a 4 by 4 card and meditated on them for another 1 -2 hours before bed.

My Favorite Healing Scriptures

Below are the 15 Scriptures and their significance to my healing:
[Please take note that all emphasis on the Scriptures are author's].

❖ **Psalm 118:17** (NKJV):

I shall not die, but live, and declare the works of the LORD.

Significance: This Scripture gave me the impetus to live in order to someday share my testimony and glorify God.

❖ **Isaiah 53:3-5:**

He was despised and rejected by mankind,... Surely he took up our pain and bore our suffering,... But he was pierced for our transgressions, he was crushed for our iniquities; the punishment that brought us peace was on him, and by his wounds we are healed.

Significance: This was a constant reminder that Jesus suffered on the Cross, so that I may enjoy good health. Thus, the least I could do was to fight to receive what was rightfully mine, and the enemy was trying to steal it from me!

❖ **Psalm 107:20:**

He sent out his word and healed them; he rescued them from the grave.

Significance: This reminded, and encouraged me that the Word of God spoken in faith was sufficient to release God's healing power.

❖ **3 John 2:**

Dear friend, I pray that you may enjoy good health and that all may go well with you, even as your soul is getting along well.

Significance: This Scripture was very encouraging. It affirmed that God was/is wishing (i.e., His will) for me to enjoy good health. It encouraged me to believe that my fight against cancer was God's will, because He desired, and still desires good health for me. He takes no pleasure when His children are sick!

- **Proverbs 3:5-8:**

Trust in the Lord with all your heart and lean not on your own understanding; in all your ways submit to him, and he will make your paths straight. Do not be wise in your own eyes; fear the Lord and shun evil. This will bring health to your body and nourishment to your bones.

Significance: This Scripture confirmed that God's Word is the best medicine for my entire body: Mind, body and Spirit, and obedience was/is the key to releasing God's perfect medicine!

- **John 6:63:**

The Spirit gives life; the flesh counts for nothing. The words I have spoken to you—they are full of the Spirit and life.

Significance: This Scripture reassured me that as I meditated on God's Word, I was receiving His life!

- **Proverbs 4:20-22:**

My son, pay attention to what I say; turn your ear to my words. Do not let them out of your sight, keep them within your heart; for they are life to those who find them and health to one's whole body.

Significance: This Scripture provided assurance, that meditating on God's Word was releasing life to my entire body, thus suppressing / killing the cancer cells in my body.

- **Isaiah 54:16-17:**

"See, it is I who created the blacksmith who fans the coals into flame and forges a weapon fit for its work....no weapon forged against you will prevail, and you will refute every tongue that accuses you. This is the heritage of the servants of the Lord, and this is their vindication from me," declares the Lord.

Significance: This was a significant assurance to me that Satan, or cancer, that enemy, could not prevail over my body.

❖ **Jeremiah 29:11-13:**

For I know the plans I have for you," declares the Lord, "plans to prosper you and not to harm you, plans to give you hope and a future..."....

Significance: This Scripture fueled me with expectation and hope for the future. It enabled me to believe that cancer was just a "temporary hurdle" in my journey, God had great plans for my future, and I was not going to allow cancer to steal my future.

❖ **Exodus 15:26:**

He said, "If you listen carefully to the Lord your God and do what is right in his eyes, if you pay attention to his commands and keep all his decrees, I will not bring on you any of the diseases I brought on the Egyptians, for I am the Lord, who heals you."

Significance: This Scripture provided added assurance that God was/is indeed, my Healer.

❖ **Romans 12:1-2:**

Therefore, I urge you, brothers and sisters, in view of God's mercy, to offer your bodies as a living sacrifice, ... Do not conform to the pattern of this world, but be transformed by the renewing of your mind. Then you will be able to test and approve what God's will is— his good, pleasing and perfect will.

Significance: This Scripture kept me "in check", and constantly reminded me that changing my thinking process to be consistent with God's Word was the gateway to strengthening my faith and receiving my healing.

❖ **Mark 9:23:**

"'If you can'?" said Jesus. "Everything is possible for one who believes."

Significance: This Scripture was an amazing "faith builder" for me, as it fostered my resolute to saturate my soul with the Word of God and strengthened my faith.

- ❖ **Matthew 9:29:**

Then he touched their eyes and said, "According to your faith let it be done to you".

Significance: This was another Scripture I called, a "faith builder", as it assured me that God will honor my faith. This Scripture also reminded me that it was not God who was withholding my healing; rather, He blesses us proportionately to how we believe in Him. With this, I knew that strengthening my faith will effortlessly align me with God's will: receiving my healing.

- ❖ **Ephesians 3:20:**

Now to him who is able to do immeasurably more than all we ask or imagine, according to his power that is at work within us.

Significance: This Scripture reassured me that as I "walked by faith" by the enabling of the Holy Spirit, God's miracle will be evident in my life beyond my imagination. This popular Scripture is often misquoted by many Christians, because they leave out this part, **"** *according to his power that is at work within us.***"** But the promised blessing mentioned in the first part of this Scripture, *"...do immeasurably more than all we ask or imagine,"* can only be evident in our lives when we activate the second part of this Scripture, "... **power that is at work within us";** which is the power of faith, working within us, as we are emboldened by the Holy Spirit Who indwells us.

As you can clearly see out of Mark 9:23, Matthew 9:29 and Ephesians 3:20, our position of faith is significant in how we receive our healing or anything else from the Lord. Due to space limitation in this book, I am unable to delve much into the topic of Bible faith. Hence, I recommend that you obtain my book titled: **Faith to Receive God's Promises: How to Walk in Biblical Faith and**

Receiving My Healing: Strengthening My Faith Through Meditation

Allow the Blessings of God to Chase You. This "how to book" will teach you how to apply the Laws of Faith as taught in the Bible and receive God's promises. This book has helped countless numbers of people; I am certain you will find it very helpful as well.

❖ **Isaiah 55:10-11:**

As the rain and the snow come down from heaven, and do not return to it without watering the earth… so is my word that goes out from my mouth: It will not return to me empty, but will accomplish what I desire and achieve the purpose for which I sent it.

Significance: This Scripture significantly assured me about the purposefulness of God's Word. As such, even when I was physically too weak to mentally comprehend God's Word coming out of my mouth, I believed in my heart that God will honor His Word spoken in faith and sincerity.

I Mentally Visualized, Saw, and Accepted Myself as Healed

I mentioned earlier how as part of meditation, you would engage all of your 5 senses (smell, touch, taste, hearing, sight). Well, as part of my practice of meditation,

//

I mentally made it a daily habit, likewise, to visualize myself as already healed by the Lord, even though I still had cancer in my body. In spite of the doctor's report of cancer in my body, I chose to refuse his report, and instead, I chose to accept God's report: I was healed on Calvary's Cross, regardless of how I felt.

//

This is so significant because before you can receive anything from the Lord, you must first perceive in your heart (deepest part of your soul) that you have first, already, by faith, received it , which is a true biblical description of faith.

If you cannot first perceive in your heart that you have already received God's promises, then no matter how much you pray, you will struggle to see it in the physical. Because when operating in Biblical faith, you have to come in agreement with God's Word, which teaches that all of His promises are already ours (**past tense**) in Christ (2 Corinthians 1:20); all we have to do is to receive them (**bringing them into the here and now**), as we trust God through our corresponding actions to complete our faith. Much more, **as part of my meditation regimen, I daily, visualized how the Lord Jesus Himself was laying hands on me, releasing His healing virtue all over my body. Thus, rather than running to another minister to lay hands on me, I used that time and mentally placed myself in the presence of the Lord, and I imagined and visualized Him laying His hands on me. Boy!** <u>This was the most powerful exercise I did daily during those initial 3 to 4 months or so of intense meditation on God's Word and I still do this today.</u>

While the above study and meditation time may appear rigorous to some of you, it was the best time I have ever experienced with the Lord. And the effects or results of my meditation practice planted indelible seeds in my soul that are still germinating results today. Besides, there are no negative side effects to God's Word, anyway! It was, and is still worth it! In spite of my dedication and best efforts at standing on God's promises, my health actually got worse. Proceed now to the next chapter to learn how I received my healing in the spirit without any physical evidence in the natural realm.

LESSONS LEARNED

- ➤ The primary way to strengthen our faith and receive our healing is by saturating ourselves in God's presence through His Word;

- ➤ To receive your healing, it is necessary that you first perceive yourself as already healed in the spiritual realm, then the visible healing will be a byproduct of what you believe — this is true Bible faith.

Recommended Resources For Further Studies:

Available At: www.DrRuthTanyi.org

*You can find more teaching on Meditation in this book:

Are You Moving Forward with Jesus? How to Excel In Your Identity in Christ.

CHAPTER 15

I Received My Healing In My Spirit and Soul

As the rain and the snow come down from heaven, and do not return to it without watering the earth and making it bud and flourish, so that it yields seed for the sower and bread for the eater, so is my word that goes out from my mouth: It will not return to me empty, but will accomplish what I desire and achieve the purpose for which I sent it.

(Isaiah 55:10-11; New International Version, NIV).

As the above Scripture in Isaiah 55:10-11 teaches, the Word of God spoken in faith will sooner or later accomplish its desired purpose. I had been doing everything I knew how to do, humanly speaking, to release my faith and God's healing power through His Word; yet, it appeared as if, at least on the surface, that my health was getting worse instead of better.

Chemotherapy Paralyzed Me

Just a few months into the Chemotherapy treatments, I was beginning to lose confidence in my ability to overcome the side effects of the Chemotherapies, as I started to experience horrible side effects. Most of the deadly side effects the Oncologist had informed me were beginning to come to pass. I began to lose weight, very fast, about 1-2 pounds a week, because during the 4 to 5 straight days of Chemotherapy infusion, I could not eat. I experienced unrelenting nausea, vomiting, and chronic salivation which led to constant drooling and spitting.

Additionally, the Chemotherapy drained all of the energy from me, and left me totally debilitated, for about 2 weeks following each treatment. Remember how I mentioned in preceding chapters that Colon Cancer had the most grueling Chemotherapy regimen? Hopefully you recall! Normally, after spending about 3 to 4 hours receiving the Chemotherapies at the Cancer Center, then another 72 hours of the continuous infusion at home, and another 3 to 5 days of shots at the Cancer Center, my body would be totally "paralyzed" from the treatment. Then, after about 1 -2 weeks of rest, depending on how I tolerated the treatment, I was scheduled for another treatment. This experience was far worse than the cancer itself!

Just after the second Chemotherapy treatment, I was not able to groom myself or walk upstairs in my home without assistance. **There were many days that I would just lay down for about 3 to 4 days in a row, unable to get out of bed, and I had to resort to bed baths. On several occasions, I would smell myself—I smelled awful!** On a bad day, it would take me about 2 to 3 hours just to get out of bed. And on several occasions, I would sit on the edge of my bed for about 2-3 hours, too paralyzed and weak to even stand up alone. I would attempt several times, but would be unable to, so I would stay in that position, all the while waiting for my friend to get to my house and assist me with grooming— it was horrible. I really do not understand how I survived those horrible days just waiting for my friend to assist me, except that, God was with me.

I was constantly drained, too tired to even read the Bible, and I began to wonder if I had made a mistake to consent to Chemotherapy; thus, I began to ask myself, "Am I able to sustain even the minimal prescribed Chemotherapy as the Oncologist had mentioned?" Even though I could not sit upright to study the Bible on these horrible Chemotherapy days, I had my 4 by 4 cards with me at all times, and I continued to meditate on God's Word with every bit of energy I had, believing that God will honor my courage.

During those days, I did not even have the energy to pray. Often, my prayers were simply me shouting, "**HELP ME**

JESUS!"; "I want to get up but I can't, HELP!". I often told myself, " God, I know you are here, watching me, I need energy, thank you." On some good days, after a prayer like that, I would, by faith, after about 2 hours, get out of bed to groom myself; but there were many other days that I just could not do so without help.

Still No Perceivable Change in My Soul

In fact, there were many days that it appeared as though I was wasting my time in studying and meditating; nonetheless, I persisted. I was patient with the process. I was not very hard on myself, as I often reminded myself how I had accumulated over 12 years of medical knowledge in my soul. Although I was believing it would take faster to cleanse and/or purify my soul with God's Word, I did not know how long it would take, so I persisted in my meditation regimen, believing that God will honor my efforts in His faithfulness, as He has taught us in the Parable of the Growing Seed (Mark 4:26-29), (more on this parable in Section 3 of this book).

Also, during those initial few months when I did not perceive any change in my soul, with the exception of meditating and emulating how the woman with the issue of blood, the Centurion, and the Gentile woman verbalized their faith aloud, I did not begin the daily habit of speaking aloud God's Word over my body. This was because I wanted God's Word to completely penetrate my entire soul and quickened my faith, that way, when I declared (i.e., spoke) it out of my mouth daily, I would truly be doing so purely from a position of unwavering faith, because I believed it, and it would come out as "rivers of living water out of me" (signifying the power of the Holy Spirit, John 7:37-39).

This is a noteworthy point because God's Word will only accomplish the desired purpose when spoken aloud out of a genuine faith (Isaiah 55:10-11). But unfortunately, some Christians are mistaken by believing that speaking God's Word aloud will just yield Godly results: NO —Rather, you have to

first believe it (i.e., the promise in God's Word) in your heart, then you would be verbalizing what you already believe. As such, you will be appropriating Scriptures such as Isaiah 55: 10-11, and Godly results will be the byproduct.

I Received My Healing Without Any Physical Evidence

After about 2 1/2 to 3 months of saturating myself with God's Word, I began to notice subtle changes in my perspective. Feelings of anxiety, fear, doubt, worry, were no longer an issue. Instead, I started to experience an indescribable sense of joy, peace, contentment, and my attention completely shifted 180 degrees from myself and the cancer, to just wanting to be in the presence of God and loving Him — It was a strange thing that was happening on the inside of me. I had never experienced anything like this before. But today, I know that what I was experiencing was the outcome of what the Lord Jesus was teaching in Matthew 6:33, when He said, "**But seek first his kingdom and his righteousness, and all these things will be given to you as well.**" So true! As we seek God first, and divert all of our efforts and energies away from ourselves and 100% towards Him, He in turn will take care of all of our needs, including the healing of diseases in our bodies.

And it is interesting how in the state of seeking and loving God with all of our mind/soul, strength, we will begin to see the manifestation of our prayers, effortlessly (Deuteronomy 4:29; Matthew 22:37; Jeremiah 29:13). Boy! If we can only learn from this, we will prevent a lot of the heartache we experience when seeking God for our needs. **God is simple and straight forward to deal with, if we just do what He says. But unfortunately, some people make it so complicated with endless "do's and don'ts", which does not impress God, Who is only after your heart and obedience, nothing else! I often say that many Christians are more religious and/or "holier" than the Lord Jesus Himself!**

Additionally, the problem many people experience today is that, they do not want to seek God wholeheartedly, and they expect quick and Godly results without taking the time to invest in a relationship with Him. Sorry, God cannot be manipulated like that, it just does not work that way in God's Kingdom! You might be able to manipulate your fellow human beings into getting "quick results", but with God, you would have to invest in a relationship with Him and grow, just like any other earthly relationship.

Noticeable Changes

As I started to notice the change in my soul, I said to myself, "Romans 12: 2 is becoming my reality."

///

I cannot describe it perfectly, and I do not know exactly how it happened. But I just remember that one day, after about 2 1/2 to 3 months of saturating myself with God's Word and meditation, I had a "knowing" that I was healed from cancer, period!

///

That was all I knew in my heart (i.e., the deepest part of my soul). I just knew it! My head was still telling me I had cancer, but I had a "knowing" that I was healed. **Today I know that, that knowing was a "spiritual revelation" that I had been healed in the spirit and in my soul.** Unlike before, that "knowing" was beyond "head knowledge", and it was accompanied by an indescribable peace and joy; and all fear, worry, anxiety, care, concern about cancer, and doubt disappeared.

There was no physical evidence to support what I was experiencing in my spirit and soul. There was still metastatic Colon cancer in my body, but by this point, it did not matter what anyone said, "I just knew it was over, I had won the battle over cancer." The doctor's report was completely irrelevant to me at this point, and I viewed it as 100% wrong. I remember telling my friend, " I am healed of cancer, but I do not know what to do next. I just know I am healed." I went on to explain to him how the Bible teaches that faith comes by hearing (also studying) the Word of God — I had experienced it practically.

The Gift of Faith

Today, I know that what happened to me was that after about 2 1/2 months of saturating my soul with God's Word, I experienced the gift of faith (1 Corinthians 12: 8-10), whereby the Holy Spirit supernaturally worked through me and strengthened me to operate in faith with absolutely no contrary emotions, such as fear, worry, anxiety, etc. When a Christian is operating in the gift of faith, contrary emotions cannot coexist concurrently. Keep in mind, this is a gift of the Holy Spirit that would flow through you, the Christian, as you prepare yourself to allow Him to work through you.

During the 8 to 10 hours I invested daily in saturating my soul with God's Word, I did not realize that I was going to experience this. I was just determined to cleanse my soul and get rid of unbelief, remember? But as I focused on God with all of my heart, soul and mind (Deuteronomy 4:29; Matthew 22:37; Jeremiah 29:13), the byproduct, result or outcome was that, I effortlessly received the gift of faith, which enabled me to receive my healing. This was such an amazing experience whereby, it was as if all "fleshy emotions", such as fear, worry, anxiety, etc, disappeared, and all I thought about was God's Word. It is hard for me to describe it. My faith was tangible— others could perceive it — I could perceive it! I was 100% single-minded, focused on God's Word, I was completely transformed!

By this point, I started asking myself, "Do I need to continue with this deadly Chemotherapy?" (more on this in Section 3 of this book). I knew I had overcome cancer "hands down", as my spirit and soul were in perfect agreement with God's Word.

My thinking had been transformed, 180 degrees, and I was 100% thinking the same thoughts as God thought of me —healed by the Stripes of Jesus!

It was the best place I had ever been in my life, as I experienced no contrary emotions to God's Word.

It Was 2 Against 1

Since God created us as tripartite beings, consisting of a mind, body and a spirit, I knew quite well that it was just a matter of time, and my physical body (i.e., the cancer cells) would succumb to the transformation that had occurred in my soul, and the physical evidence of my healing would manifest soon. **The cancer had no choice, as my spirit and soul were in perfect alignment with God's Word. Here is the illustration: My born again spirit , representing God's perfect Word and Light, and my transformed soul (i.e., 2 parts of my being/existence) were against 1 (my physical body, i.e., the cancer cells). Thus, by virtue of the majority (my spirit and soul) being against the minority (the cancer cells), I knew beyond a shadow of a doubt, that the life of God from my spirit and soul had to overcome the cancer cells, and the physical result was imminent.**

But as I would find out later on, the manifestation of my healing would be the most challenging, difficult, and scariest part of my fight, as I had to fight the lies from Satan, my "flesh", and the environment for over 5 years. Now proceed to Section 3 to learn how I overcame this most difficult part of the journey with cancer and how my physical healing manifested, in Jesus name! Take heart, you can be healed too!

LESSONS LEARNED

➢ Many times, we receive the answer to our prayers in the spiritual realm first, before we see the visible evidence;

➢ Not seeing the visible answer(s) to your prayer right away does not mean that God did not answer your prayer: Many times, there is a waiting period;

➢ Learning to overcome doubts from Satan, and the lies from your "flesh" and environment are the initial steps in you receiving your healing.

Recommended Resources For Further Studies:
Available At: www.DrRuthTanyi.org

1. How to Overcome Doubt and Receive God's Promises. 10 Life-Changing Lessons Learnt from Overcoming Metastasis Colon Cancer. By Dr Ruth Tanyi (**A 2-Set Audio CD** teaching).

2. What Are the Gifts of the Spirit? By Dr Ruth Tanyi (**A 2-Set Audio CD** teaching).

SECTION 3

WAITING FOR THE VISIBLE MANIFESTATION OF MY HEALING!

CHAPTER 16

THE MENTAL TORTURE OF WAITING

Jesus also said, "The Kingdom of God is like a farmer who scatters seed on the ground. Night and day, while he's asleep or awake, the seed sprouts and grows, but he does not understand how it happens. The earth produces the crops on its own. First a leaf blade pushes through, then the heads of wheat are formed, and finally the grain ripens. And as soon as the grain is ready, the farmer comes and harvests it with a sickle, for the harvest time has come."

(Mark 4:26-29; New Living Translation, NLT).

I had received the revelation that I was healed from cancer about 2 1/2 to 3 months into my rigorous regimen of saturating my soul with God's Word. It was no longer a "head knowledge" — it was now a reality to me — the Holy Spirit had opened my spiritual eyes, and I saw my personal healing through Christ. However, there was no physical evidence to corroborate what I had received in my spirit and soul. All of my symptoms persisted; and in fact, they became worse (more on this a little later in this chapter). What I did not quite realize was the fact that the principles in the Parable of the Growing Seed taught by the Lord Jesus, which is popularly known as the principle of Seed, Time, and Harvest (Mark 4:26-29), had to run its course in my fight with cancer.

Seed, Time, and Harvest

In the parable of the Growing Seed, the Lord teaches on how the Kingdom of God operates. Because Christians are indwelt by God's Spirit, we have the Kingdom of God living on the inside of us. From this perspective therefore, I will discuss this parable in light of our "walk" with God. In this parable (i.e., a story told in order to illustrate a moral or spiritual lesson), the Lord Jesus was using farming to illustrate a spiritual principle (see Mark 4:26-29). The Lord teaches how the farmer in this story scatters (i.e., spreads out, distributes; plants) his or her seed (**implying the Word of God**) in the ground, night and day (**implying at all times**), and the earth enables the seed to start producing crops on its own without the farmer even realizing, knowing, or understanding how it happened (**implying faith**).

Then, the scattered seed begins the process of growth and germinating its harvest; and initially, the "*...leaf blade pushes... then the heads of wheat..., and finally the grain ripens*" (**suggesting the passage of time**, which is a process). Now take a closer look at verse 29, " *...And as soon as the grain is ready, the farmer comes and harvests it with a sickle, for the harvest time has come*" (**implying the full** harvest of that seed which the farmer scattered, and through the process of time, is ready to be harvested).

Now, let us approach this parable from a spiritual perspective before I even continue. Keep in mind that often times in the Bible, the word **Seed** is used as an illustration to describe or represent the Word of God (e.g., 1 Peter 1:23; Matthew 13:1-23, Mark 4:1-20, and Luke 8:4-15; Genesis 3:15-16 [see NKJV]; etc). Thus, in this parable, the Seed represents the Word of God (i.e., referring to how applying the Word of God in our lives will reveal the way things operate in the Kingdom of God). So from a spiritual perspective therefore, below **are four major lessons** and applications we can learn from this parable.

Practical Lessons From the Parable of the Growing Seed

1. When we are studying and meditating on the Word of God, we would be scattering (i.e., planting, distributing, dispersing) God's Truths all over our souls;

The Mental Torture of Waiting

2. The Seed in our soul(s) starts to work instantly (depending on our choices), at the time it is planted, day and night, even though we do not know how (implying faith in trusting God with the process);

3. Once the Word of God (i.e., the Seed) is scattered into our souls via the practice of meditation as an example, we have to allow some time before expecting visible results. And the process from when we plant the Seed until we see visible results depends on many factors, such as, but not limited to: our relationship with God, our maturity in faith, our ability to overcome unbelief, the amount of quality and quantity time spent in the presence of God; the intentions in our hearts; etc, etc, which are all things that can affect the timing of the visible results (i.e., the full harvest).

I am aware that this notion is not very popular, because there are people who are mistaken to believe that God's timing is God's timing, period, regardless of our actions! But it is not so, and the Bible does not teach that, because our actions (i.e., obedience, acting out our faith, etc) in accordance with God's Word have a lot to do with either (a) delaying the visible manifestation of God's promises, or (b) aligning us with God's perfect timing. God is humble, and He will not force His will upon us; He will honor our choices, whether good or bad, although our bad choices hurt Him and negatively affect our relationship with Him;

4. The harvest or visible manifestation of the promises often begins in subtle but noted stages, and the full manifestation is evident in God's perfect timing. This also depends on many factors such as, but not limited to our level of faith and maturity, our motives, etc, etc.

Please keep in mind that there are some instances in the Bible whereby it may appear as if this process of Seed, Time and

Harvest, might have been bypassed, such as in cases with most of the individuals who received their healing instantaneously from the Lord. However, as discussed in preceding chapters, that was not the case. The fact that the Bible does not tell us how long some of those individuals had been waiting in order to receive their healing does not imply that they did not go through this process. God is consistent, and does not, will not, and cannot, violate or contradict His own ways as described in the Bible, such as how His Kingdom operates.

Even today, in the 21st Century, those who claim to have received their healing from the Lord instantaneously still go through this process, somehow or the other, because this is how God has designed His Kingdom to operate. For instance, if you were to ask those who have received instant healing when hands had been laid on them, they will agree that they had been believing God for the healing (i.e., planting the Seed in their souls), praying and expecting to be healed (i.e., the process of time), and finally, they received it (i.e., the harvest or the healing). And as already explained, for some individuals, the harvest (i.e., manifestation of the visible results) can happen rather quickly, while it may take longer for others. <u>Recall, it is not God who is delaying the visible manifestation. Our obedience to God's Word has a lot to do with the timing of the visible manifestation of His promises in our lives.</u> Also, as the Lord Jesus clearly taught, we receive in accordance to how we believe (Matthew 9:29), which is another major principle in God's Kingdom that we cannot avoid.

Unfortunately, to the natural person (i.e., an unbeliever), and sadly, to the carnal Christian (i.e., one who is still led by their emotions rather than by God's Spirit and His Word), the notion of believing and verbalizing to have received God's promises such as healing without any physical evidence is considered a lie! But, it is not a lie!

Because in God's Kingdom, as already described, we receive our blessings in our hearts first by faith, before we can observe it physically. In fact, the Lord Jesus Himself put this principle of Seed, Time and Harvest into practice when He cursed the fig tree with His Word (the Seed), and it instantly died (i.e., the answer), but it was the next day (i.e., a process of time), when the visible result was evident (Mark 11:12-25).

My Harvest, Longer than Expected

I had overcome the battle with the surgery and rehabilitation at home. The process of renewing my mind (i.e., changing my thinking patterns) was yielding abundant fruit in my soul and outlook; and through the Holy Spirit empowering me, I had experienced the gift of faith and received my healing in the spirit and soul. Nonetheless, the laboratory and diagnostic test results still showed no evidence of me being healed. I knew that the harvest (i.e., the visible healing of the cancer to be evident via medical testing) was imminent. But as I later found out, it would take much longer than I would have ever imagined, about 6 years, to see the visible results.

A New Battle, A "New Devil"

As Christians, it appears that after overcoming one battle, we have to fight even harder to overcome the next; hence the saying, "a new battle, a new devil." This is not implying that there are many "little devils" going around. Rather, it means that as we mature in our ability to apply God's Word and overcome trials and tribulations (i.e., battles in this life), Satan takes notice, and with each subsequent battle, he fights us even harder; but God is always available to enable us overcome again, and again, Hallelujah! For me, the next battle was that of "waiting."

The Mental Torture of Waiting

The battle in fighting any advanced cancer is usually packed with unexpected twists and turns. The diagnosis of any type of cancer is accompanied by a multitude of emotions, such as fear, worry, anxieties, etc; then the Chemotherapy poses a different type of a major hurdle to overcome. **For those who survive the initial year of cancer, waiting for the laboratory and diagnostic test results to show " no evidence of cancer," is the most frustrating, fearful, and exhausting period. In fact many cancer survivors will agree that the period of "waiting" was/is the worst. To undergo this period of waiting, the cancer patient must have the will to live and fight, prepare his or her mind to fight like a "tiger", and hang on as a "dog would hang on to a bone for dear life".** It was/is an unbelievable psychological fight, that unfortunately, many cancer patients who perceive that they do not have a purpose to live simply just "give up", and succumb to their deaths.

In my situation, the psychological trauma was no different from what many cancer patients with a dire prognosis experience, except that I was willing to live and fight, because, if you recall, "How can I let Jesus down?". As a matter of fact, my period of waiting was worse than the majority of cancer patients in similar situation. This was because I had received my healing by divine revelation just 2 1/2 to 3 months into my battle, while I still had many more prescribed Chemotherapy treatments to take.

Conversely, many cancer patients do not even begin to think they are close to being healed until years after Chemotherapy. Most Oncologists would confirm that traditionally, a patient with any type of metastasis cancer is not declared as "cancer free" until after 5 years following the diagnosis/medical treatment; although in some instances, some patients may be considered to have, "no evidence of metastasis disease" after 2 years. So that 2 year "land mark" was/is a "big deal" for many cancer patients waiting to hear those encouraging words from the Oncologist.

Nonetheless, in many cases, especially in patients with advanced cancers (i.e., metastasis cancers), there is a very high probability that the cancer will recur within 2 years, even after Chemotherapy; and even after the 2 years, there is still a very high probability of the cancer recurring within years 3 to 5. This explains why Oncologists usually prefer to wait until after 5 years to pronounce most patients as "cancer free." But in my situation, I was already believing I was "cancer free" within 2 1/2 to 3 months into my battle, which made it a very, very difficult waiting period, compared to others with similar prognosis.

A New Mental Game

What some Christians may not understand is the fact that the Holy Spirit can flow through them, at His discretion, at anytime (as He flowed through me), and supernaturally embolden them to operate in His various gifts such as faith, healings, miracles, etc, in order for them to receive whatever they are believing God for, and/or for them to intervene in the lives of others (1 Corinthians 12: 8-10). And God the Holy Spirit could flow through any spirit filled believer who is available and submissive to His promptings, in order to meet the needs of others at any given time. Thereafter, the Christian would still need to operate in faith daily, and depend on God for sustenance and for the visible manifestations of His promises. That was the case with me because after that initial supernatural empowering from the Holy Spirit, I had to "walk" by faith daily, and trust God with the visible manifestation of my healing, and it was tougher than ever to fight.

Mentally, the dynamics changed, and by the middle of Fall season 2009, it was as if I was fighting a brand new battle, except this time, I was believing God for the cancer and its damages to my entire body to leave, period. In essence, I knew that physically, according to the medical report, cancer was still in my body, but I started to believe God for complete restoration of my physical body and for a brand new immune system. It was tough!

Lies From Satan!

I started noticing that my mind was being bombarded with thoughts such as, " You will never see the physical evidence"; "It is a lie, you are not healed, it is in your mind". I was also bombarded with thoughts such as, " Who are you to be healed this fast when others are waiting for up to 5 years to believe they are healed?". It was very interesting because the fear of cancer, worry, care, etc, about the prognosis seemed to have disappeared when I received the revelation that I was healed; but then, Satan started to attack my mind with doubts. This was especially scary because physically I felt sick, and according to the Oncologist, I still had cancer in my body.

Whose Report to Believe?

Boy! This is where the "rubber meets the road" for the Christian journey—was I going to believe what my body was telling me (i.e., all of the symptoms), the Oncologist's report, or what the Word of God says, which had been confirmed in my heart?

The Bible teaches that we walk by faith, meaning, we live out our lives as Christians primarily based on what God has revealed to us in the Scriptures, and not by what our five senses are telling us (2 Corinthians 5:7). And, the Bible admonishes us that if we "walk" primarily in accordance to the flesh (i.e., our senses), it leads to death (fear, worry, anxiety, etc), but when we live by faith (i.e., what the Bible teaches), it leads to life (peace, joy, healing in our soul and bodies, etc) (Romans 8:6-10). So again, in this new battle, I had to decide whose report I was going to believe: God's Report or what Satan was attacking my mind with, and/or what my diseased body and laboratory reports were showing?

Thus, by the middle of Fall season 2009, I realized that I had entered a new season, with a new battle (waiting for the visible results), and I needed new tools to fight that battle. I was surprised that shortly after I had operated in the gift of faith and received my healing, thoughts of doubts started to resurface. **But this is exactly how Satan operates: planting doubtful thoughts in our minds** so that we would question God's promises, become fearful and paralyzed, thus hindering the manifestation of God's blessings in our lives. And in spite of my diligent efforts appropriating the Word of God, I got sicker. During a particular Chemotherapy treatment session around this time, even before leaving the Cancer Center, I got violently ill: trembling, vomiting, drooling, and there was shooting pain all over my body. The nurse then decided to reduce the continuous infusion rate to the lowest level, and sent me home.

My Symptoms Became Worse

I arrived home still feeling sick. Some level of mild to moderate sickness was expected following Chemotherapy treatments for up to 10 to 14 days, at times. However, my symptoms were out of the ordinary, severe; there was something different about this particular treatment. I went to bed feeling the most miserable I had ever felt, and upon awakening, it was as if my mouth was "shut tight". There was severe pain and tingling all over my body. Just being exposed to cold temperatures caused severe, unbelievable pain all over my body. I could not even drink fluids or eat. It was as if I became allergic to fluids. The nurse later came to my home and discontinued the 72 hours continuous Chemotherapy infusion without me even getting the maximum dosage. Thereafter, the Oncologist was concerned and decided to run some blood tests.

I Went Into Liver Failure

There are various components in assessing damage to the liver. Usually, when there is damage to the liver, an enzyme called Alanine Aminotransferase (ALT), which is specifically made by the liver cells will leak into the bloodstream, creating an elevated abnormal blood test level when measured in the laboratory. Normally, depending on the laboratory used, normal range for ALT is between 6-29 units per liter (U/L). But in my case, my ALT blood test level was triple digits, over 350 units per liter (U/L), positive for liver failure. Besides the ALT, other blood tests used to detect liver failure include evaluation of other enzymes such as Aspartate

Aminotransferase (AST), (normal range between 10-35 U/L) ; Alkaline Phosphatase (ALP), (normal range between 33-130 U/L); Bilirubin total, (normal range between 0.2-1.2 Mg/dL, etc. In my situation, with the exception of my total Bilirubin, the AST and ALP were in the triple digits as well.

A Paradox, on the Surface

All of the above liver studies showed I was in liver failure. As Christians, sooner or later, we will encounter this seemingly intriguing paradox, whereby, we are standing in faith in accordance with God's Word, praying, and doing everything right to the best of our ability, and we know beyond a shadow of doubt that God is with us; but then, our disease, circumstance or crisis gets worse, instead of better. Personally, I call this the "Daniel Syndrome". The Old Testament prophet Daniel was doing everything right before God, yet the manifestation of the answers to his prayers were delayed, as the "king of Persia" (a personification of Satan himself), fought him for about 3 weeks. This kind of scenario can be very frustrating to the Christian, but it happens frequently.

This is not implying that Satan is stronger, and/or that he can stop our prayers from manifesting—NO! God is stronger than Satan! However, Satan can work through people, thereby causing a delayed response to our prayers, especially if certain individuals are involved in God's manifestation of the promise; because God cannot force His will upon people, He has to work through people who will obey Him. Of course, I am not implying that every delayed response to our prayer is due to Satan's influence, NO: because at times, multiple factors, such as praying outside of God's will, unrepentant sin, wrong timing etc, can be in operation, thus causing a delayed response to the visible manifestation of God's promises in our lives.

As I contemplated on how worse my health was becoming in spite of my diligence and consistency in "sitting at the feet of Jesus," saturating my soul with His Word, I had no other choice but to wholeheartedly rely on God's faithfulness to reward my faith. I

The Mental Torture of Waiting

started wondering if Satan was behind the worsening of my health, just like he was behind the delayed answer to the prophet Daniel's prayer? I also wondered if things would get worse before they actually improved. I have heard some ministers say that, when we are believing God for a promise and our problem(s) begin to get worse, it is probably a good indication that the manifestation is very imminent, but Satan might be fighting harder to prevent it from happening. I actually believe there is some truth in this. **In my case, medically speaking, "things" appeared almost hopeless on the surface. Nonetheless, I knew that as a child of God— nothing can, and will ever be hopeless in my life; thus, that thought encouraged me!**

Proceed now to the next chapter and find out how, "What Man considers as impossible, is possible with God!".

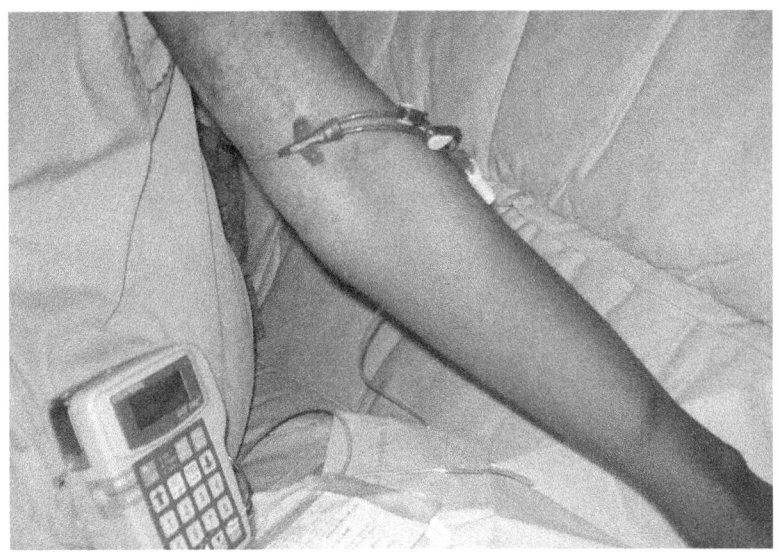

72 hours continuous home infusion chemotherapy bag

LESSONS LEARNED

- ➢ Regardless of what we, as Christians, are believing God for, there is a period of "waiting" for the visible manifestation of the promise. During this period, our actions such as, but not limited to obedience, display of faith, etc, can negatively or positively affect the length of time we wait for the manifestation;

- ➢ No matter how dire our circumstances may appear on the surface, the Bible admonishes us to always choose God's report (i.e., His solutions/promises in the Bible), above all others — the choice is ours.

Recommended Resources For Further Studies:

Available At: www.DrRuthTanyi.org

Did God Really Say that? How to Overcome Doubt and Receive God's Promises: 10 Life-Changing Lessons Learned from Overcoming Metastasis Colon Cancer: **A 2-Set Audio CD Teaching.** By Dr Ruth Tanyi.

CHAPTER 17

ONLY JESUS!

...but those who hope in the LORD will renew their strength. They will soar on wings like eagles; they will run and not grow weary, they will walk and not be faint.

(Isaiah 40:31; New International Version, NIV).

For the person whose hope is in Christ Jesus, there is never, and there will never be a hopeless situation in this life and in all eternity. *I often say it like this: for a Christian undergoing adversities, it is a win-win situation because if he or she dies prematurely, well, it is a gain, because he or she will go and be with the Lord, which is far better* (Philippians 1:20-21). However, if the Christian overcomes the adversity, then, it makes for an awesome testimony to glorify God and "shut the devil up"— indeed, it is a win-win situation, always! Such was the case with me when the Oncologist perceived that my situation was dire, due to the liver failure. But I knew that with God, there was/is always hope!

A Hopeless Situation, Medically

After all of the blood tests were drawn, I returned to the Oncologist's office for the results. As the Oncologist examined my liver enzymes, he looked at me, and with a very, very sad countenance, said something I will never forget, " We have to stop Chemotherapy, your body is failing the treatment, you are in liver failure." He then advised me to go home, and follow up with him in about 1 week or so for further examination. **At this point, my body had started to reject Chemotherapy: my organs were shutting down, and cancer was still in my body, and now major organs were being affected.** The Oncologist was very concerned, so he scheduled frequent visits to see me. He noted that some liver damage is possible as a result from Chemotherapy treatments but my situation was very dire, and he was unsure whether or not I could continue the treatment regimen, because it would require several weeks to months for the liver to recover, if it even does.

I Was Not Afraid

For some reason, which I still cannot explain today, that news from the Oncologist did not scare me. I was not afraid, whatsoever! It was as if God had prepared me to handle this bad news. Today, I know that it was all of the countless hours I had spent in the presence of the Lord, "giving healing to others" (more on this later), speaking aloud faith filled words and Scriptures over my body, etc, that anchored my soul with peace. Even though I heard very well what the Oncologist said, his words did not penetrate my soul—I was unfazed!

I got home from the Cancer Center that afternoon and in a very nonchalant manner, explained everything to my friend. He was not concerned either — we had consecrated ourselves into a prayer of agreement with the Lord; I had been faithful in doing my part, meaning, saturating my soul with God's Words and acting in faith, there was nothing else for me to do, except to continue to trust God! While waiting for my next appointment, I got sicker with constant abdominal pain, persistent nausea and vomiting, extreme fatigue, weight loss, etc. Getting out of bed was extremely difficult, and I needed much help with performing basic grooming and with ambulating.

Refusing to Focus on the Symptoms; Choosing to "Fix" my Eyes on Jesus, The Healer!

As I was experiencing the abdominal symptoms, etc, associated with the liver failure, I started to also experience extreme clotting of blood vessels with just the slightest exposure to cold. Just opening the refrigerator would cause extreme sharp, burning and shooting pain all over my entire body, and my fingers would turn almost white and then blue, very painful.

During this period or so while I was waiting to revisit the Oncologist, I would get up every morning and tell myself, " I am healed, so I will live this day by faith, and not by what my symptoms are telling me." I refused to focus on the symptoms; rather, I chose to fix my eyes on Jesus, the Healer. Boy! It was not easy.

There was nothing else for me to do, except to continue doing what I had been doing. **I reminded myself daily to ignore the symptoms. I would say things such as, "Jesus, You Know about these symptoms. You will not allow me to suffer beyond what I can bear, You have already healed me, I have received my healing, I won't be afraid, thank you God!."** I carried on with my daily regimen of studying the Word of God, meditating on Scriptures and speaking faith filled Words over my body. Because of the extreme fatigue I was experiencing by this point, I could not sit upright to open the Bible (I was mostly bedbound). Good thing I had memorized all of those Scriptures listed in chapter 14 in this book, and I knew all of the healing stories in the ministry of the Lord by heart. So on several occasions, I would just close my eyes and meditate on the Scriptures I knew by heart. **Additionally, I continued to visualize and imagine myself in the presence of the Lord Jesus, as He was laying His hands on me.** Doing all of these took my mind away from myself, and I stayed focused on Jesus.

Only Jesus!

It is interesting how during this time when I was sent home to essentially "die", since there was nothing else the Oncologist could do, except to wait and see, I did not even consider to engage in activities such as fasting. Additionally, because of extreme fatigue,

I could not even pray for up to 5 minutes, so I resorted to more meditation, visualization and imagination of being in the presence of Christ, with Him laying His hands on me.

In a way, it was a blessing in disguise because had I had enough energy to fast and pray for extended periods of time, I would have probably made the mistake that many Godly Christians make — to focus and depend more on spiritual activities such as fasting and praying for extended periods of time, calling a prayer line and asking dozens of people to bombard heaven with prayers, and even considering how they had been "holy" in serving the Lord, etc, rather than totally focusing on the Lord Jesus 100%. It is critical that we focus completely on Jesus — The Healer of All Healers, and completely avoid to depend on our "religious self-righteous works" as a way to receive healing or any other promise from God—self righteousness will pose a major barrier to you receiving your healing.

//

The amazing thing was that, my meditation, visualization and imagination were all forms of prayer, in faith. And the best thing was that, this form of prayer enabled me to take my eyes off of myself, and to fix it solely onto Jesus, my Healer.

//

As I was undergoing intense suffering, I started wondering, and I asked myself, "What was the worst thing that could happen?". The answer was straight forward — death! But then, when I thought about death, I realized that, I needed to have a better Scriptural perspective about heaven; thus, with every little energy I had, I started meditating on Scriptures on heaven.

By this point, I had mastered the art of meditation, and within just a few days, my soul was being saturated with the beautiful imagery and scenery of heaven, such as streets of gold, the pearly gate, the perfect worship and music, etc (see Revelation chapters 21 and 22). As such, I started desiring to be with the Lord, and all concerns about dying disappeared. Whoa! Amazing, what meditating on the Word of God will do to our souls; no wonder, the Bible admonishes us to meditate on the Word daily.

The Bible teaches that the moment we die, we go straight into the presence of our Lord and Savior, Jesus Christ (2 Corinthians 5:8; Acts 7:54-60; Luke 23:43), so I had reached a place where it was okay with me if I died. I figured that, I had fought a good faith fight in accordance with God's Word, and I believed God was pleased with my efforts in Christ, thus there was nothing else for me to do. With that mind set, when it came time for me to return to the Oncologist office, I had no concerns. I had surrendered to the situation, and was ready to die and meet the Lord, if that was His will.

Another Miracle

I arrived at the Cancer Center and my blood was drawn, and after a brief wait, I was called to see the doctor. I will never forget the look on the faces of the doctor and the nurse. The doctor had been discussing the blood test results with the nurse, and they both turned and looked at me with expressions of surprise or shock! I did not know what to think, I just sat quiet. Then the doctor looked at me and said, "Your blood test came back normal." I asked him to explain further, and he said, "Your liver enzymes are back to normal." He then looked at me and asked, "What happened?" And the nurse said, "This is a miracle!".

The doctor later explained that he was shocked by how fast **the liver enzymes returned to normal levels within a week with no medical intervention.** As I heard his comments and those of the nurse, I was emotionless, with a "blank stare". Then I softly uttered, "Jesus did it!" They sat quiet, and the nurse nodded her head to indicate, yep! Then I thanked the Lord for that miracle.

After my liver enzymes returned to normal, all of the

associating symptoms stopped. But, after the investigation of my other symptoms, it was noted that I had developed Raynaud's disease. This disease is characterized by narrowing of arteries in the body with subsequent decrease of blood flow to various areas such as the fingers and toes. Then, when these body parts are exposed to cold temperatures, there is numbness, pain, tingling, changes of color of the digits, etc, exactly what I was experiencing. It was a miserable condition, and I was advised to wear protective clothing and gloves when exposed to anything cold, such as the refrigerator, touching a glass of cold drink, etc.

Things did not make sense, at least on the surface! I received one miracle, then another disease? It was one battle after another; yet, the biggest battle, the cancer, was still in my body, the Oncologist believed. The Oncologist had decided to put Chemotherapy on hold for a few weeks, as he wanted to recheck my liver enzymes to be certain they were remaining within normal levels. After a few weeks, blood tests were rechecked and everything was still normal; thus he decided he wanted to try another dose of Chemotherapy (adjusted). And, still being uncertain about a sense of direction from my spirit, I agreed with his plan.

It Was A Mistake

It was around early December of 2009, and I proceeded to receive yet another Chemotherapy treatment. Towards the beginning of that treatment, it appeared as if "everything was caving in" on me —every organ of my body was affected and I was debilitated. I started trembling, vomiting; I experienced sharp headaches, vertigo, drowsiness, my mind became foggy, there was severe tingling in my extremities. I was not tolerating the treatment. I started to groan, in discomfort. The nurse called for help, and another nurse came over to help, and they injected "something" into my IV line (I was later told they were giving me other drugs to combat the reactions I was experiencing).

Thereafter, the nurses immediately stopped the infusion to

give me a break, and after a short while, they restarted it at a very reduced dosage/rate. The nurses began to be concerned that I would not finish the treatment session. During this incident, the nurse had to stop and restart the treatment several times, it was miserable. I really do not remember the details because I was so foggy and drowsy. But in that drowsy state, I saw my friend and some nurses wheeling me into the car. We got home close to 930PM, about 2 hours later than usual. The 72 hour infusion was in place, at the very lowest dosage possible. By this point, I was not even getting the full dosage of the prescribed Chemotherapy.

I Chose Death

That night was the worst night I had experienced. I was so miserable, restless, and sicker than ever before. And in that condition, I decided that being with the Lord was better than living in such profound misery and suffering. I did not want to go through such suffering all night. **So I started asking the Lord to take me. I said something like this, "Lord, I am sorry that I am giving up. I don't want to fight anymore, I am tired. Please forgive me. I want to die."** I continued, "Please Lord, don't let me go through this tonight, I can't handle this anymore, I am sorry, I am ready to die." I felt so bad giving up, thus I kept asking God to forgive me, because if you recall, the Lord had spoken to my heart these words, "spiritual warfare", and I had been determined not to "let Jesus down", remember? But now, I could not continue the fight, so I felt like I was "failing" the Lord, thus I asked for His forgiveness.

For the Christian, death is far better than living in constant agonizing pain and suffering. And many people do not realize that the human will to live, in spite of adversity, is paramount to survival. **Once a person gives up his or her will to fight, death is usually imminent, sooner or later. Although, in His love, compassion and grace, God will provide multiple opportunities for the person to choose life (Deuteronomy 30:19) in order to prevent a premature death, because it is always God's will that we, His children, live a full long life.** However, if the individual persists to choose death,

God, in His love, will honor the individual's choice. This is a critical point because God has given us a Free Will, and He will not violate our will and force His will upon us; He will respect our choices, even though they may not be best for us.

In my situation, I truly believed I was going to die that night. So I wrote a note to family members and placed it on my night stand. The interesting thing was that when I made that decision to die, my symptoms started to diminish; I do not understand how this works! I went to bed that night and, to my amazement, I awoke in the morning. And for a brief moment, I was not sure if I was in heaven or earth. I looked around and realized I was in my bedroom, still alive. In fact, I had had the best sleep ever, and I experienced no pain and suffering during the night—I had slept through the night with no problems whatsoever, amazing! Once I realized I did not die, I figured that I needed to live, and not die; hence I felt revitalized to fight and kept my promise to the Lord.

Until today, I really do not understand why I did not die that night. The only explanation I can offer is that, I had already been healed in the spirit and soul, and since, " ... **God's gifts and his call are irrevocable**" (Romans 11:29), I reasoned that in God's nature of faithfulness, my visible healing had to manifest, one way or another, period! After 72 hours, the nurse came and disconnected the continuous infusion, and it was time to go back to the Cancer Center for almost 1 week of more shots. I received the first shot and came home. But, after about 30 minutes of getting home from receiving that shot, I started to experience unbelievably intense itching all over my body. Within just a few minutes, there was diffuse rash "spreading" all over my body, and my entire body was turning red. Then my fingers and legs started to swell, then there was pain all over. This was happening so fast; I started to scream, "I am dying, help, Jesus help". As I was screaming, my voice started to become faint, and I started to experience difficulty breathing. My throat was feeling as if there was a huge lump there, preventing me from talking. I knew I was dying, I felt faint, but before I fainted, I reached to my phone and called the emergency number for the

Only Jesus!

Cancer Center.

Still Another Miracle

As I started to describe to the nurse on the phone what was happening, as if by a supernatural divine appointment, my friend was just walking into my home. Then in that exact moment, I started to fall on the floor with the phone still in my hand. He got on the phone, and the Oncology nurse advised him to immediately administer emergency medications I had, and he did. All these were happening very fast, within a timeframe of less than 5 minutes. Then, within minutes of receiving the emergency medications, my breathing started to improve. But the intense itching, redness, and pain continued for another hour or so. Shortly thereafter, he took me to the Cancer Center and I was told I had experienced an anaphylactic reaction to the Chemotherapy shot, and had my friend not come into my house at that exact moment, it would have led to a full blown Anaphylactic Shock, and I would have died.

An Anaphylactic shock is an extreme life-threatening medical emergency whereby in the presence of a potent allergen, the individual's immune system releases chemicals that would suddenly flood the entire body, causing significant drop in blood pressure, narrowing of breathing airways, with subsequent sensation of lump in the throat, swollen tongue, lips, wheezing, etc, which were all symptoms I was experiencing. Without immediate medical or divine intervention, death would ensue in just minutes. Or, if a person survives the shock, major complications to different bodily organs may ensue.

Friend, had God not intervened by placing my friend at my home at the perfect time, right when I was beginning to fall (i.e., fainting), I would have gotten into a shock and died, because there was no one home with me, remember? Boy! God was/ is awesome! He was really rewarding my faith in visible ways, and others were actually taking notice. **Again, another miracle from God, Halleluiah**! By now, it was obvious that the Chemotherapy was threatening to kill me more than the cancer itself, and I started to sense that I would not be able to continue with the treatment.

Proceed to the next chapter to learn how God's Word provided the fortitude I needed to endure the wait, and how I started to use my mouth as a weapon to release healing into my body.

LESSONS LEARNED

- We should never lose sight of the fact that our Godly endeavors such as prayer, fasting, serving God, etc, are not reasons why we will receive our healing from God — Our focus should be on Jesus only;

- At times, in the life of a believer, things might get worse before they actually improve. Hence, we should not use our circumstances or problems to decide whether or not God is with us, because He is always present, regardless of how "things" may appear on the surface.

CHAPTER 18

ENDURANCE THROUGH THE SCRIPTURES WHILE WAITING

For the word of God is alive and active. Sharper than any double-edged sword, it penetrates even to dividing soul and spirit, joints and marrow; it judges the thoughts and attitudes of the heart.

(Hebrews 4:12; New International Version, NIV).

I believe the majority of Christians would agree that it takes faith to wait for God's promises to manifest in their lives. Many times, the waiting period can be good for us, as it can strengthen our faith and help us to stay focused on God, if we choose to. For me, I had absolutely no choice but to wait! Again, I had to rely on God's Word to provide the fortitude while waiting. Hebrews 4:12 is one of my favorite Scriptures about the power in God's Word — as it teaches, the Word of God is alive— it energizes and strengthens us, if we choose to depend on it.

While I continued to meditate on all of the other Scriptures discussed in the previous chapters, **I selected 5 additional Scriptures** which I meditated on daily, as part of my meditation regimen. These Scriptures provided the supernatural strength I needed to endure the wait.

Endurance Through the Scriptures

Below are the 5 Scriptures and their significance: ***Please note:*** *All emphasis on Scriptures are author's.*

❖ **1 Corinthians 10:13:**

No temptation has overtaken you except what is common to mankind. And God is faithful; he will not let you be tempted beyond what you can bear. But when you are tempted, he will also provide a way out so that you can endure it.

Significance: This Scripture helped to reassure me that there was "nothing new under the sun". Others had gone through what I was going through and God's grace was/is always available to enable me to overcome the temptations to doubting God's Word.

❖ **2 Corinthians 10:5:**

We demolish arguments and every pretension that sets itself up against the knowledge of God, and we take captive every thought to make it obedient to Christ.

Significance: This Scripture really admonished me to evaluate every thought that came to my mind— if it was not consistent with God's Word, then I knew immediately it was either the cancer symptoms or Satan attempting to lie to me. This Scripture was like a "gauge" that helped me to continuously assess my thinking processes, thus I learnt to readily recognize when contrary thoughts about seeing the visible manifestation of the healing were attempting to come to my mind.

❖ **Isaiah 40:31:**

But those who wait on the LORD Shall renew their strength; They shall mount up with wings like eagles, They shall run and not be weary, They shall walk and not faint.

Significance: This Scripture encouraged me that waiting has significant benefits. And as I waited patiently for the visible evidence of my healing while abiding (focusing, relying) on Christ for strength, and at the same time studying and meditating on God's Word, I remained hopeful. That hope was an anchor that fueled me with the necessary strength to wait.

- ❖ **Galatians 6:7-8:**

Do not be deceived: God cannot be mocked. A man reaps what he sows. Whoever sows to please their flesh, from the flesh will reap destruction; whoever sows to please the Spirit, from the Spirit will reap eternal life.

Significance: This Scripture encouraged me that God will honor my time of waiting while focused on Him, as I continued to sow spiritual seeds (i.e., studying, meditating, prayer), into my soul. I was encouraged that one way or the other, and someday, I would reap Godly results.

- ❖ **Galatians 5:16-18:**

So I say, walk by the Spirit, and you will not gratify the desires of the flesh. For the flesh desires what is contrary to the Spirit, and the Spirit what is contrary to the flesh. They are in conflict with each other, so that you are not to do whatever you want. But if you are led by the Spirit, you are not under the law.

Significance: This Scripture reminded me to be faithful in walking by faith rather than minding what the doctor's report and my bodily symptoms were telling me. It also reassured me that as I walked by faith (i.e., focusing more on God's Truth that I was healed), it would be difficult for my bodily symptoms to rule over my thoughts.

The above Scriptures fueled me with a new purpose to "wait" on the Lord for the visible evidence of my healing. Besides adding the above Scriptures to my daily regimen of studying and meditating on God's Word, I started to make a deliberate effort to set aside about 30 to 45 minutes in the morning, and again at night, to speak aloud God's Word over every part of my body.

Using My Mouth as a Weapon

While waiting for the visible evidence of my healing, I started to:

1. Speak aloud Scriptures all over my body;
2. Release healing into my body by faith in the name of Jesus;
3. Command healing to manifest by faith in the name of Jesus; and
4. Minister healing to others.

Let us now examine the details of how I did these.

1. Speaking God's Words Over My Body

Keep in mind that by this point in my journey, I had 100% confidence that I was healed from the cancer without any physical evidence. Thus, because I truly believed it in my heart, every Word of God that came out of my mouth was purely from a position of faith —I believed 100%, beyond a shadow of doubt, that those words will come to pass, period! In keeping with my morning and evening routine, I faithfully spoke aloud all of the Scriptures cited above, in addition to those listed in chapter 14 of this book, all over my body. This habit went on intensely during the initial 2 years of waiting, and continued until the sixth year of my fight and even today; although the intensity, duration and frequency have significantly reduced. But it is a habit I still rely on to overcome battles in other areas of my life.

2. Releasing Healing into My Body by Faith, in Jesus Name

Besides speaking God's Word over my body, I would, by faith, release healing all over my body by verbalizing what

I was expecting to see manifest. Recall, as children of God, we have power and authority in the name of Jesus to bring into existence things that are not seen in the physical (Romans 4:17-18), because there is power in our words when spoken by faith in the name of Jesus. Our words can either release life, such as joy, peace, strength, healing, etc (John 6:63; Galatians 5:22-23) into our bodies and circumstances, or death, such as fear, anxieties, worry, etc (Proverbs 18:21).

Healing Out of My Mouth

The Bible teaches that our words can release healing and life into our circumstances (Proverbs 15:4). From this biblical perspective therefore, I used my words and released **healing all over my body by saying something like this, " I release the healing power of Jesus all over my body, right now, and my body is receiving it, thank you God". I would also say, "My cells are responding to the Word of God, in Jesus Name, I am healed".** I often stated, " I believe, and I am declaring that cancer cells are dead in my body, and they have left, never to return, in Jesus name"; " My immune system has been fully restored, functioning perfectly, healthier and stronger, and I believe in these things, in Jesus name". I would also speak to the symptoms by saying, "Symptoms, you have no power or authority over me, so I command you to respond, right now, to the Word of God and STOP", etc, etc.

3. Commanding Healing to Manifest, in Jesus Name

//

Additionally, on a daily basis, in keeping with my studying and meditation regimen, I would speak to every organ of my body, calling each one by name, and release life into it, and then I would command healing to manifest, in the name of Jesus.

//

I would say something like this, *"Colon, in the name of Jesus, I command perfect healing to all of your cells, and I curse cancer, never to return anymore, thank you God, I receive the answer"*. I would also say something like this, *"Immune system, in the name of Jesus, I command you to produce and multiply healthy antibodies, right now, to nourish the cells of my body and produce healing, in Jesus name, thank you God, it is done, Amen!"*. A lot of times, I would do all of these (commanding healing to manifest in my body in the name of Jesus) upon awakening, first thing in the morning, before I even get out of bed.

I would remind my body that at the name of Jesus every knee shall bow (Philippians 2:10-11) and I would say something like this, " Cancer, you are a name, and My Healer says you must bow down to Him, so I command you to bow down and leave my body, now, in the name of Jesus, leave!" I would also talk to cancer and say, "Cancer, I am not afraid of you, because my God who lives on the inside of me is greater than you, so you are no threat to me" (1 John 4:4).

I would go on like this to speak to every organ of my body, calling its name, commanding the organs to function perfectly, speaking to the cells and arteries to obey my words, in the name of Jesus. And after each prayer as mentioned above, I will end by thanking God in advance, that it was done! I reminded God that I was believing in His Words which are flawless (Proverbs 30: 5). Even though God already knew my heart, it was important for me to still verbalize (i.e., remind Him of His promises) that I was in agreement with Him, because He has told us that He is bound by His Word (Psalm 89:34; Psalm 138:2). Which meant the manifestation of my healing was imminent because God is faithful and consistent 100%.

Some of you may find it weird to speak to your body, but guess what? Jesus teaches that we should do so. The Gospels recorded that after the Lord Jesus had cursed the fig tree and it withered the next day, His disciples were shocked, and then He used that as an opportunity to teach them about the prayer of faith and speaking faith filled words over our problems, *"Have faith in God," Jesus answered. "Truly I tell you, if anyone says to* **this mountain***, 'Go, throw yourself into the sea,' and does not doubt in their heart but believes that what they say will happen, it will be done for them..."* (Mark 11: 22-26), emphasis author's. The "mountain" the Lord is referring to here is not a physical mountain, but rather, it represents our daily problems, trials, tribulations, etc.

Speaking Directly to the Disease By Faith in Jesus Name

The Lord has set a precedence for us to speak directly to our problems, by calling the exact problem by its name, in His name. At times, some Godly Christians make the mistake of not appropriating their inherited authority in the name of Jesus to speak directly to their problems. **God already knows our problems — we do not need to chronically remind Him — rather, there are times when we are to appropriate our authority in the name of Jesus, act in faith, and directly speak to our "mountain" (i.e., our problems) and expect results.** Unfortunately, some Christians do not have a revelation about their authority in Christ, and/or how to use that authority; as such, they waste so much time begging God for help, rather than using their authority. God has already told us to use the power and authority in the name of Jesus and speak directly to the problem (more on this in Section 4 of this book).

Additionally, medical science supports this notion which was already laid down by the Lord as noted in Mark 11: 22-26, that our bodies will respond to stimuli from the environment. Thus, when you speak directly to an organ of your body and command it to be healed in the name of Jesus, the cells and other organ tissues will respond to that command. Besides, Jesus Christ, in His Deity as God, created your body anyway (Colossians 1: 15-23), and He has Absolute

Sovereignty over His creation, right? <u>Thus, your body will respond to the name of Jesus, in faith.</u> This notion of speaking to your "mountain" directly is powerful, and it works! **But remember, on your own ability, you cannot command even a fly to die, but in the name of Jesus, standing in faith, nothing is impossible!**

4. Ministering Healing to Others

Sometime in December 2009, as I arrived at the Cancer Center for another treatment, I made a conscious decision to start "giving healing away to others" (i.e., laying hands on anyone who wanted me to; praying for healing for others, etc). Remember, I mentioned earlier how during one of my earlier visits to the Cancer Center, the Lord had placed the desire in my heart for me to start ministering healing to the other cancer patients there, I hope you recall this? I had already started to do this in the last few months before December of 2009; but this time however, I started asking more patients at the Cancer Center if they wanted me to pray for them. Everyone I approached said yes; thus, **I would lay hands on some of them and pray for their healing. Some of them even gave me their contact information, and on off Chemotherapy days, I met with them and discussed the Lord, healing, the revelation about Jesus being their Healer, and I would pray with them.**

It was amazing how I started to look forward to going to the Cancer Center just to pray for some of them. This decision to "give healing away to others" made a significant difference in my healing. It was as if I was "walking through the fire without being burnt". I was peaceful, joyful, and all thoughts of cancer left my mind during those days when I ministered healing to others — My focus shifted from myself onto others.

//

Today, I now know that this is a powerful way to receive your own healing, based on the biblical principle that every kind [Seed] will produce according to its kind (Genesis 1:24), and the other biblical principle that we reap exactly what we sow [same kind of Seed planted is what is reaped or harvested]

(Galatians 6:7).

//

In the natural, this principle is very easy to understand. As an example, if you plant tomato seeds, you will in turn reap tomatoes, right? A tomato seed cannot germinate apples, you get the point, right? In the spiritual realm, this principle is equally applicable, such as it was in my case. I wanted to see the visible evidence of my healing, so I ministered healing to others—same kind of seed. Much more, when we help others even when we are in need ourselves, God will be certain that He takes care of us. Here is how Proverbs 11 puts it, *"The generous will prosper; those who refresh others will themselves be refreshed"* (v. 25), (emphasis author's).

It was now around early Winter of 2010. I made it through 2009! It was a new year! I was still alive! As much as I was steadfast in standing on God's Word and walking by faith, I still felt sick daily because I had experienced multiple organ failures, it was getting worse. Hence, I was feeling very confident that I would not continue with any medical intervention.

Multiple Organ Failures and Subsequent Diseases

The Raynard's Disease had gotten worse, to the point that I was wearing protective gloves most of the day, almost every day. I had also developed Polyneuropathy, a condition whereby multiple peripheral nerves become damaged, causing tingling pain, discomfort and even difficulty walking, etc. **Everything was getting worse; yet, there were no visible signs of being healed from the major disease: The cancer**. I had been diagnosed with severe Irritable

Bowel Syndrome (IBS), a disorder that affects the large intestine, with subsequent cramping, abdominal pain, bloating, gas, diarrhea and/or constipation. IBS is a chronic condition with long term treatment, so I was prescribed several drugs to take. Later on, I was diagnosed with premature infertility, and prescribed multiple drugs. The doctors feared that the premature infertility might lead to severe long term medical problems. I also suffered from Leukopenia (chronically dangerously low White Blood Cell count) and Absolute Neutropenia. Neutropenia is a condition with abnormally low levels of Neutrophils. Neutrophils are a type of White Blood Cell important in fighting infections — particularly bacterial infections. As a result of all these, I was advised to be on reverse isolation (meaning, protecting myself from others' germs) because my immune system was damaged; my body could not protect itself against germs.

In spite of my worsening health by this point, I attempted to continue with my daily routine of studying and meditating on God's Word. Then it was around Winter Quarter of 2010, time for me to officially begin my academic preparation to become a Minister. By this time as well, I was already taking correspondence courses from Charis Bible College out in Colorado, and I had already been accepted at Loma Linda University School of Religion (their Non Seventh Day Adventist (SDA) Program) to begin my Master's Degree in Ministry. It was the day of my first New Testament course. I was very excited and looking forward to attending class to honor my calling as a Minister. But there was a problem: I had just had another Chemotherapy treatment, and I was hooked up to the 72 hour Chemotherapy continuous infusion.

God Spoke Through His Miracle

I was advised not to leave the house except if necessary, if I was able. Plus, I was experiencing the paralyzing side effects from Chemotherapy, and I was very sick from the other diseases I was suffering from by this point. I had not eaten in about 5 days; I was exhausted. I was experiencing constant nausea. In my determination to attend class, I gave myself an anti nausea medication rectally because I could not swallow any liquids or eat. I had severe and painful tingling all over my body, mouth, fingers — it was horrible. Yet, I wanted to attend class. I was praying to God for energy.

Class was at 6pm, but then around 3pm, on the same day, I started to experience a paralyzing fatigue and unbelievable drooling and spitting, with foul odor. And I looked at myself in that condition and said, "There is no way I am going to class in this manner." My friend knew it was my first day to attend school. So around 4pm, he came to check on me, and I told him I would not go to class. In spite of my best efforts, I had succumbed to the paralyzing side effects of Chemotherapy. I was defeated, and I accepted it, so I refused to leave the house. As such, I started experiencing thoughts of doubts about everything, including my ability to trust God for the visible evidence of my healing — it was scary.

Then, my friend looked at me straight in the eyes and said, "Don't you tell me you will not go to your first class to honor God! You have to go, period!". I then looked at him and said, " Look at me, all the spitting, it smells, it is disgusting to be around me, much more sit in a class room." He persisted and said 5 words that changed everything. He simply said, **"Just go and honor God."** I paused for a few minutes to evaluate what he had just said. Then I asked him, "What do you mean by that?". He said, " *If it is God who has called you into Ministry, then He will sustain you through the 4 hour session while in class."* The moment he said that, it was as if something on the inside of me rose up (I now know that, that was the power of the Holy Spirit quickening me). And I said to him, "Okay then, I will trust God and go to class, regardless of how disgusting I appeared."

Overcoming The Doubts

With that boldness that rose from within me, I reminded myself that the only way to deal with the spirit of doubt that was coming at me was to go to class, by faith, regardless. So by faith, I decided I would drive myself to school. Keep in mind, I was not supposed to be driving during treatments. But I was determined to act on my faith. Being that it was the Winter season, I dressed in heavy winter clothing to disguise the continuous infusion and my IV tubing. I got into my vehicle, and continued with the spitting. Then, I prayed a simple prayer and asked God for two things: **Firstly,** I asked Him to supernaturally stop the increased salivation, drooling and spitting, as it was disgusting and unsightly for others; then **Secondly**, I asked Him for energy to sit upright in class for 4 hours. With that prayer, by faith, I got into my vehicle and began to drive to school. It was only about a 15 minute drive, but it took me about 30 minutes or so to get there. When I arrived , it took a while just to walk upstairs to the classroom, where there were about 12 other students already seated.

A Miracle Happened!

As I took my seat, I quickly noted that the New Testament professor was also a medical practitioner like myself, he was a medical doctor. Right away, I was encouraged, as he was extremely awesome in his teaching. Then, less than 10 minutes after I sat down, I immediately noted a very dry sensation in my mouth; then, the increased salivation immediately stopped. I said to myself, "What is going on?". Then, about 20 minutes or so into the lecture, I experienced an amazing "influx of energy all over my body", and for the entire 4 hours in class, all the side effects of Chemotherapy supernaturally left my body.

Amazingly, during the break, I had enough energy and I went downstairs to the vending machines and purchased dried fruits and other snacks. And for the first time in about 5 days, I ate all of the snacks and fruits with absolutely no nausea, drooling, spitting, tingling in my mouth whatsoever. It was such a miracle, and during class, I kept thanking God underneath my breath. My first class was awesome! I enjoyed every second of it, and it was a solid confirmation to me that God had indeed called me into ministry — He wanted me to attend that class and begin my academic preparation for ministry; He answered my prayer exactly as I requested it! And most importantly, God had honored my faith, when I stepped out in my misery and trusted Him. With this noted miracle and reward of my faith, those doubtful emotions that were beginning to attack me dissipated.

Once more, I was reassured and encouraged, that God's presence can be tangible in the midst of my problems. And just like the Psalmist said, " **God is our refuge and strength, always ready to help in times of trouble. So we will not fear**" (Psalm 46:1, NLT). This Scripture has become a reality to my existence. Indeed, God is always present to help us! He was indeed with me through it all! The most interesting thing was that as I entered my home that evening after class, the increased salivation, drooling and spitting immediately started again. Boy! I learnt a big lesson not to limit God with my specific request in prayer, because He might answer it exactly as asked, as I found out in my situation. Since God's grace is sufficient for each day (Matthew 6:34), I realized that I needed to depend on His presence and miracles on a daily basis. For the rest of that evening, in spite of the return of my symptoms, I was awe struck because of God's love, compassion, and presence in my life.

Around this time as well, I was scheduled for another CT Scan and further blood tests to evaluate the cancer. By this point, I had been doing CT Scans about every 3 months to reassess the cancer. However, the CT Scan at that time was of utmost importance because of the other diseases I had been diagnosed with. Additionally, other diagnostic testing such as Intravaginal Pelvic Ultrasound was ordered because I was in premature menopause, and the previous CT Scan had suspicious spots in the pelvic area. MRI, Mammogram, etc were also ordered.

It was like a fulltime job going to and from the hospital to get these tests done. It was amazing how all of the doctors' appointments, blood and diagnostic testings kept me extremely busy. All of the testings were done, and they showed that the cancer was "unchanged," no improvement or progression from the last testing. It was time for me to make a life changing decision—stop conventional medications and trust God or continue with medications and suffer more? Go to the next chapter to find out more.

LESSONS LEARNED

- ➣ As Christians, we have inherited power and authority in the name of Jesus. Thus, by faith in the name of Jesus, we can command and expect healing to manifest in our bodies. We can also use our mouths as a "weapon" to release healing into our bodies by faith in the name of Jesus;

- ➣ Even when we are sick and dying, we can still minister healing to others because it will be God working through us. In fact, ministering healing to others while you are sick will position you to receive your own healing.

Recommended Resources For Further Studies :

Available At: www.DrRuthTanyi.org

Can I trust the Bible as God's Word? How do I Know? What Is the Evidence? By Dr Ruth Tanyi.

CHAPTER 19

No More Medications!

My son, pay attention to what I say; turn your ear to my words. Do not let them out of your sight, keep them within your heart; for they are life to those who find them and health to one's whole body.

(Proverbs 4:20-22; New International Version, NIV).

I want to begin this chapter by clarifying that taking conventional medications does not make a person a weak Christian. Each of us as believers, are at a different "place" in regards to our faith walk with the Lord. So do not feel like you are less of a Christian if you take prescription medications to manage a disease —absolutely Not! **However, in my situation, I had continued Chemotherapy even after I received the revelation that I was healed from the cancer. Ever since then, I had been seeking God's direction regarding when to stop taking medications.** Well, that time came when I finally believed in my heart it was time to stop medication therapy, period! As noted in the Scripture above (Proverbs 4:20-22), God's Word is medicine, without any side effects, as I have stated before. Thus, after suffering from all the horrible side effects from conventional medications, it was an easier decision for me.

Finally, I Refused to Take Prescribed Medications

At the time I was diagnosed with all of the diseases discussed in the preceding chapters, I was prescribed over 5 different medications to manage each of these problems. At this time as well, even though I had not received the optimal prescribed Chemotherapy regimen, I had matured in my faith "walk", and I had peace with my decision. It was time to stop the medications. In fact, the Oncologist was also ready for me to stop, so it worked out! It was as if God spoke to his heart at the right time, and just about when I was ready to tell him I would stop all of the medications, he himself stated it was time to stop Chemotherapy! Whoa! I was happy —I did not have to convince him about my decision. I did not hear an audible voice from God, not at all. Rather, I just had a sense of knowing in my spirit and soul that it was time to stop.

That decision to stop all medications was a significant turning point in my fight with cancer. I reasoned that, at the time I was diagnosed with cancer, I had no chronic disease but with each Chemotherapy dose, I got sicker, and sicker, and it had gotten to the point where I had suffered multiple organ failures. It was obvious, the medications were causing more problems for me. And in spite of all of the mishaps with Chemotherapy: the adjusting, stopping, restarting, reducing the dose, etc, etc, the Oncologist and the entire nursing staff actually considered me as one of their "heroes", for surviving that process. They were so encouraged by my faith and fight, they gave me an award certificate with very encouraging words (see Appendix A, back of this book).

What made me to comfortably reach that "place" of refusing prescribed medications was because I was losing the battle while on medications. Thus, I took a chance, and reasoned that "maybe it was not God's will for me to be healed with medications". **I did not know for sure, but because I experienced peace with my decision, and I was not afraid to die, I went ahead and refused further medications. Additionally, I did not want to deal with the long term side effects of depending on medications, because I believed it [medications] would be a temporary solution to a long term problem.** I know many cancer survivors (some of them my patients) who ended up with horrible permanent medical complications from all of the medication regimen they were taking during their fight with cancer. I did not want that for my life, so I chose to take a chance and trust God instead. And most significantly, with any kind of healing from God, there are no side effects to be concerned about!

The Doctors Became Concerned

On my next appointment with the various specialists I was scheduled to see for all of the various diseases I had developed, **I honestly looked at each doctor straight in the eyes and said, " I have not filled the medications prescribed. I have decided not to take any more medications." When each of them asked why? I simply said, " I will trust Jesus."** I remember that the GI doctor turned and looked at me as if I was crazy, then he said, "Well, be careful!" Then he reminded me to at least take supplements; he was the most encouraging of them all.

The Gynecologist appeared upset, and said, "Then, why did you come to see me if you won't take medications?" I responded, "Because the Oncologist said I should, and out of respect, I came". She rolled her eyes in disbelief and said, "Okay then, come back in 6 months, if you want to, for your physical exam and breast Ultrasound." I respectfully agreed , booked my 6 month appointment and left. The Primary Care doctor did not want to get involved with anything that had to do with the cancer, thus he referred me back to the Oncologist.

Later on, the Oncologist referred me to see a Psychotherapist —I suppose I was considered to be in denial and/or mentally/ emotionally unstable— But I was not! In fact, the Psychotherapist turned out to be a blessing in disguise, she was a Christian lady. I went to see her, and it was a very peaceful atmosphere. I spent about 75 minutes in her office and explained my story. She listened attentively to me and then concluded that nothing was wrong with me. Well, I knew that already! She noted that I did not have to see her again. She forwarded her report to the Oncologist and that was the end of that.

The Symptoms Persisted

It was now Spring season of 2010, and I had already stopped all medications by now; nevertheless, my symptoms did not stop, in fact, they persisted. I had to figure out a "New Normal." By now, I was able to get out of bed without assist, groom myself and even drive short distances, although there were many days I was disabled because of chronic fatigue, neuropathic pain, and just a generalized sense of not feeling well. I had lost a significant amount of weight —I did not look healthy at all.

The Oncologist recommended I should file for disability benefits, because He did not want me to work for about 2 years; and thereafter, he only wanted me to work part time for several years. **He was very concerned; he did not want me to deal with the extra stress from working, or to be exposed to germs (remember, my immune system was damaged). I was told to also wear a face mask continuously as part of the reverse isolation, which by faith I refused, and trusted God instead.** Also, I turned down the Oncologist's kind offer to apply for disability, and by faith, I returned to work 1 day a week. By this time as well, I was attending Charis Bible College via correspondence, while pursuing my Master's degree in Ministry, concurrently. With a full school schedule and back to work 1 day a week, I was still spending over 8 hours a day, saturating myself in God's presence and meditating. I was very excited. I was finally, preparing to be a Minister, and the hours I had to spend each day in school, plus doing my homework got me deeper and deeper into God's Word. Even though I was still sick, my academic preparation to become a Minister became my primary focus, which reenergized me daily — I was hopeful!

In the preceding year, I had spent countless hours in the presence of God, and while in school, I was in the classroom with other students on a regular basis and via correspondence, sharing and learning from others, including Bible scholars. It was an exciting time, and I sensed a new purpose to live and fight until I observed the visible evidence of my healing from cancer. **Medically, the doctors believed I was not yet "cancer free", but that was their report — I believed a different report: God's report, regardless of how I felt, that was my position, spiritually, emotionally and mentally!**

Given my background in lifestyle medicine, Bible knowledge and revelation from the Holy Spirit, I decided to come up with a new regimen while waiting for the visible manifestation of my healing.

A New Regimen: Laughter is Good Medicine

In my academic research while pursuing my degree in Lifestyle Medicine/Preventive Care, 4 other doctors and I investigated lifestyle remedies to overcome depression and improve healthier emotions. The focus of our research was to better understand the interconnectedness between the mind and body, and how bodily cells communicate with one another via selected pathways, thereby improving our mood. Our research showed that activities such as meditating on God's Word and laughter, significantly reduced depression and improved overall mood (these research findings have been published in an academic journal elsewhere).

Hence, being that I had studied the positive effects of laughter, nutrition, sleep, healthier relationships and their effects in optimizing the immune system, I decided to schedule about 20 to 30 minutes daily sessions to watch comedy shows in order just to laugh. As noted by a plethora of medical research, I knew that, that amount of laughter a day over a period of just a few months could have significant benefits in improving my immune system and overall health. Most significantly, the Bible teaches that laugher is good medicine (Proverbs 17:22), so I knew that I was doing something that had been prescribed by God Himself for our health.

By now, I knew all of the healing Scriptures and many other Scriptures by heart, and it had become much easier for me to meditate on them. Every morning, I would study God's Word for a few hours, and studied the healing Scriptures again; then, I would spend over an hour or so meditating on all of the Scriptures, including the various healings in the Lord's ministry. Thereafter, I would confess Scriptures, including confessing what I was expecting to see happen (i.e., complete healing from head to toe) all over my body.

Even while I was away from the house and at work or at school, I made it a habit to speak aloud Scriptures all over my body and released healing into my temple (i.e., my entire body) , and by faith, commanded healing to manifest in the name of Jesus.

///

It was as if, if you touched me, the Word of God would come out of me; that was how I had the Word of God in my heart and around me during every waking hour.

///

Then every evening, I would watch comedy shows on DVDs for about 30 minutes. Also, about 1 to 2 times per week, I went back and started to re-watch those testimonial DVDs (from Andrew Wommack's Ministries, remember), focusing on those individuals who waited on the Lord and finally saw the visible manifestation of their healings — this really quickened my faith!

While my regimen may appear to be "a little bit too much" to some people who may be looking for a quick "fix"; in God's Kingdom, things do not always happen as quickly as we want. Hence, while waiting, we would be wise to be creative on ways to stay focused on Him. **Besides, I would rather allow God to take me through this process, than depend on medications which will definitely bring about more and worsening medical problems in the future.**

During this time as well, it was still very difficult for me to eat a regular meal, as my "gut" was not functioning properly, yet. Also, I had major damages to my taste buds, and suffered from chronic nausea for almost 2 years. At times, just looking at certain foods caused me to vomit; as such, I could not maintain my Vegetarian diet; thus, I resorted to eating anything (of course, healthy food) that I could tolerate. I had also began to exercise regularly , slowly but surely, and had resumed my habit of taking Vitamins, such as Vitamins C, D, Multivitamin daily, in addition to a baby Aspirin in order to boost my immune system. So, I was utilizing different methodologies, except prescribed medications, to allow my body to heal itself completely while trusting God with the restoration.

Even though I was barely functioning independently, with the exception of my friend, older sister and medical team, I still had not informed anyone about my medical condition. Nonetheless, after much prayer, I decided to inform one of my brothers, who agreed to keep the secret, and he remained faithful to that promise. This was actually a wise decision because this brother ended up providing a lot of financial assistance to me during this period.

A Financial Miracle

Financially, life was tough! Nonetheless, I was " getting by," and my older brother was helping, plus I had returned to work about 1 day a week. Even though life was not easy financially, I had been managing, by God's grace. Then one day, I received a letter from the hospital and a follow up call that simply stated that, I had exceeded my medical allowance from my health insurance, a long time ago. At the time of my surgery, hospital stay and initial treatment, I was still under the student health plan from the University because I had barely graduated when I got ill, remember? And this student health plan only allowed a few hundred thousand of dollars for medical expenses; thereafter, the student would incur out of pocket expenses.

Well, my surgery alone, the multiple emergency room visits and hospitalizations, blood and diagnostic testings, plus just a few visits to the Cancer Center exceeded the allowable maximum of that health insurance plan. So I ended up owing the hospital over twenty-five (25,000) thousand USA dollars. When I received that phone call, it was as if, "my heart sank straight into my belly." I felt sick immediately, and I plainly explained to the representative, a lady on the phone that, I was unable to pay, for obvious reasons. The lady was very kind and pleasant. She asked me to write a letter, addressed to the hospital board of directors and explain my situation, and why I was unable to make the payments. Upon receiving my letter, someone would get back to me within a few weeks, she added. After sometime praying and "surrendering" the entire situation to the Lord, I wrote a heartfelt letter which explained my situation, disability and inability to pay back what I owed. I asked for their mercy and understanding. I personally dropped off the letter at the designated location at the hospital.

Only God!

A few weeks thereafter, I received a phone call from the same lady who originally contacted me. She said they have received and reviewed my letter, and unanimously decided to cancel all of my debt. She added that I was the kind of individual that the hospital liked to assist as much as possible. She added that she was praying for me, and prayed that God was with me. When I got off the phone, I was dumbfounded for a few minutes. I sat down for a little while to allow what I had heard to "sink" deep into my soul.

Thereafter, I went on with my day, in awe of God's faithfulness, love, grace and compassion in my life. Only God could have orchestrated such a financial breakthrough! The financial cost of just treating any kind of metastasis cancer alone can easily run close to half a million US dollars, including lost time from work, etc. And I have heard of countless stories, and I personally know people who have had to borrow, sell their homes, properties, etc, in order to supplement their financial expense from the cancer treatment; this kind of financial stress alone does contribute to making the cancer worse, for many people. **Hence in my view, that financial miracle had equal importance as being healed from the cancer itself! I felt blessed and reassured — God was with me, through "thick and thin," as He had promised to me, His beloved child, in His Word.** God is so good, and I was about to experience even more of His miracles.

Other Miracles of Healings!

Even before the end of Summer season of 2010, without any medical intervention, I received complete healing from Raynaud's Disease, Polyneuropathy, and IBS. Recall that, these were diseases

No More Medications!

I had been diagnosed with in the preceding months. **The doctors had anticipated long term complications as normally seen in these medical conditions, but to their amazement, I was completely healed, without medications or other medical interventions whatsoever, until today.**

People often ask me if I did anything special to receive all of these healings—and the answer is NO. I just continued to do what I had been doing in the preceding year, even though I still experienced all of the symptoms. I stood by God's promises, refused to focus on the symptoms, and refused unbelief any entrance into my soul; I totally surrendered the diseases to the Lord Jesus 100% —with absolutely no reservation.

//

I was going to either live or die, with a fixed gaze (i.e., focused) onto Jesus, period! And as I did that, without me even knowing how or when, I received these healings!

//

Remember, the "parable of the growing seed?" Seed, Time, and Harvest— I hope you recall !

Still No Medically Visible Healing of the Cancer!

Towards the end of 2010, multiple CT Scans and blood work had been done, and there was still no change in the cancer prognosis. Being that I was healed from many other diseases by now, the frequency of doctors' visits had significantly reduced. I was now seeing the Oncologist about every 3 months, and the GI doctor about every 6 months. My visits to the surgeon, PCP, and other specialists had been reduced to yearly, or as necessary. By the end of 2010, I was becoming very exhausted with the frequency of the CT Scans and the constant exposure from radiation, and I decided I would ask the Oncologist if we could "slow down" on that, since I was confident about my healing.

In the mean time, my immune system was not improving. It was as if "nothing" was working. My White Blood Cell (WBC) count was chronically below 4,000 (cells per micro liter of blood) and had even gone as low as below 3,000 cells per micro liter (although slightly different with each Laboratory, normal range of WBC is between 3,500 and 10,500 WBC per micro liter of blood). At the rate mine was staying low, my body could not fight off germs, and I was chronically exposed to all sorts of germs. And in spite of my continuous habit of studying and meditating on God's Word, speaking healing Scriptures and faith filled words over my body, in addition to my laughter regimen, a healthy diet and Vitamins, I continued to experience worsening and progressive worsening of my immune system, at least on the surface. **Yet, during all these, I contracted no infection, even though the doctors had prophesied that I would — they were wrong! God's Word, which was/is medicine to my entire body, protected me through it all! Hallelujah!!**

Worsening Immune System

As my immune system progressively declined, the Oncologist started to become very concerned, and in one of my visits with him, he stated he would be ordering a Bone Marrow Biopsy to rule out Leukemia, if my blood test did not improve. A Bone Marrow Biopsy is a test whereby specimens are aspirated from the Bone Marrow (usually from a location in the back of the pelvis bone), and they are then examined to rule out certain cancers, such as Leukemia.

Leukemia is a type of cancer of blood forming tissues, including the bone marrow, with symptoms such as chronic fatigue, weight loss, infections, chronically abnormal WBC, etc, which were all symptoms I had been experiencing. The moment I heard his words, I immediately came against them and told him, **"I do not want to undergo that test". I went on to release my faith by stating, "I have no Leukemia, in Jesus name."** He then responded by saying,

"I understand, it is a very invasive and painful test, so let's see what happens."

//

I walked away from the Oncologist's office thinking to myself, " that cannot happen, I am taking my daily medications [God's Word], it [Leukemia] cannot happen. God's medicine is the only perfect medicine and I am taking it every day."

//

I just kept reassuring and reminding myself how God had brought me through the end of 2010, and in His faithfulness, He will preserve me, regardless of what laid ahead.

Proceed now to the next chapter to find out what happened at my 2 year cancer check up. Recall that I discussed the significance of that 2 year check up previously, that "land mark," which many patients with metastasis cancers patiently look forward to. In the next chapter, I discuss what happened to me during that check up.

LESSONS LEARNED

➤ As Christians, we are not defined by the diseases "attacking" our bodies; rather, our identity is found in Christ;

➤ The Bible teaches that laughter is good medicine for our bodies. When we laugh, our inbuilt immunities are released, thus strengthening our immune system. Thus, scheduling regular times of laugher is highly recommended, in accordance with God's Word.

Recommended Resources For Further Studies :

Available At: www.DrRuthTanyi.org

1. Are You Moving Forward with Jesus? How to Excel In Your Identity in Christ: By Dr Ruth Tanyi.

2. Who is the Real Jesus? Answers to 25 of the Toughest Questions About the Real Jesus: Simple & Straight forward to the point answers that will change your life! By Dr Ruth Tanyi.

3. The Heart of True Christianity: The Gospel Message of Jesus Christ: Answers to 10 Major Questions Pertaining to Your Salvation in Christ Jesus. **A 5-Set Audio** CD Teaching: By Dr Ruth Tanyi.

CHAPTER 20

Christ-Like Perspective In Suffering

... And we boast in the hope of the glory of God.... because we know that suffering produces perseverance; perseverance, character; and character, hope. And hope does not put us to shame, because God's love has been poured out into our hearts through the Holy Spirit, who has been given to us.

(Romans 5:2-5; New International Version, NIV).

It was the end of 2010, and I was still looking forward to seeing the visible evidence of being healed from cancer. Nonetheless, I was being taunted with persistent chronic fatigue on a daily basis. Even though by this time I had resumed about 50% of a normal life, and redefined a "New Normal" for myself, it appeared as if the suffering was endless. As Romans 5:2-5 teaches, I had to rely on Scriptures for the supernatural hope to endure my suffering. As I did so, I was able to maintain a Christ-like perspective throughout my suffering. The Scriptures teach that the Lord Jesus endured the Cross , looking forward to the joy ahead (Hebrews 12:2). Likewise, I believed my suffering was short-lived, knowing that joy would come in the future.

Finding Hope in Suffering

I had figured out a new way to eat small frequent meals so as to minimize post surgical problems of bloating and abdominal discomfort; it would take up to about 7 years for my Colon to start functioning close to the way it did before that major surgery and trauma I had experienced back in 2009. Even though I had been slowly exercising, I had to fight through the chronic fatigue and a general sense of feeling sick on a daily basis.

It was horrible because for a period of about 6 years, I awoke every morning feeling sick because of my diseased immune system. Notwithstanding, by faith, I determined to "press on" daily, and continued with my daily regimen as I stood on God's Word faithfully, knowing that my suffering was engendering patience and hope , which I desperately needed while waiting for the visible manifestation of my healing.

What really encouraged me throughout my suffering was the inspiring and encouraging writings in the Bible from the Apostle Paul about suffering. With the exception of our Lord Jesus, it is my opinion that the Apostle Paul went through the most suffering, compared to any other Christian, dead or alive, combined (see 2 Corinthians chapters 1 and 6; Book of Acts). Yet, he had an amazingly Christ-centered perspective about his suffering, which was, and is still extremely encouraging to me.

As an example, just go back and study the entire book of Philippians. Can you imagine that, under the inspiration of the Holy Spirit, the Apostle Paul penned down those inspiring and encouraging words while he was in prison? In this book, the Apostle exhorts us to rejoice, always, in the Lord, and not to be anxious (see Philippians 4: 4-9). Amazing, for someone who was in prison (a dungeon, not like the improved prison conditions we have today in the 21st Century), awaiting possible execution. Then, in Romans 5:2-5, the Scripture cited at the top of this chapter, he encourages us to find meaning in our suffering (that is to say, to be hopeful and persevere through the suffering, which could engender Godly character, if we allow God to work through us during our sufferings).

While it can be tempting for us to blame others, God, or our circumstances for the suffering; in my situation, I was determined, just like the Apostle Paul, to maintain a Christ -centered perspective, regardless of how severe and lasting my suffering would be. This was essential because I believed that, "someday, all things would work out and make sense" (Romans 8: 26-28), even though I could not understand how.

God is Not Glorified by our Suffering

And, **it is most important for me to explain that I never considered the lie that my suffering from cancer was glorifying God: absolutely Not — My healing was what would glorify God, and not my suffering from cancer. It is a lie from the enemy, which unfortunately, some Christians have believed, that when they are suffering from a disease, God is being glorified.** Friend, if you believe this lie, STOP IT! The Lord Jesus took all of your diseases and its subsequent pain and suffering upon His sinless body on the cross — He wants you to be well! Thus, your suffering does not, it cannot, and it will not glorify God, so stop believing this lie from Satan, which will keep you in bondage, preventing you from receiving your healing (more on this in Section 4 of this book).

Finally, that 2 Year Check Up

The year 2011 came and I was still alive, even though according to the doctors and medical report, I still had cancer in my body. Nonetheless, in spite of no visible evidence of my healing, I had considered myself healed, as such, I continued with my life.

By Faith, I Chose to Act Healed

Even though by faith I had been acting healed all along since I received that revelation through the gift of faith that I was healed; but it was in 2011 that I made a decision to completely REST in the Lord! By resting, I rededicated my healing again to the Lord, and I accepted whatever the outcome will be. With this decision to REST, I determined to engage in life 100%, regardless of the doctors' prognosis. This was significant because as explained earlier, the Bible teaches that faith without corresponding actions is useless (James 2:14-26). So I knew that it was time for me to engage in life 100%, so as to align my actions with my belief that I was already healed. Also, take note that "RESTING" in the Lord does not imply that you "fold your arms" and do nothing. Rather, using my example, I surrendered to the process, accepted whatever the outcome would be, and then I proceeded to engage in life 100%.

Additionally, recall that in 2009 and 2010, by faith, in spite of the daily symptoms I was experiencing, and without seeing the visible evidence of my healing, I was already acting as someone who was healed; meaning, my actions were already corresponding with my belief that I was already healed. For example, by faith, I had (1) refused to sign up for disability benefits, and instead, I returned to work 1 day a week against doctor's advice; (2) refused to take prescribed medications; (3) refused to implement the reverse isolation to fight germs; (4) been "giving healing away" to others, etc, etc.

But, in 2011, the major difference was that, I made a decision that regardless of what happened, life must go on, fully. **I am not giving you a recipe to refuse doctor's recommendations. Rather, in my situation, I was only acting in accordance with what I had come to believe.** With the decision to fully engage in life, I officially opened my private integrative medical practice in San Bernardino, California. Even though I had been, slowly but surely, seeing patients at this practice towards the end of 2010, by the middle of 2011, I started seeing patients about 2 to 3 days per week, totally against the Oncologist's advice, who was concerned about the extra stress work might have on my body; I kept it a secret from him.

Much more, I was still pursuing my academic degree in Ministry and taking Bible College courses concurrently (part time); it was a hectic schedule. Additionally, I started holding regular Bible studies at various locations on weekends, and at times on weekdays in my office, and I became more involved at serving God at my local church on Sundays. Still at that time, besides my older sister, brother, the friend who had been with me from day one (plus another friend in Minnesota whom I later told, but without the details), and the medical team, others still did not know my diagnosis and prognosis.

A Divine Purpose

My life was 100% focused around the Lord, and there was no turning back at this point. I started to meditate, on a regular basis, on how God had been gracious to intervene in my life for a uniquely divine purpose, thus I chose to love and serve Him wholeheartedly, every opportunity I had while I was still alive. Remember, I had not yet seen the visible healing of the cancer — I was living life purely by faith, counting on God's grace, love and compassion! **Even though I was not doubting God for the visible manifestation of my healing, I was ready for whatever the outcome would be. As such, I decided that if I were to die, let me at least start pursuing my calling; because at that point, I had come to the realization that God had called me to be a Bible Teacher.**

I often tell people that regardless of how dire our circumstances may appear on the surface, one way or the other, some good can still come out of it if we keep an open mind, get rid of anger, bitterness and all pseudo methods of self preservation; and instead, trust God with the process. In my situation, it took being diagnosed with cancer and a wholehearted surrender to God for me to discern that all along, God had called me into ministry, as a Bible teacher. After this realization, I plunged into my calling 100%, until today —there was and there is no turning back, period! In the last several years, many individuals have mentioned that, God allowed the cancer so as to "wake me up" about my calling as a Minister. **I do not agree with this; rather, I believe it was me, who was unable to perceive my calling because of the "fast -paced" life I was living, and cancer "slowed me down", causing me to evaluate my true (i.e., eternal) purpose and calling in life, and in that process, God confirmed it in my heart.**

That "Spirit of Fear", Again

Finally, it was July of 2011, about 2 years after that initial diagnosis of cancer, and it was time for that "famous" 2 year cancer check up. It was the "big one", meaning the testings. Recall how

I mentioned earlier that cancer studies and research have shown that the probability of metastatic cancers returning within 2 years is extremely high? In fact, I have read several studies that concluded that up to 85% of all metastatic cancers return by 2 years from the date of the original diagnosis; that was scary, and is still a crazy and dire prognosis! So according to medical science, the thinking is that, if a cancer patient will survive the disease, that 2 year "land mark" will start to provide some hope, and a sense of direction.

Boy! What a scary experience! And every patient who has survived any kind of metastatic cancer will agree that reaching that 2 year "land mark" came with a flood of mixed emotions —feelings of dread about the cancer advancing, and/or feelings of hope, of the cancer either staying unchanged or (in "remission," using the medical terminology), because after just 2 years, most Oncologists would be extremely reluctant to use the words, "cancer free".

The heightened stress, mental torture, and emotional agony during this 2 year "land mark" is unbelievably unbearable for the cancer patients who survive till then. Until today, I really do not know how people cope during this period without the Lord Jesus.

For me, that demonic spirit of fear I thought I had overcome started to resurface, flooding into my thoughts all over again, just about 1 week before undergoing the testings. It was major testing, which included diagnostic and blood testings, CT Scans, plus my very first Colonoscopy. A Colonoscopy is an examination of the inside of the colon (large intestine or large bowel), whereby a long and flexible Colonoscope (with a tiny video camera at the tip, to allow visualization of the colon), is inserted into the rectum, and the examiner, usually a Gastroenterologist, evaluates the inside of the colon to evaluate the presence of a disease, including any suspicious growth that may be cancerous .

Christ-Like Perspective In Suffering

I had been doing the same thing in the last, almost 2 years: studying the Word of God, meditating on the Scriptures, speaking Scriptures and faith filled words over my body, eating healthy, exercising, plus carrying out my laugher regimen faithfully. But about 3 days before undergoing the testings, the Oncologist's words about the chances of the cancer spreading more within 2 years began to resurface in my soul. **And unfortunately, all of the other cancer patients I had met at the Cancer Center had all died within 2 years. I was the only one still alive!**

Satan's Opportune Time

The spirit of doubt started to torment me with thoughts such as, " **You are finished! Shame on you, you thought you were strong and stopped the medicines, now cancer has spread all over."** I heard thoughts such as, "**You won't make it, you should have relied on the medications."** Satan brought Scriptures in my mind such as, *My Father's house has many rooms; if that were not so, would I have told you that I am going there to prepare a place for you?* (John 14:2); and in return, I would yell "NO", quoting Scriptures right back, *"I will not die but live, and will proclaim what the Lord has done* (Psalm 118:17), emphasis author's. It was amazing how these thoughts were so real, and constant, and I was beginning to be paralyzed by them. About 2 days before undergoing the testings, I was so sick and paralyzed with fear, I could not function; I could no longer spend time in God's Word or carry out my usual daily activities. I called my older sister overseas, and I was crying nonstop. And in a very gentle manner, she said, "It is okay, you have been planting Godly seeds, it will be fine." She continued to remind me of the victories I had overcome.

I was shocked by what was happening to me, as I thought I had dealt with all such emotions in the past. But as the Bible teaches, Satan will leave us alone for a season, then at the opportune time, he will revisit us with his lies (Luke 4:13). That 2 year "land mark" was Satan's opportune time in my life, to attack and attempt to deceive me with his usual tricks — planting doubtful thoughts and lies about

God's Word into my soul; reminding me about all of the other cancer patients who had died, so as to frighten me that my end was also near; and also reminding me about the dire survival statistics for metastatic Colon cancers; etc, that way, I would succumb to his lies and begin to doubt God.

Fighting Against Satan's Lies

After a few days of being paralyzed with fear, it reached a point where I was unable to focus on God's Word; the fearful thoughts were beginning to affect me severely. So with that realization, the evening before the testings, I started walking around my house like a "crazy woman", reading aloud all of the Scriptures on fear, and all of the other Scriptures I had written on a 4 by 4 card. Even though I had memorized all of these Scriptures, I could no longer rely on my memory. Hence, I resorted to reading them aloud, over, and over, and over, and over, again over a period of about 2 to 3 hours (while breaking in-between to rest), until I was exhausted.

At night time, I went to bed feeling a little better, but still taunted by a "little" fear. Upon awakening, I experienced less fear. **Even though I had fought fear before and I knew what to do, I realized that the moment a fearful thought comes at you, you must come against it immediately with the Truths in God's Word, lest it would start to sink deep into your soul and thoughts. Truly, fear is just a shadow. Today, when I teach on fear, I describe it as: F= False , E = Evidence, A = Appearing, R= Real. In other words — False Evidence Appearing Real — Fear is really just a shadow, but we have the real thing: Jesus Christ.**

Additionally, I now teach people that another mistake many individuals make when fighting fear is that, they believe that all of the fearful emotions must leave before they can act on God's Word in faith, which is absolutely FALSE. In fact, the courage to come against fear must be executed, using God's Word, while you feel the fearful emotion. Do not wait until the fear emotion subsides, because it will not without you doing something about it. Rather, you must come against fearful thoughts with The Truth—God's Word. And as you do so, the fearful emotion will then subside — that is how you overcome fear, in Jesus name, Amen!

It is amazing how as finite beings, we will always have to deal with such ungodly emotions of fear and doubt, etc. Satan, our environment, our past, etc, will always present various opportunities for us to doubt God's Word. Therefore, we have to learn how to quickly recognize those emotions and quickly apply God's Word to overcome them. **For those of you needing help with overcoming these emotions that can prevent the manifestation of your healing or other promises from God, I have put together several audio CD teachings on how to overcome these emotions. These teachings continue to help hundreds of people daily, they will help you likewise.** So if you would like, check out the resource list at the end of this chapter and obtain some of these teachings. By the day of the testings, I had already spent several hours applying God's Word to overcome those fearful thoughts; hence, I proceeded to undergo all of the testings with much confidence. It was a full day venture at the hospital.

And The Results Were....?

The day came for me to receive the results. Interestingly, I was no longer afraid, rather, I was emotionless, part of that was being too tired from fighting. I sat in the Oncologist's examination room, and while waiting, I continued to mutter Scriptures underneath my breath, over my body. He came in, in his usual calm and pleasant manner and sat down to examine a plethora of blood and diagnostic tests he had ordered.

Unbelievably Scary!

While he was doing that, my heart was beating so fast, I thought I was going to faint. But underneath my breath, I continued to softly speak aloud faith filled words and Scriptures, and I visualized, and placed myself in the presence of Jesus, and imagined Him laying

His hands on me. I was also meditating on the stories in the healing ministry of Jesus, doing everything I had been doing, just to calm myself down. It only took about 10 minutes or so for him to review all of the results, but it seemed like an eternity. While sitting there and waiting for him to review the results, it was very emotionally painful, disturbing and mentally exhausting. Then finally, he turned and looked at me and said, "Congratulations!, there is no further spread of the cancer". Then I asked him, "So what's next?", even though I knew what he would say.

He explained that I was not "cancer free" yet, but the cancer is not spreading. Thereafter, my visits to him was reduced to about every 6 months, and further diagnostic and blood tests were scheduled for the upcoming visit. I expressed my concern to him about the frequency of the CT Scans and radiation exposure.

Then I proceeded to confidently tell him, "I have already been healed of this cancer, it is not coming back, do I still need to do these frequent CT Scans?".

He noted that he admired my attitude, but he wanted to do a few more CT Scans, and if negative, he would schedule them for about every 6 months. I agreed with the plan, and off I went out of his office to come back again in another 6 months.

According to Oncology medicine, I had to wait for another 3 to 4 years for them to be certain I was indeed cancer free. But for me, life moved on. In the next chapter, I discuss activities that enabled me to stay hopeful while waiting for the visible evidence of my healing, proceed there to learn more.

LESSONS LEARNED

➢ Our suffering does not glorify God — He is glorified when we, His children, succeed in every area of our lives. But during intense suffering as Christians, our best option is to seek hope in God's Word, and to remember that God will not allow us to suffer beyond what we can bear. Most importantly, we should remember that God is always with us, through our pain and suffering;

➢ For the Christian, fear is just a shadow! You have the "real thing": Jesus Christ! The best time to demolish fearful thoughts with God's Word is immediately such thoughts come to your mind.

Recommended Resources For Further Studies:

Available At: www.DrRuthTanyi.org

1. Live Above Your Fears & Overcome Sicknesses and Diseases: **A 2-Set Audio CD Teaching** By Dr Ruth Tanyi.

2. Did God Really Say that? How to Overcome Doubt and Receive God's Promises: 10 Life-Changing Lessons Learned from Overcoming Metastasis Colon Cancer: **A 2-Set Audio CD Teaching** By Dr. Ruth Tanyi.

3. Be Anxious No More. **A 2-Set Audio CD Teaching** By Dr. Ruth Tanyi.

CHAPTER 21

THE VISIBLE EVIDENCE: CANCER FREE!

Do not be deceived: God cannot be mocked. A man reaps what he sows. Whoever sows to please their flesh, from the flesh will reap destruction; whoever sows to please the Spirit, from the Spirit will reap eternal life. Let us not become weary in doing good, for at the proper time we will reap a harvest if we do not give up.

(Galatians 6:7-9; New International Version, NIV).

As noted in Galatians 6:7-9, we reap whatever we sow! If we invest time in Godly activities, we will in turn reap an abundance of "spiritual harvest", but if we invest in the "flesh", we will reap pain and suffering. Since my dire diagnosis and prognosis in 2009, I had been diligently planting Godly seeds into my life, and I believed that God, in His faithfulness, was taking notice.

It was around Fall of 2011, and I was continuing to trust God as I moved on with life, believing that sooner or later, my diagnostic and blood tests would confirm, "cancer free," just so that the Oncologist and my medical team would stop "concerning themselves" so much about me. They were still treating and approaching me as a cancer patient, and I did not like that — I was healed, and living life by faith, period!

By this point in my journey, my primary focus for wanting the visible medical evidence to corroborate with my healing was for the medical team, so that they would believe what I had been telling them all along: that I was healed.

Led by the Holy Spirit

Also by this time in 2011, my daily regimen was becoming almost legalistic, meaning, I felt a sense to speak aloud Scriptures and faith filled words over my body for a set period of time daily, and if I did not do so, I started to experience a sense of frustration and a little "guilt". Boy! I quickly noted that, that subtle feeling of frustration and guilt was not from God. With that realization, I decided to "tweak" my daily routine so as to still spend significant amounts of time in the presence of God studying, meditating, confessing Scriptures and faith filled words over my body only as led by the Holy Spirit, rather than doing so on a prescribed schedule like I had been doing.

As I allowed the Holy Spirit to guide the process, I realized that there were many days whereby I did not have to speak aloud all of the dozens of Scriptures I had memorized, but instead, I would be focused on just 1 or 2 Scriptures, and those Scriptures would nourish and sustain me for the rest of the day. With this, the process became extremely enjoyable and more meaningful —I suppose I had grown to the extent whereby, those Scriptures were so ingrained in my soul, hence, it was time for me to approach the process with "quality" in mind, versus attempting to accomplish quality and quantity concurrently. Additionally, I started to delve into other aspects in my relationship with the Lord, which made a significant difference in sustaining me after that initial 2 years while waiting for the visible results, since my medical team needed to see that before believing I was healed.

An Added Dimension with Much Hope

I often tell people that fighting cancer is a very, very long, emotionally, mentally, and physically daunting fight! And through the years, every cancer survivor has to keep redefining a "New Normal". For me, that "New Normal" was coming up with other ways to keep trusting God and grow in Him. Next, are the added activities I carried out on a daily basis which enabled me to sustain with much hope while waiting for the blood and diagnostic results to corroborate with the fact that I was already healed in the spirit and soul.

Other Activities That Drew Me Closer to God

- ✓ I started to study about **the love of God,** and to meditate on His unfathomable love for me. The Bible teaches that perfect love casts out all fears (1 John 4:18). **As I meditated on God's unfathomable love for me, it started to become difficult for me to even consider the option that I would not see the visible evidence of my healing.** As I received a deeper revelation of God's love for me through studying the Scriptures, I was reenergized, and I embraced a deeper Christ-centered perspective about waiting as I stay focused on Jesus. It was an amazing mental relief!

- ✓ I also started to study, and to gain a better revelation of my **identity in Christ.** A lot of times people take this (their identity in Christ) for granted; hence, they do not fully appreciate what Christ Jesus did for them on the Cross. As such, they are, unfortunately, not knowledgeable about who they have become in Christ.

///

Sadly, without knowing who you are in Christ, you will not know the power and authority you have inherited by faith in Christ, much more know how to enforce that authority and expect Godly results.

///

For me, delving into the Scriptures and gaining a richer revelation about my identity in Christ was an eye opener, which in fact, led me to write the book: **Are you Moving Forward With Jesus? How to Excel in Your Identity in Christ.** This book, which came out in October of 2017, continues to help hundreds of people; I believe it will help you as well.

When this book came out, some individuals were surprised because I did not publish the book of my healing from cancer first. To some of them, I had to explain that having a revelation of their identity in Christ is sufficient to receive any kind of healing and/or to overcome crisis in every area in their lives. **As I delved further into the Scriptures and learnt more about my identity in Christ, and the authority and power I had inherited by faith in Him, I was emboldened, and my confidence "went off the roof."** If people could only understand and operate in the power and authority they have inherited in Christ, most of them would not "put up" with as much, especially from the devil, as some ignorant people do today and allow the enemy to keep them in bondage.

- ✓ The Bible admonishes us to **examine (i.e., to evaluate in light of Scripture) ourselves** if we are "walking" and living out our lives in accordance with God's Word (2 Corinthians 13:5). **Boy! This is something that some Christians often ignore; and they would examine everybody else, except themselves.** Yet, this is a powerful admonition that will help to "keep us in check". For me, it was absolutely essential that I examined my life, relationship with God and others, frequently, to be certain there was nothing in the way, preventing the visible manifestation of my healing. I was not going to allow Satan any inroad into my life through my lifestyle or other relationships, period!

Thus, I made it a habit to frequently examine all of my relationships, actions, and speech, to be certain they were in synch with God's Word. **I examined and made certain there were no ungodly emotions of unforgiveness, resentment, anger, envy, jealousy, bitterness, etc in my heart towards anyone**. I also made sure I was not in strife with anyone. In essence, I made certain I was not harboring any sort of ungodly emotions in my heart that the enemy could use against me (I discuss more about how these emotions can prevent the manifestation of healings in Section 4 of this book).

✓ Given my medical background and biblical studies, I had gained a richer understanding about the relationship between healthier emotions and health. As such, I made it a daily habit to "walk" in the Fruit of the Spirit: love, joy, peace, forbearance, kindness, goodness, faithfulness, gentleness and self-control (Galatians 5:22-23). **To do this therefore, regardless of how I felt, I listened to praise and worship music and then spent quality and quantity time in worshipping and praising the Lord, thereby activating the joy of the Lord in my spirit.** I made it a daily habit to practice and express unconditional love towards others, and refused to allow my emotions to direct my attitude, behaviors and mannerisms towards others.

As I purposefully practiced and activated these Godly emotions that were already in my born again spirit, it was amazing how I was able to easily focus more on God, and His peace flooded my soul. When we choose to walk in these Godly emotions, we in turn allow our bodies to generate inbuilt medicines to heal itself and revitalize us (see Nehemiah 8:10; Isaiah 26:3; Proverbs 14:30; Proverbs 15:30; Proverbs 17:22). I used the phraseology, "choose to", because like everything else with the Lord, it is our choice whether or not we choose to walk in the Fruit of the Spirit, thereby activating the benefits. For those of you interested in learning more how to allow the Holy Spirit to enable you to "walk" in the Fruit of the Spirit, check in the resource list for my audio CD teaching titled: **Holy Spirit-Led Healthy Emotions and Your Health**, and obtain that teaching.

The end of 2011 came and passed, and there was still no visible medical evidence of my healing. Nonetheless, I moved on with life, still feeling sick on a daily basis from a damaged immune system. By now, my visits to the Oncologist had reduced significantly. They had gone from weekly visits, to monthly, to every 3 months, and now, I was only seeing him about every 6 months, which was a good indication that I was doing better, from the medical perspective.

Other Noted Miracles

The Miracle of Fertility

By the middle of 2012, during one of my visits to the gynecologist, she ran various laboratory and diagnostic tests which confirmed that I was 100% fertile— I had been healed from that premature medical menopause (infertility) I was diagnosed with! Again, another miracle from the Lord. Towards the end of 2012, my White Blood Cell count levels were still below normal limits. Thus I started to become very frustrated, especially as I still felt sick on a daily basis; as such, I started to inquire from the Lord about the "status quo" of my immune system. For a period of about 2 weeks thereafter, I intensely sought the Lord in prayer about the issue, and about my decision against the Bone Marrow biopsy.

The Vision, a Confirmation

Then, one night during those two weeks of my intense discussion with the Lord about my immune system, I had a dream with a vision that confirmed everything. In this dream, I saw a vision of a doctor seated in his examination room examining my blood test. I was in the room with this doctor, as he explained how my White Blood Cell count was getting better. In the dream, he added that my Red Blood Cell count results showed a family history of Thalassemia (which I was already aware of), an inherited blood disorder which causes fewer Red Blood Cells and less hemoglobin, leading to anemia, fatigue, etc, and other related symptoms. He went on to explain that I would not need the Bone Marrow biopsy, as he was no longer concerned about Leukemia.

I awoke from that dream with a sense of indescribable peace, a sense of "knowing," and, an assurance that God had spoken to me.

I was very aware that the Bible teaches us not to rely on dreams and/or visions as a way to hear from God, because the primary way God speaks is through His revealed Word in the Bible. And if God is to speak directly in our hearts, through any other means such as a dream, vision, audible voice, or through others, etc, it will be consistent with His revealed Word — because God is 100% consistent, and He will not speak to us outside His Word nor contradict His revealed Word. I was also aware that our enemy, Satan, can manifest himself in dreams, visions, etc, and deceive us, if we do not know the Word of God (2 Corinthians 11:12-15); thus, God's Word remains the most reliable way to know and hear from God.

It Was God!

But what convinced me that God had spoken to me through that dream was the "knowing" and the indescribable peace I experienced, and all concerns about Leukemia immediately left upon awakening. Then, on my next appointment with the Oncologist just a few weeks after that dream, he repeated, verbatim (i.e., word for word), exactly what I had heard in that dream. It was like an "aha moment", and I concluded that it was indeed God, Who had spoken to me in that dream, to reassure me that all was well.

At the Oncologist's office, when I got there for my follow up visit, he sat at the same location I had seen the vision of a doctor in my dream. Then the Oncologist went on and explained how my White Blood Cell count was improving, and although my Red Blood Cells showed a history of Thalassemia, there would be no need for the Bone Marrow biopsy as he was no longer concerned about Leukemia. As he explained all that to me, I was 100% certain that, God, in His love, compassion and grace, had spoken to me through that dream and answered my prayer that there was no Leukemia. I left that Oncologist's office that day reassured and comforted. And that was the end of the Leukemia issue.

By the end of 2012, although I still felt sick on a daily basis, and I was still struggling physically to engage in life fully, I continued doing so by faith. My overall White Blood Cell count was getting better, but my White Cell count was still under 4000 WBC per micro liter of blood. It is amazing, the damage that metastatic cancer can have on the body, and how long the road to complete recovery was for me.

January of 2013 came and I was still alive, and there was still no medical evidence of my healing from cancer. Also, although my White Blood Cell count still stayed abnormally low, that feeling of sickness that plagued me on a daily basis was less frequent. I carried on with my regular regimen of attending school in preparation for my degree in Ministry; I was still seeing patients part-time; holding Bible studies; actively involved in my local church, and still studying and meditating on Scriptures faithfully as led by the Holy Spirit. Throughout 2013, the CT Scans, laboratory and other diagnostic tests by the Oncologist showed no change in the status of the cancer. Nonetheless, I continued to see him (the Oncologist) about every 6 months.

It Was Time to Speak Out

There is a time for everything under the sun (Ecclesiastes 3:1; John 7:6), and by late Summer of 2013, **I was beginning to sense that it was time to, " let the cat out of the bag", meaning, to tell my entire family, friends and others what I had been going through in the preceding 4 years.** I had not been declared "cancer free" yet by the Oncologist, but I felt as if the Lord was leading me to move on and start sharing my story with others. I proceeded to share this with my friend who had been with me from the beginning, my brother who later knew about it, and my older sister.

While my friend and brother agreed, my older sister was still reluctant about me telling others, yet. Nonetheless, I felt "very compelled in my spirit," to start sharing and helping others.

Interestingly, as I considered the option of not sharing my story at that time, I experienced a sense of "dread", which I still cannot explain until today. But it felt as though the only way to overcome that feeling of "dread" was to start telling others, regardless of what the future held! **Recall, by that time, the Oncologist had not yet declared me "cancer free", but, I believed it was God's time for me to move on, and by faith, I had to obey, period, in spite of no visible medical evidence for others to corroborate my healing! —Boy! I had to really go by faith and trust God that all would be okay!** It was a tough decision, as I had a "gut" feeling that some people would doubt my healing without medical evidence. With that strong discernment in my spirit to proceed, I decided to tell my family first before anyone else. Hence, I held a telephone conference with some family members here in the USA, and told them everything about the cancer diagnosis and prognosis, and where I was in my journey at that time.

And their Reactions Were…?

Different family members expressed different reactions, as expected. But overall, I could sense fear, doubt, worry, care, etc, exactly what I had avoided in the very first place. But by that point, their reactions of fear, doubt, care, etc, could not penetrate me. By far, my mother was the most concerning to me, which was the primary reason my older sister did not feel comfortable with me telling her, yet. Upon hearing the news, my mother immediately started to cry, and she remained saddened throughout that day, and I had to constantly encourage her to "snap out of that mood". As expected, my other siblings were shocked, remained dumbfounded and expressed sadness. **Again, I had to encourage every one of them that I was not afraid, and I would not tolerate any fear, doubt, or care about the prognosis.**

It was amazing how, even though I waited over 4 years to tell my siblings and other family members about my story, the fear, doubt and care in their voices was as if I was dying in the very next month or something. Boy! That C word has a way of paralyzing people. I had to spend significant amounts of time in just reassuring my siblings and family members that I was not dying, and I had to literally beg some of them not to act as if I was dying —it was horrible, just to watch their different reactions. The very next day after telling my family, I said to myself, "It was the best decision not to tell my family about my diagnosis and prognosis", because of their depressing and discouraging reactions, which would have engendered unbelief and allowed Satan inroad into my life.

Thereafter, I proceeded to tell friends and others as the opportunity presented itself. Dear reader, believe it or not, peoples' reactions were just like those of my siblings and other family members. **Again, I had to constantly encourage and reassure others that, " I was cancer free! I was not going to die! I would live, even though the Oncologist had not declared me 'cancer free' — I would insist to them, I am going by God's report".** And eventually, God's report proved to be true, making every other report a lie, as the upcoming years would reveal.

Finally, Visible Evidence, Cancer Free

The 5 Year Cancer Work-Up

It was late Spring in 2014, and the scheduled blood and diagnostic testing, including a Colonoscopy for my 5 year major cancer follow up was soon approaching, in July of that year. By this time as well, my visits to the Oncologist had been reduced to yearly check-ups, until today (the time of the writing of this book). Unlike during the 2 year cancer work up, this time however, I experienced little or no anxiety whatsoever. By this time, I had already had multiple Colonoscopies and CT Scans which were all negative.

Before my scheduled appointment date, I proceeded and had all of the testings done. Then, a few weeks or so thereafter, I went to see the Oncologist. I was very calm and confident during this encounter. Upon his evaluation of all of my blood and diagnostic tests, he simply said, " There is no cancer, just low WBC", that was

The Visible Evidence: Cancer Free!

all. Then I asked him, " So what's next?". He then explained that moving forward, he would continue to schedule my appointments yearly. I asked him if medically, I was "cancer free", he reluctantly explained that after 5 years, the chances of the cancer returning are less than 5%, but there is still a slight chance of recurrence. It was interesting how he did not want to use those words, "cancer free". Nevertheless, by then, I was not depending on the Oncologist to tell me that, as I had already "let the cat out of the bag", and everyone knew I was cancer free; although, some people did not believe as they were waiting for the doctor's report.

///

How interesting, and in my opinion, sad, that some Christians would trust and honor a doctor's word over God's report.

///

Finally, 6 Years After The Diagnosis...!

I returned for my annual follow-up with the Oncologist in September of 2015, it had been slightly over 6 years since that initial diagnosis of cancer. And upon examining all of the blood and diagnostic tests, he then, finally, said, " You are cancer free!". "Oh well!", I thought to myself, " I've known this all along". Also, at that point, his words were not as meaningful to me, as God's report had proven to be true, all along. **I was amazed how from the moment I received that revelation in my spirit and soul about 2 1/2 to 3 months into my fight with cancer, I was instantly healed; however, it took several years for the visible evidence of that healing to show in my blood and diagnostic tests.**

Why So Long...?

I have often wondered why it took so long in my case? Others have asked the same question. Friend, I wish I have an easy answer for you, but I do not! The only possible answer I have considered is that, perhaps, (1) the Seed, Time, and Harvest was prolonged because I needed to grow in my faith? I do not know! Or, (2) it could be that, given the significant damage to the various organs of my body, major restoration had to take place, and it just took longer? I still do not know! Or, (3) maybe because I had to overcome so many other diseases in between the cancer, my faith was only strong enough to overcome one battle at a time? Or, (4) maybe my mind/soul was so "messed up" with medical facts, I needed more time to renew my mind? I do not know! **Whatever the reason(s), which in my view is insignificant, one thing is certain — today, in 2018, over 9 years when I was originally diagnosed with metastasis Colon cancer and given a very dire prognosis, I am 100% Cancer Free, healed by the Stripes of Jesus — you can be healed too, if you believe!**

Moving Forward

Today, I am functioning 100% in the life God created for me to enjoy. The pain and suffering I endured have been redefined within the context of biblical perspective, as I am now a full time Minister, helping others to know the love, compassion and grace of God. I am 100% cancer free and disease free. **Unlike many other cancer survivors (those with similar prognosis like I had) who end up with major complications and other chronic diseases, I have absolutely no disease in my body, and my White Blood Cell count is perfectly normal — Glory to God! My entire medical team considers me a miracle, and indeed, I am a miracle of God!** With the exception of Vitamins which I continue to take, I take no prescription medications, and I plan not to do so — **I continue to rely on God's Word daily, as my only/primary Medicine!**

Others Have Been Healed Too!

Ever since I started to share my testimony with others, I have seen many others healed as well. I have prayed and stood in faith with countless individuals and believed God for their healing, and I have witnessed, and continue to witness many of them healed from all sorts of diseases, using the same principles I have taught in this book.

In the few years I have been holding healing conferences (I continue to do this yearly), I continue to teach others about these same principles and recommendations I have shared in this book, and I have witnessed several individuals receive their healing as well. Even as a former Prayer Minister with Andrew Wommack's Ministry, I have seen countless people healed of all sorts of diseases, based on the same principles and recommendations shared in this book;

//

Because God is no respecter of persons—in the same way I received my healing by standing on His Word with unwavering faith through the power of the Holy Spirit, you can be healed too, if you so desire! God is willing for you to be healed; but, do you want to be healed?

//

Proceed now to the last section of this book where I discuss (1) some common barriers, right from the Bible, that can prevent many Godly Christians from receiving their healing; (2) how you can receive your healing too; and (3) some "do's and don'ts" when ministering healing to others.

LESSONS LEARNED

➢ God is not mocked — when we plant spiritual seeds such as, but not limited to: spending time in His presence, prayer, meditating on His Word, praise and worship, etc, He will be certain that we reap an abundance of harvest in His perfect timing, if we do not give up;

➢ Having a deeper revelation of God's unfathomable love for you is a potent antidote against any attack from the enemy;

➢ For the true Christian, hope is found in only one person: Jesus Christ.

Recommended Resources For Further Studies:

Available At: www.DrRuthTanyi.org

1. Holy Spirit-Led Healthy Emotions: The Fruit of the Spirit and Your Health. **A 2-Set Audio CD Teaching** by Dr Ruth Tanyi.

2. Did God Really Say that? How to Overcome Doubt and Receive God's Promises: 10 Life-Changing Lessons Learned from Overcoming Metastasis Colon Cancer. **A 2-Set Audio CD Teaching** by Dr Ruth Tanyi.

3. Who is the Real Jesus? Answers to 25 of the Toughest Questions About the Real Jesus: Simple & Straight forward to the point answers that will change your life! By Dr Ruth Tanyi.

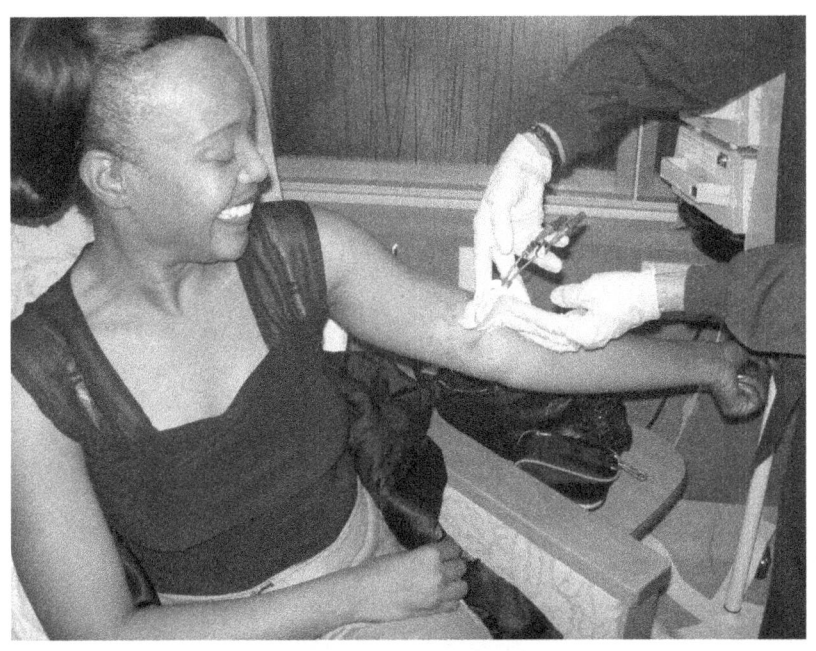
Nurse caring for chemotherapy IV site

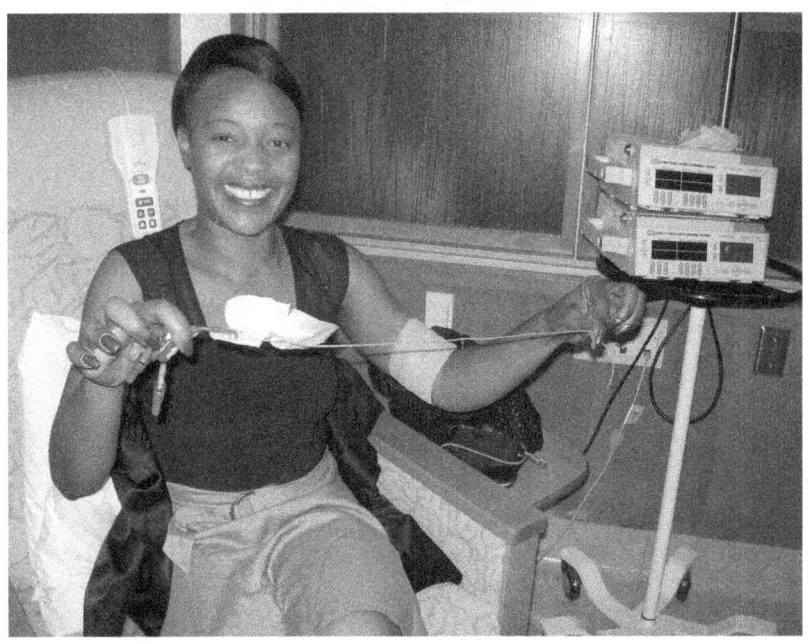
Chemotherapy IVs coming off after treatment stopped

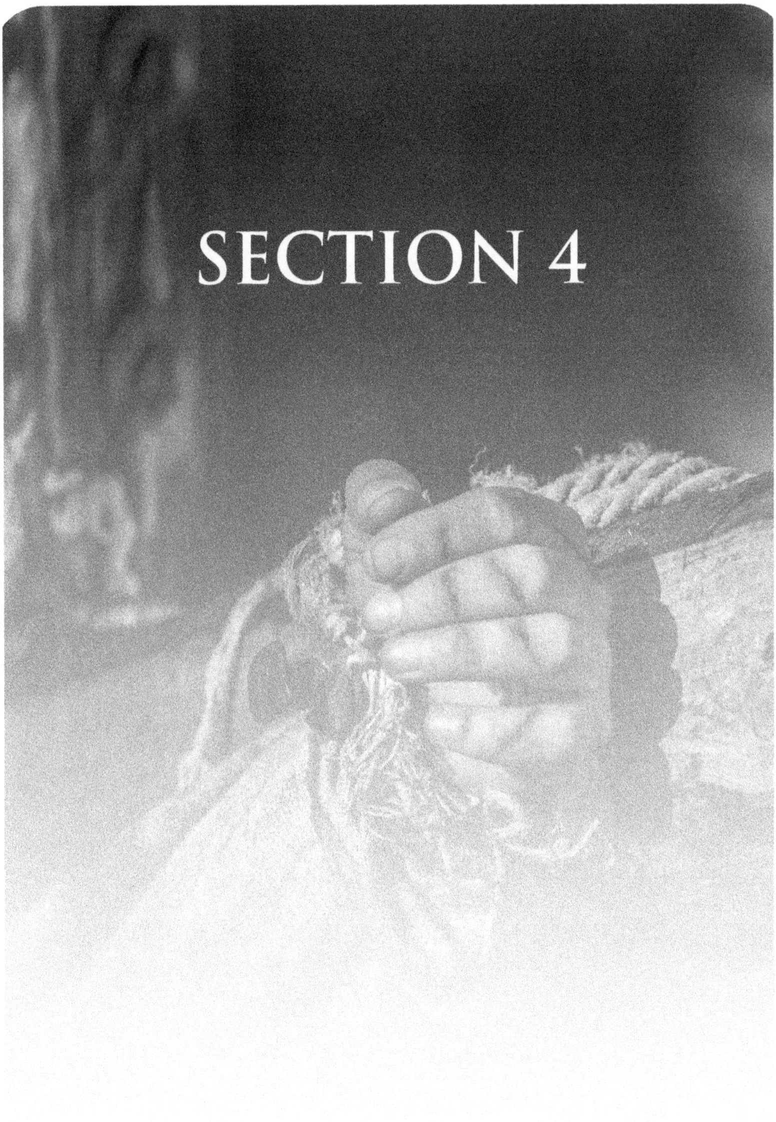

SECTION 4

YOU CAN BE HEALED TOO!

CHAPTER 22

BARRIERS TO RECEIVING YOUR HEALING

"PHYSICAL" BARRIERS

PART A

Do you not know that your bodies are temples of the Holy Spirit, who is in you, whom you have received from God? You are not your own; you were bought at a price. Therefore honor God with your bodies.

(1 Corinthians 6:19-20; New International Version, NIV).

As I have explained throughout this book, the Bible teaches that the Lord Jesus not only died for the forgiveness of our sins, He also died for physical healing of our bodies, and He has delivered us from the Kingdom of darkness, thus we can prosper in every area of life, if we choose to. And, I have also explained throughout this book that, although healing was/is part of the Lord's atonement on the Cross, many individuals are either ignorant about this Biblical Truth, and/or they refuse to accept it for various reasons already discussed in preceding chapters. Nonetheless, one thing is certain — **the fact that some people do not receive their healing after they have prayed does not imply that it is not God's will to always heal!** At times, there are many barriers or hindrances which individuals often ignore, and as such they are unable to receive their healing.

In spite of the fact that the Bible teaches about various barriers that can prevent God's healing power, presence, and other miracles from manifesting in our lives, I have heard so many people pose the argument that, if it is God's will to always heal, then, why do some people not receive their healing? **Firstly**, that question is problematic, because it assumes that we, as finite human beings, can perceive into people's hearts. **Secondly**, this question is also assuming, incorrectly, that God's will always comes to pass. This line of thinking is grossly incorrect and unscriptural, because the Bible clearly teaches that God's will does not always come to pass, because we have a Free Will. And sadly, people often use their Free Will against God's wisdom, and as such, hinder God's perfect will from manifesting in their lives.

The Bible has so many examples of individuals using their Free Will against Godly wisdom, hence thwarting God's perfect plans from manifesting. For example, the Old Testament is replete with examples of how the first generation Israelites used their Free Will and rebelled against God, and as such, they did not get into the Promised Land, which was God's perfect plan for them; instead, they all died in the wilderness, with the exception of Caleb and Joshua who survived (see the Book of Numbers). So, yes, we have a role to play in allowing God's perfect will to manifest — which is obedience to God's Word and allowing the Holy Spirit to direct our paths.

We Do Not Have All of the Answers

Before I even discuss some of the common barriers that can prevent you from receiving your healing and/or deliverance in any area in your life, I want to emphasize that, as finite human beings, we do not have all of the answers!

Therefore, in the upcoming 2 chapters, I will only discuss those barriers that are evident (as taught in the Bible), which can hinder the manifestation of your healing or other promises from God; yet, these barriers are often ignored by some Christians.

Also, the barriers I am about to discuss can hinder the manifestation of God's promises in every other area of your life, such as, but not limited to your finances, relationships, etc, etc, besides your physical healing.

Please keep in mind that, **these barriers are not intended to be legalistic (i.e., "a do's and don'ts" list); but rather, should serve as "pointers or guide posts" that can assist you to evaluate yourself in light of Scripture, and to recognize areas in your life where you can grow and receive your healing, deliverance, other promises from God, etc, which the Lord died for you to enjoy**. Besides, the Lord is after your heart! He desires a heartfelt relationship with you, and not "do's and don'ts", which He despises (1 Samuel 15:22; Psalm 51:16-17).

I decided to begin this section of this book with these barriers; that way, when you get to **chapters 24 and 25** which will focus on "how to receive your healing", you might, hopefully, have already begun the process of discerning any barriers to you receiving your healing. This is essential because discerning and overcoming these barriers is the initial step towards your ability to receive any promise from God.

For purposes of simplicity and to enhance understanding, I have categorized these barriers into **4 major categories**: (1) Physical; (2) Emotional; (3) Spiritual; and (4) Demonic, although the end result is the same — a hardened heart towards the Lord — Unbelief, which will prevent His power from flowing in your life. Also, take note that there is some overlap, as some of these barriers can easily fit into multiple categories. In this chapter, I will discuss the physical barriers which are straight forward and easily noticeable. Then in the next chapter, I will discuss the other barriers, which I call "hidden" barriers. Below are the physical barriers and their explanations.

Physical Barriers

These are issues pertaining to the physical realm in the lives of individuals.

- *Not Really Wanting to Get Well*

In the Gospel of John chapter 5 verses 1-15, we are told a very interesting story about a man who had been invalid for about 38 years, and when the Lord saw him at the Pool of Bethesda, He asked him if he wanted to get well. This was an interesting question which the Lord Jesus asked that man, and is still a very valid question to ask people today. You would be amazed, by the number of people, who on the surface, are professing that they are trusting God for their healing, but upon further evaluation, some of them really do not want to get well. As a doctor, I have met hundreds of patients like these. **They enjoy the attention they are getting from being sick (*by the way, a wrong and pathological way to get peoples' attention*);** they are lazy and want the disability benefits, and they want people to sympathize with them, etc, etc, and as such, they "put up a show", trying to impress others that they really want to be well; but at heart, they do not.

Just by virtue of the fact that the Lord asked this question of this man, it validates that there are people who really do not want to get well. God knows your heart, period! (Psalm 44:21; Luke 16:15; Acts 15:8). **Hence, if you are lying to others, but God Who sees the heart knows that you do not really want to get well, then, you will not receive your healing from Him.** So you might as well stop calling upon the name of the Lord, making Him look bad. So today, I am asking you the same question the Lord Jesus asked that invalid man: ***Do you really want to get well?*** If yes, then truthfully start seeking God's help, stop the deceit, and trust God. If no, then stop pretending and causing others to wonder why God is not answering your prayers. This type of deception is sin against God, so STOP it (if you are doing this), and repent! God loves you, and He wants to help you!

- **Dependence on Modern Medicine**

There are those Christians who are more dependent on modern medicine (i.e., medications) and are not honestly trusting God with their healing. **But unfortunately, they give a false impression that they are solely dependent on God, when all the while, they are**

more dependent on drugs. In essence, they trust their medications more than God, primarily because of fear! There is nothing wrong with taking medications, as long as you do not do so because you are afraid to trust God for your healing.

Unfortunately, there are individuals who are suffering from horrible side effects from modern medicines, and it is obvious that the medicines are not effective; but yet, they are afraid to stop the drugs and give God a chance with their healing. **The issue here is not the action of taking medicines, but rather, the motive behind taking the medications — If your motives are purely fear-based and/or laziness to trust God, then, this will become a major barrier in you receiving your healing from Him.** Again, if you do this, STOP it! And if fear is the reason you are more dependent on medications, then, may I suggest that you seek God's help to overcome that spirit of fear. As previously mentioned, I have teachings that can help you to overcome fear and trust God more, if you are interested in this.

God sees through your heart, and no matter how you lie to others, you cannot lie to Him. Hence, if you are dishonest, this deception will pose a major barrier to you receiving your healing directly from God. Again, there is nothing wrong with taking medications if that is where your faith is: God can still work through modern medicine, but be honest — where is your faith? — 100% dependent on modern medicine or God?

- **Neglecting Your Physical Body**

The issue of neglecting to care for God's temple, which is your physical body, is something that unfortunately, many Christians are guilty of, even though the Bible is very instructive that we should care for our temples (1 Corinthians 6:19-20). There are people who do absolutely nothing to care for their health: (1) They eat very poorly and as a result become obese, which is a sin against God (Deuteronomy 21:15-20); (2) they do not exercise regularly; (3) they do not practice good sleep hygiene; (4) they are emotionally and mentally undisciplined and immature, yet they choose to do nothing about it.

When people develop a disease because they have purposely neglected their physical bodies and health needs, and they continue to do nothing about it, but instead, expect to automatically receive their healing from God, it will not happen. I am sorry to say so! God will not bless disobedience, laziness or a rebellious attitude, period! To overcome this barrier to you receiving your healing, you would have to, by faith, initiate the process of being responsible in caring for God's temple: Your physical body and health needs. Think about this for just a minute. If you were to receive healing, right now, say from Diabetes, without you being responsible to care for your health needs, it will not benefit you in the long run! This is because you can be healed of diabetes, but if you do nothing to prevent diabetes from coming back, guess what? Diabetes will come right back, with a vengeance! Why? Because our lifestyles have a significant influence in the expression of most chronic diseases!

I am not implying that a healthy lifestyle habit will be a 100% guarantee for excellent health and/or long life: NO, that is not what I am saying! This is because at times, our healthy lifestyle practices will not automatically prevent all diseases and promote longevity; things are not perfect in this life. However, we would be wise to care for our physical bodies in accordance with God's Word, that way we will be doing our part to maintain our health and resist diseases.

We live in a "fallen world", and things are not as perfect as God originally created the earth. Thus, all kinds of diseases abound, but our lifestyle practices to care for our temples in accordance with God's Word will prevent the majority of chronic diseases. Likewise, being in disobedience and neglecting to care for our bodies will engender a host of chronic diseases: The choice is ours, and not God's! These physical barriers are straight forward and easy to fix. God wants you to be strong and healthy, that way you can be of more use to Him, yourself and others. Hence, I hope you can start, today, to take your health seriously. Proceed now to chapter 23 to learn more about the other barriers.

LESSONS LEARNED

➢ God has given us an ordinance to care for our physical bodies, thus, neglecting to do so is sin against God;

➢ With the power of the Holy Spirit, we can overcome chronic diseases that are attempting to dwell in our bodies, even when we have a genetic predisposition to these diseases.

Recommended Resources For Further Studies:

Available At: www.DrRuthTanyi.org

1. 13 Reasons Why People Get Sick: A Biblical Perspective & Remedies: **A 2-Set Audio CD Teaching**. By Dr Ruth Tanyi.

2. *Daily Habits For Your Soul:* Daily Biblical & Lifestyle Remedies to Prevent Sicknesses and Diseases: **A 2-Set Audio CD Teaching**. By Dr Ruth Tanyi.

CHAPTER 23

Barriers To Receiving Your Healing
"Hidden" Barriers
Part B

But if you are bitterly jealous and there is selfish ambition in your heart, don't cover up the truth with boasting and lying. For jealousy and selfishness are not God's kind of wisdom. Such things are earthly, unspiritual, and demonic. For wherever there is jealousy and selfish ambition, there you will find disorder and evil of every kind.

(James 3:14-16; New Living Translation, NLT).

Spiritual, emotional, and demonic hindrances are not easily noticeable, hence I call them "hidden" barriers, because people mistakenly believe they can hide them from God and others. **Also, because these barriers are not readily observable, people erroneously conclude they are "safe" in harboring these issues in their hearts** —well friend, this is a lie from Satan. Whether or not you are caught and/or exposed, these "hidden" barriers, which God knows all about, will still prevent you from receiving your healing, as clearly explained in the cited Scripture above, James 3:14-16. Let us now examine these barriers.

Spiritual Barriers

These are barriers pertaining to the spiritual realm.

- ***Practicing Sin***

    This one is pretty obvious, right?

//

The God of the Bible, Who is The Only True Living God, is 100% holy; and He will not, or cannot, and will never fellowship with an unrepentant sinful man or woman.

//

Sin is the original and primary reason that man's relationship was severed from God (see Genesis chapter 3), and sin remains the primary reason a person's relationship is severed from God Who is 100% holy, and as such, sin cannot abide in His presence. So, if you are practicing any kind of sin, and expecting to receive your healing from the Lord; well, I am here to categorically tell you that it will not happen. You must repent, before fellowship can be restored with God. And, if you are a true Christian, God has already made provisions for the cleansing of your sin. He has told us that if we (1) acknowledge our sins and take full responsibility for it; (2) confess the sin; and (3) stop practicing the sin, in His love and grace, the blood of Jesus will cleanse us, and restore us back into fellowship with Him (1 John 1:9). Once you repent of any sin in your life, God in His love and grace, will start to answer your prayers.

- o *Unbelief*

I have already described what unbelief looks like in preceding chapters, so refer there for details. But briefly, unbelief is multi-factorial and include, but is not limited to: **(1)** chronically doubting God's Word (e.g., James 1:7-8); **(2)** ignorance and/or a willful refusal to accept God's Truths as already revealed in His Word (Hosea 4:6); **(3)** elevating the opinions of others, including yours, above God's Word (e.g., John 5:44; Proverbs 29:25); **(4)** double-mindedness (e.g., James 1:7-8); etc; etc.

Sadly, as already described, unbelief was the primary reason that many people did not receive their healing from the Lord while He was here on the earth. And unfortunately, unbelief remains the primary barrier preventing countless amounts of people from receiving their healing today! **But the great news is that, this problem of unbelief can be easily fixed, if you are willing to keep an open heart, and allow God's Word to fill and heal your soul — it is your choice!**

o *Harboring Unforgiveness*

This subtle, but deadly, ungodly emotion is far too common among Christians. I have ministered to countless Christians who are deceived into believing that God will still answer their prayers, even though they harbor unforgiveness towards others in their hearts. Friend, I am sorry to say that it will not happen. The Lord Jesus vehemently teaches that if you stay unforgiving towards others, then God will not answer your prayer, period! (Matthew 6:15). So, if you are believing God for His healing power to flow in your life, and you harbor unforgiveness in your heart, you must repent, confess it, forgive the other person, and then ask God to forgive you of this sin of unforgiveness. Doing this will cleanse you from this barrier to you receiving your healing from God, today!

o **Spiritual Laziness, Being Passive**

The issue of being utterly passive towards the things of God, such as not praying, studying the Word of God, seeking spiritual discernment and counseling, etc, is far too common among many brethren in the body of Christ. **There are many who are erroneously believing that God's will for their lives will "just come to pass", automatically, which is FALSE and unbiblical. As I have discussed throughout this book — you have a role to play — obedience, walking by faith, knowing God's Word and applying it in your life, etc**. Also, keep in mind that this spiritual laziness I am referring to here is a hardened heart towards God — which is considered disobedience.

If you are spiritually lazy, then it will pose a major barrier to you receiving your healing. God will not violate your Free Will. By being lazy and not seeking Him, you will limit His ability to manifest in your life. Spiritual laziness and not resisting the devil go hand-in-glove. As Christians, we have inherited power and authority, by faith, in the name of Jesus to use our mouths as weapons and speak faith filled words and Scriptures over our bodies, circumstances, etc, and expect deliverance. Unfortunately, some Christians are passive, mistakenly believing that because they have prayed, God's promises will automatically manifest— Friend, this is not the case some of the times. You have an enemy, Satan, who can fight you in the spiritual realm, delaying God's answers to your prayers. So we have to be alert to the enemy's schemes, and quickly come against any hindrances to our prayers. A classic example of this in the Bible is the Old Testament Saint, Daniel, who had to fight Satan for 3 weeks after he prayed (see Daniel 10: 1-15).

In fact, there are many other circumstances in our lives whereby God wants us to enforce our authority in the name of Jesus by faith, and trust Him with the results. As an example, there are many people who have come to Christ, and as such, have been immediately delivered from generational curses in their families such as alcoholism, addictions, thievery, etc; yet, they are extremely passive about the consequences of these things, and thus are allowing Satan to still torment them about their past. Rather, stand up in faith in the name of Jesus, resist the lies from Satan, enforce the power and authority you have inherited in His name, and curse those generational curses and their consequences out of your life and family. Thereafter, speak "life" and healing into your situation and trust God with the result.

God has already delivered you from generational curses; but by faith, you can overcome the consequences of your past by enforcing your authority in Christ while trusting the Holy Spirit for help. To illustrate further, you can remind Satan, daily, that your past has no authority over you, and then use your mouth to speak health into your life, in Jesus name! But, if you are one of those passive Christians, then, your passivity will be a major barrier to you receiving your healing. The Bible teaches that faith without

Barriers To Receiving Your Healing: "Hidden" Barriers (Part B)

corresponding action is dead, useless! (James 2:14-26). So if you just pray, refuse to enforce your authority in Christ and/or act in accordance with your faith, then you will struggle with receiving your healing.

Additionally, there are those individuals who are "indifferent" about physical healing, considering it as a "non essential" to their relationship with God, because we will receive new (glorified) bodies in heaven. Well, I agree, that physical healing is not an essential doctrine of the Christian faith (proclaiming the Gospel Message of Christ Jesus and making disciples are the most essential doctrines). However, all of the other doctrines taught in the Bible, including physical healing, are significant in how we live out our Christian life and serve God. As an example, being chronically sick will limit your physical ability to serve God to your fullest. Thus, being "indifferent" will pose a barrier to you receiving your healing.

Emotional Barriers

In my opinion, **emotional barriers, such as gossiping, jealousy, envy, etc, are by far the major killers of God's children today. Unfortunately, these are the most "hidden" barriers too — Yet, God sees through it all.** And countless brothers and sisters in Christ are dying daily from these emotional maladies. As a Doctor and a Minister, I continue to minister and counsel dozens of brethren with these emotional issues, and many are being set free. Since the majority of Pastors/Ministers are not medical professionals, they themselves do not have an in-depth understanding about the connectedness between these emotions and diseases. Nonetheless, God's Word has told us so, and medical science has a plethora of studies validating the deadly effects of these emotions to your health, hence we should take heed to God's advice. Due to space limitation, I am unable to expound more on this, **but for those of you interested, I have over 7 hours of teachings on this topic on audio CDs that have set many people free.** You can obtain these resources to supplement this section of the book.

- **Strife, Gossiping, Harboring Bitterness, Anger, Resentment, Envy, and Jealousy**

    Besides harboring unforgiveness which is a major barrier to you receiving your healing from God, these other toxic and ungodly emotions of being in constant strife (i.e., being contentious, argumentative, etc); gossiping, harboring bitterness, anger, resentment, envy, and jealousy in your heart will absolutely prevent you from receiving God's healing. This is because we serve a God of love and peace, Who desires unity! **God flows through His love and compassion to heal us, and He will not operate contrary to His nature or character. Hence , in the presence of these contrary emotions, you will limit His ability to flow through you.**

    These ungodly and demonic emotions are major barriers that have prevented many Christians from receiving their healing. Believe it or not, people who are unforgiving are also bitter, envious and contentious. Those who gossip are often liars, very contentious and frequently cause division among others, which is something the Lord abhors (see Proverbs 6). The type of individuals who display these ungodly emotions would chronically argue and fight over nonsensical issues "at the drop of a hat", cause division, lie, etc, and then turn around and believe God for their healing. Yet, they fail to realize that all of these behaviors are contrary to God's character of integrity, love, unity, and peace. And, **the Bible is very instructive in teaching that the power of God is quenched, and all kinds of evil work from Satan will be evident in the presence of these toxic ungodly emotions (James 3:16).**

    Besides the fact that you will be sinning against the Lord when you harbor these emotions, medical research has confirmed that these ungodly emotions will trigger the release of potent stress hormones, which will eventually dampen your immune system. As a result, all existing chronic diseases will get worse, you will become sicker, and even modern medications will not work effectively in your body. For those of you needing help in this area, I have an audio CD teaching titled: **Daily Habits For Your Soul**, that goes into depth, explaining the connection between these emotions and your Health, and how you can overcome them. I also recommend my audio CD teaching: **Holy Spirit-Led Healthy Emotions and Your Health**. In this teaching, I further explain how to activate the Fruit of the Spirit and allow healing to manifest.

- o *Chronic Fear, Worry, and Care*

By care, I am referring to the tendency to focus more on your disease and problems, than on the solutions found in God's Word; chronic in this context implies few weeks in duration. No matter how much you pray and/or love God, if your energy is spent more on worrying about the disease and its outcomes; rather than focusing on the solutions as already prescribed by God in His Word, that is to say, meditating on God's promises, then, this habit will hinder you from receiving your healing, period!

Alongside the habit of care, are the ungodly emotions of fear and worry, which go hand-in-hand. As previously described, fear and worry are never from God, and fear is accompanied by torment (1 John 4:18). Also, keep in mind that in the presence of fear, the power of God is always quenched, because God Who is love, will not flow through fear, period!

Love and fear are two opposite emotions that cannot coexist—they are mutually exclusive — when one emotion is in operation, the other cannot dominate. So you, and not God, gets to decide which emotion will dominate your soul.

Because God is love in His essence, He flows through compassion and love, and not fear! (1 John 4:7-21). So if you invest your energy in being chronically fearful, and you choose to do nothing about it, then your actions will prevent God's healing power from flowing through you, and your enemy, Satan, will rejoice! And medically speaking, chronic fear, worry, care, etc will lead to a host of preventable diseases, such as High Blood Pressure, Heart Burn/ Acid Reflux, Anxieties, Depression, Headaches, etc, etc.

- *Pride*

Pride comes in many forms, such as (1) self-righteousness; (2) displaying a "know it all" attitude; (3) displaying a "familiarity Complex" attitude, etc. Let us now examine these types of pride in this section. The Bible teaches that God hates pride (Proverbs 6:16-19). And in fact, pride leads to self-destruction, but God honors humility (Proverbs 16:18-28; 18:12). **Friend, it is sad, but there are many people who are too proud and/or ashamed (which is a form of pride) to depend on God for their healing**. And there are those who are too proud to even pray to God for their healing, or ask a Minister or others to pray for them. I have ministered to many people like these, who did not even perceive that they were prideful, but yet their comments were a tell-tale sign! As an example, I have heard people say, *"Well, even if I ask, is God going to answer? If not, I might as well keep doing what I know works!"* Whoa! A statement like this, while it may appear subtle and ignorant, reveals a person's heart— **they are self-absorbed, which is a form of pride, exalting their ways above God's Word, period!**

Then, another form of pride is seen in those who think **"they know it all"; yet, they have no clue how to go about receiving their healing.** People like these are not sensitive to God's inner promptings, and are often impatient and quick to say, "I already know that"! Or, they would say something like this, "I've already tried that and it didn't work!". This type of a heart attitude is horrible, because even God is unable to reach them in His love, humility, and grace.

I remember talking to a lady who called me and was asking for prayer about her failing health. But it was sad because each time I attempted to minister to her over the phone even before our scheduled meeting, she would interrupt me by saying, " I already did that with my mother who is a Pastor", etc. The more I attempted to minister to her, the more I noticed that she would interrupt me to say, "We've already done that!". Then finally, I said, "Well, it appears as if you do not need me then, because you are not listening to me, but rather, you want to let me know about your "spiritual prowess." When I said that, she then realized how arrogant she had been, and she softly said, "Well, it is okay, I can always use more prayer". I was disappointed, to say the least. An attitude like this is a significant barrier to people receiving their healing from God Who is humble.

In this lady's case, it was obvious that whatever she and her mother were doing was not yielding results, because she contacted me, but her pride was in the way. If you are like this lady, arrogant about your 'spiritual prowess' rather than humbling yourself and listening to God and/or a minister who wants to believe God and pray with you, then your attitude will hinder God's power from flowing.

Self-righteousness: A Major Killer!

The pride of self-righteousness — viewing yourself as "holier than thou" and/or stupidly believing that God owes you "something" because you are a "good" Christian, will absolutely prevent you from receiving your healing or anything else from God.

In my view, this is by far the worst, in God's eyes. I have even heard stories of so many Christians who have said, "Well, I am going to stop serving God because He didn't do so, and so", etc. <u>Boy! If this is your attitude, I am sorry to say that God does not need you — He will use someone else</u>. Why are you blaming God? This type of misplaced unrelenting chronic anger towards God is from the devil, I believe. Can you ever pay God back for what He has done for you —dying that excruciating and humiliating death for you? I get so angry (i.e., holy anger) when I hear this from Christians. If people could only meditate on what the Lord Jesus did for them on Calvary's cross, and God's grace towards us, they will not make such ignorant statements!

Also, **Self-righteousness can be very subtle. As an example, I was ministering healing to a lady a few years back and she made a statement that was a "tell- tale" sign of her pride. She said, "I have prayed, fasted, read my Bible, and I am still not healed". The moment she said that, I told her right away, " That is why you are not receiving your healing because, you are pointing to your 'good works' rather than what Jesus has already done for you." She was shocked by my response and she quickly repented. Friend, we must take our eyes off of ourselves and focus on Jesus, the Ultimate Healer**, period!

Then, there is the pride that comes with the **"familiarity Complex"** phenomenon, meaning, people who know you personally may disregard or "put down" your ability to help them with their problems. This was what happened to the Lord Jesus during His earthly Ministry. Sadly, people who know you the most may be too proud to even ask you to lay hands on them — how stupid, this attitude of pride! If you are struggling with asking people you personally know to pray and to lay hands on you, you may be limiting God's ability to reach you. God always works with what is available at hand—it may be that relative or friend you do not like, yet he or she is the person available, willing, and ready to be used by God.

o *Ashamed of Jesus*

Being shameful to call upon the Lord publicly is another destructive form of pride. If when among your intellectual friends you are ashamed to announce that you are depending on God for your healing, but then, when in church or among fellow Christians you give the impression that you are trusting God with your healing, then this major barrier will prevent you from receiving your healing.

As already discussed a little earlier, God sees your heart, so you might as well "come clean" and stop deceiving yourself. The Lord Jesus is not ashamed of you in front of God the Father, why would you be ashamed of Him in front of others? Think about this! But, if you remain ashamed to call upon the name of Jesus publicly, then, He too will not intercede to God the Father on your behalf (Luke 9:26). **And remember, Jesus is the Only Mediator between God and us, Mankind, period (1 Timothy 2:5)!**

Demonic Barriers

These are issues pertaining to the demonic realm. As Christians, we have inherited power and authority in the name of Jesus to overcome any kind of demonic activity. **But regrettably, some Christians do not know how to go about this, as such, they have believed the lies from Satan, and he is oppressing and suppressing them — Not resisting the devil is one major reason why some Christians are unable to overcome their diseases.**

- *Not Resisting the Devil*

A major barrier to receiving your healing is your inability to resist (i.e., come against) the lies of the devil, especially if you discern that your disease is "demonic" in origin. The Bible teaches that when we resist Satan, he will flee from us (James 4:7). God is stronger than Satan, this is obvious! However, when Christians purposely and/or ignorantly neglect to enforce their authority in Christ (i.e., put to practice by calling upon the name of Jesus) and refuse to resist the devil due to spiritual laziness, then, it will pose a barrier to them receiving their healing. Although the majority of diseases are not demonic in origin, some of them are! But unfortunately, some Godly Christians are unable to discern whether or not their sickness and/or disease is demonic in origin.

And, some Christians are not, by faith, enforcing their authority in the name of Jesus to command healing to manifest in their bodies. I remember teaching a Catholic lady how to enforce her authority in Christ, and it was amazing how after just a few months, she called me and was screaming, "It is working, I am seeing results", and I could not help but laugh at her amazement. Friend, by faith, you have inherited power and authority in the name of Jesus, so use it, and you will be amazed (just like that Catholic lady was), at the results you will start to see in your life!

As you submit to God through obedience and start enforcing your authority in Christ, you will be appropriating James 4:7, and you will experience visible results. As an example, call the disease attacking your body by its name (i.e., cancer, heart disease, diabetes, etc), and command it to leave your body in the name of Jesus, and then tell the disease it has no authority over you, a child of God.

o **Occult Practices**

There are two Spiritual Kingdoms in existence today on the earth: The Kingdom of Light, belonging to God [The True Kingdom], and the kingdom of darkness, belonging to Satan [The False Kingdom]. **By using the word "Kingdom" in association with Satan, I am not implying that he has equal power as God: Absolutely NOT. Satan has been defeated "hands down" by the Lord Jesus on the cross. The underpinning of Satan's kingdom is false, 100% lies, evil, etc, leading people to hell.** <u>These two Kingdoms are mutually exclusive, and the Bible is extremely clear that children of Light, belonging to God, have no business with the Kingdom of darkness</u> (2 Corinthians 6:14).

Unfortunately, there are those who claim to be Christians, but yet, are still involved in the occult, such as witchcraft, sorcery, psychic powers, palm reading, etc, which are practices that the Only True living God vehemently abhors, and has already told us that those who delve into the occult are not His children (Leviticus 19:31; 2 Chronicles 33:6; Galatians 5:19-21; Revelation 21:7-8), and they will send themselves to hell.

Occult practices are an abomination to the Lord, and anyone who is involved in this should evaluate if he or she is genuinely a true Christian? If not, you can change this right now by asking the Lord Jesus to come into your heart by faith, and He will accept you, regardless of your past. So if you are involved in these demonic practices, and at the same time calling upon the name of the Lord, you must STOP, repent, ask for cleansing and forgiveness. Thereafter, start to believe God for your healing.

There is Always Hope For Change

There are many other environmental barriers such as (1) "bad influence from hanging out with ungodly friends," (1 Corinthians 15:33); (2) toxic environmental influences; (3) internal barriers such as erroneously believing that your disease is glorifying God; etc, which can all pose major barriers in you receiving your healing. **God has given you a Free Will —so it is up to you, and not God, to overcome these barriers with the help from the Holy Spirit, and receive your healing in the name of Jesus. Choosing not to overcome these barriers have contributed to the premature deaths of many individuals who love God.**

Regardless of the barrier(s), they all lead to one ultimate problem— Unbelief! Unbelief is a choice: You can change that today, right now, if you sincerely want to receive your healing from God. If you are struggling with any of the common barriers discussed above, God's Word is available to you, right now! You can begin by searching the Scriptures for yourself, and allowing God's Word to cleanse your soul, like it did to me; that way, you can be emboldened by the Holy Spirit to start the process of overcoming these barriers. **God is readily available to help you, right now, but are you ready for His help**? (Psalm 46:1). With this thought, proceed now to the next chapter and learn how you can be healed too!

LESSONS LEARNED

- As much as God wants us to receive our healing, we have a choice in the matter— We must obey Him, come in agreement with His Word, and overcome common barriers that can prevent us from receiving our healing;

- It is up to us, and not God, to enforce the power and authority in the name of Jesus and excel.

Recommended Resources For Further Studies:

Available At: www.DrRuthTanyi.org

*All Audio CD teachings by Dr Ruth Tanyi.

1. 13 Reasons Why People Get Sick: A Biblical Perspective & Remedies.

2. Unforgiveness and Other Toxic Emotions: How to Walk in Forgiveness.

3. Live Above Your Fears & Overcome Sicknesses and Diseases.

4. Be Anxious No More.

5. Daily Habits For Your Soul: Daily Biblical & Lifestyle Remedies to Prevent Sicknesses and Diseases.

6. *Faith to Receive God's Promises: How to "Walk" in Biblical Faith and Allow the Blessings of God to Chase You.*

CHAPTER 24

RECEIVE YOUR HEALING: FOUNDATIONAL TRUTHS ABOUT HEALING
PART A

Dear friend, I pray that you may enjoy good health and that all may go well with you, even as your soul is getting along well.

(3 John 1: 2; New International Version, NIV).

Throughout this book, I have discussed how it is God's will for us, His children, to enjoy good health, as cited above in 3 John 1:2. And to my satisfaction, I have used various Scriptures to support this notion — I hope your spirit has been quickened. Sadly, there are some Bible teachers who are claiming that Scriptures such as 3 John 1:2 has nothing to do with our health. Well, friend, that is not so. If you were to take some time to study 3 John 1:2 in multiple translations, it will become obvious that this Scripture is indeed saying what it is saying in regards to God's desire, which is His will, for us to enjoy good physical health too!

As an example, let us take a closer look at how the Amplified Bible (AMP) version renders 3 John 1:2: ***Beloved, I pray that in every way you may succeed and prosper and be in good health [physically], just as [I know] your soul prospers [spiritually].*** What I like about the AMP version is that it includes multiple definitions of words in the English language from the original language, in this case, Greek, and it offers explanatory readings in brackets in order to enhance understanding. With this thought, go back and take a closer look at how the AMP Bible version renders 3 John 1:2. It is very obvious that this Scripture pertains to our physical health as well, right? I hope you can see this, and you are in agreement with God's will. Most significantly, I hope you are in agreement that it is always God's will for us, His children, to be healed, although it does not always happen for various reasons, some of which I have already explained.

Before I even begin the discussion of how to receive your healing, I want to establish some foundational biblical truths pertaining to healing, that will determine the outcome of your endeavors in seeking God. Thus in this chapter, I will discuss **7 Foundational Truths**, straight from God's Word, that are critical to you receiving your healing. It is essential that you make a decision with regards to where you belong regarding these foundational truths I am about to discuss. Without doing so, it might pose a problem with you receiving your healing. Below are the biblical truths:

Foundational Truths About Healing

    ಙ **Firstly, it is absolutely essential that you come in agreement with God that physical healing of your body was/is part of Christ's atonement on the cross**

The Bible teaches that, how can two walk together if they do not agree? (Amos 3:3). If you do not agree with God that His Only Son, the Lord Jesus has already purchased your physical healing on Calvary's Cross when He died, then you will struggle in this area of receiving your healing. This is crucial because you cannot approach receiving your healing from God as something that you are expecting to see happen in the future: NO! **Rather, God had already healed you over 2000 years ago on Calvary's cross (past tense). Most significantly, keep in mind that today in the 21st Century (until the second coming of the Lord), people are receiving their healing from God, rather than begging and waiting on Him to heal them, as God's healing power has already been released on the Cross when the Lord Jesus died for us.** In fact, the apostle Peter highlighted this Truth by penning it down in the past tense. Under the inspiration of the Holy Spirit, he wrote, "*He* *himself bore [**past tense**] our sins" in his body on the cross, so that we might die to sins and live for righteousness; "by his wounds you have been healed"* [**past tense**] (1 Peter 2:24), emphasis author's.

//

If you are constantly begging God to heal you, then it may mean that you do not quite understand and/or have not come in agreement with His Word that, He had already healed you over 2000 years ago. It is like a 180 degree change in mind set to come from a perspective of expecting that God will heal you, and believing that He has already healed you.

//

Here is the major difference. The former position (i.e., **placing the healing in the future**) can engender doubting and wondering whether or not God will heal you. Conversely, the latter position (i.e., **placing the healing in the past**) is consistent with God's Word, engenders faith, minimizes doubt, fear, wonder, etc, as it will be appropriating what is already available, and the biggest hurdle will be for you to learn how to receive it — this is the True biblical position (2 Corinthians 1:20).

Also, from the latter position (i.e., **viewing your healing as already accomplished**), it will be very difficult for Satan to deceive you, because you would have already believed that it [your healing] was achieved on the cross. **This position in and of itself will even change the way you pray — it will enable you to pray a prayer of faith, with boldness and confidence, since you will be praying in agreement with God's will, which is His Word.** However, from the former position, expecting that God will, maybe, might (i.e., **viewing your healing in the future tense**) heal you, can potentially open the door for Satan to plague your thoughts with chronic doubt, fear, wonder, whether or not you are worthy to receive the healing. You know why? **Because this [placing the healing in the future] is**

a position of unbelief, ignorantly or intentionally, hence it might open the door for Satan to come in and plague your mind with tormenting thoughts. Do you get the picture here? I hope you do, because for some people, this alone is setting them free right now, in Jesus name! The Lord Jesus said, if you adhere to His teachings, you will know the Truth and the Truth will set you free; so start adhering to His teachings today and be set free (John 8:31-32).

I am not saying that you cannot receive your healing if you are not in perfect agreement with God's Word: you might. **God, in His love and compassion, can still work through others who are in agreement with Him and are standing in faith on your behalf, in order for you to receive your healing. The difference here is that, <u>you will receive your healing through others, and not directly from God, because you are not in agreement with Him!</u>** Do you see the difference? However, God's best is for you to receive your healing directly from Him, if you are in agreement with His Word.

> ❧ *Secondly, it is essential for you to agree that you have a role to play in receiving your healing*

As described in multiple places in this book, God has given you a Free Will, and He will not violate that. I also want to clarify that your actions do not, and will not move God: He already moved on the cross over 2000 years ago. However, your part has to do with you acting out your faith in accordance with God's Word, so as to position yourself for His will to manifest in your life. In other words, you have to believe God's Word, then by faith, act on it, then trust Him with the results. As already discussed, spiritual laziness and/or passivity will guarantee no results from God. Additionally, as part of your role, you have to, so to speak, "clean up your act", that is to say, evaluate your internal and external environments for any unbelief and/or barriers to you receiving your healing. **You do not have to be perfect, none of us are! But God wants you to be honest with your weaknesses, and He will help you — He specializes in helping the weak and the strong alike.**

ಐ Thirdly, your "Godly works" or actions will not cause you to receive your healing

By "Godly works/actions", I am referring to the tendency of you depending more on your spiritual activities and/or engaging in activities such as fasting; endless hours of prayer and/or putting together a prayer team to pray unceasingly, boasting of your holiness, spiritual activities or good standing in church, etc, as a way to receive God's healing. **These Godly activities are good if practiced within the proper context, meaning, out of a genuine heart as led by the Holy Spirit because you love God; <u>but never do these as a means of gaining God's favor.</u>**

God is very clear in His Word that He is after our hearts first, then everything else is secondary (Psalm 51:17; 1 Samuel 15: 22-23). Besides, there is absolutely nothing you can do to "buy" God's love or favor. As a genuine believer of God through Christ, you are already in good standing with Him because of your relationship with the Lord Jesus. You already have favor with God, so stop trying to earn it; doing so is called works of self- righteousness, which God considers as filthy rags (Isaiah 64:6). **This foundational Truth requires that you approach God on the merit of your relationship with the Lord Jesus only, and nothing else!** This leads me to the very next foundational truth, which is a struggle for many self-righteous people to comprehend and accept, because of their futile efforts to "buy" God's love.

ಐ Fourthly, God loves you! He is on your side, and He wants you to overcome this battle and "walk" in good health

This foundational Truth is very essential to keep in mind, especially when your circumstance appears bleak and it seems as if everything is "caving in" on you! Never lose sight of the fact that God is with you, fighting this battle with you, and for you. He is on your side, whether or not you perceive His presence! He is there, right now (Psalm 46:1-3; Romans 8:31), count on that!

ඝ **Fifthly, God's grace is available and is more than sufficient for your problems**

A lot of times, many individuals easily give up because they evaluate their disease or circumstance based on their human ability. But, it ought not to be this way. **For the true Christian, God's grace will always be present through His Holy Spirit, at the exact time to assist him or her to overcome any crisis, regardless of how severe the diagnosis or prognosis is.** Most importantly, keep in mind that God provides His grace for the problem at hand, and not for your future problems. When future problems come, God will be there likewise, providing His grace for you to endure and overcome. This foundational Truth alone is enough to assist you to overcome any fear, anxieties, etc about what tomorrow will bring or about what the prognosis will be. **God will not provide tomorrow's grace today. He is an ever present God. He is The God of NOW! His name is " I AM", RIGHT NOW! (Exodus 3:14).** So accept this foundational Truth and avoid the temptation of trying to figure out how you will handle the news from the doctor tomorrow or whenever. God's grace will be available tomorrow, deal with NOW! Trust God with NOW!

ඝ **Sixthly, God is Not punishing you with a disease**

This lie from Satan has sent so many ignorant Christians to a premature grave. This is one of the worst lies I have heard with regards to healing. **Friend, why would God, in the person of the Lord Jesus, die on the cross for you to enjoy good health, and then turn around and punish you with a disease? Does this make any logical sense to you? Have you thought through this line of thinking before? It is 100% contrary to the nature of the loving, compassionate and gracious God of the Bible.** Many people are suffering from various diseases today because of their poor choices —God has nothing to do with bringing on your disease!

Besides, the Bible clearly teaches that there is no guilt and/or condemnation if you are a follower of Jesus (Romans 8:1-2). So why would God condemn or punish you with a disease? God is not the author of confusion (1 Corinthians 14:33), Satan is! Like I explained earlier, God uses His Word to correct us into all righteousness and truths, and not diseases (2 Timothy 3:16). God will not, and He cannot punish you with a disease or any crisis to "teach you a lesson", this will be 100% contrary to His nature and Word.

Unfortunately, Satan uses this lie to deceive ignorant Christians, that way he will render them ineffective and/or powerless to fight against him and the disease. Think through this with me please, if you foolishly agree that God is punishing you with a disease, then there is no need to fight, right? Because, how do you fight with God? You cannot! As a result therefore, you will easily adopt a passive "victim mentality", accept the disease, become ineffective and powerless! — And guess what? Satan wins, and you suffer or may even die before your time. You see how this lie from Satan can lead many God loving Christians to an earlier grave? I hope you do not allow Satan to deceive you likewise. **This foundational Truth alone has been sufficient to set many Christians free to receive their healing from the Lord!** I hope you can be set free too, in Jesus name!

    ಐ **Seventhly, God is always with you! I mean always!**

This foundational Truth was very comforting to me during my battle. I hope it can bring comfort to you as well. **God is The God of comfort. He is an ever present God** (Psalm 46:1), whether you perceive His presence or not. He specializes in making Himself known in times of crisis, so call upon Him, count on Him hearing you, because He is always available! I mean always present—believe this Truth! Embrace this Truth!

I hope you are in agreement with the 7 foregoing foundational Truths from God's Word. Hopefully, that is so; I want to now proceed to offer some recommendations that will better position you with God's will, so that you will receive your healing. Proceed now to the next chapter to learn these recommendations.

LESSONS LEARNED

➤ For the true Christian, we have the assurance that God will never punish us with a disease, because the Lord Jesus took all of our sins and its punishment on His sinless body on the cross;

➤ Even though healing of our physical bodies was/is a part of Christ's atonement on the cross, we, His followers, have a role to play in receiving our healing;

➤ Our Godly activities such as fasting, serving God, etc, cannot cause us to receive our healing. We can only receive healings because of God's grace and our relationship with Christ. Thus, choose to focus on Jesus, and not on your "self-righteous works."

~~~~~~~~~~~~~~~~~~~~~~~~~~~~~~~~~~~~

**Recommended Resources For Further Studies:
Available At: www.DrRuthTanyi.org**

*All by Dr Ruth Tanyi.

1. The Heart of True Christianity: The Gospel Message of Jesus Christ: Answers to 10 Major Questions Pertaining to Your Salvation in Christ Jesus. **A 5-Part Audio CD Teaching.**

2. *Are You Moving Forward with Jesus? How to Excel In Your Identity in Christ.* ***Also available in Audio CD.***

3. *Can I trust the Bible as God's Word? How do I Know? What Is the Evidence?*

4. Faith to Receive God's Promises: How to "Walk" in BIBLICAL FAITH and Allow the BLESSINGS of GOD to Chase You. ***Also available in Audio CD.***

CHAPTER 25

RECEIVE YOUR HEALING: YOU CAN BE HEALED TOO! PART B

He sent out his word and healed them; he rescued them from the grave.

(Psalm 107:20; New International Version, NIV).

Hopefully, you are in agreement with God's Word that He desires for you to overcome your disease and thrive. Therefore, all that is necessary from you is to learn how to receive your healing. But unfortunately, some people do not know how to operate by faith and receive God's promises because they have not been discipled (i.e., taught) how to do so. At times, even those who claim to have been discipled make the mistake of attempting to appropriate God's promises by relying on a formula.

But there are no formulas when it comes to receiving from God — it does not work like that in God's Kingdom. Some of you may be looking for a list of "do's and don'ts" on how to go about receiving your healing. But sadly, such a list does not exist in God's Kingdom.

As already explained throughout this book, everything we receive from God is based from a genuine heartfelt relationship with Him because of His grace, and our relationship with the Lord Jesus and the empowering from the Holy Spirit.

Hence, the recommendations I will discuss in this chapter

are therefore not intended to be dogmatic; rather, I want them to serve as a guide to assist you with positioning yourself to receive your healing. **These recommendations are all biblical truths—I will not be presenting any new information here.** Rather, I will only make recommendations based on God's Word, and offer to you sort of a "pathway", so to speak, on how you can apply them into your life and expect Godly results. **Plus, these recommendations are not "head knowledge" — I am a living testimony that they work!** For God's Word is medicine, and He has already sent forth His Word to heal us, as the Scripture cited above at the top of this chapter (Psalm 107:20) is teaching — this is the absolute truth —I am a living testimony to this truth!

Because I have discussed most of these recommendations in preceding chapters in depth, I will simply list them here, then offer practical "tips" as a way to guide you through the process of receiving your healing. Then, I want to add that, as a Bible teacher since 2006, I always make it a habit to ask people to take the time and study the Word of God for themselves. Thus, I am asking you to conduct an honest evaluation in light of Scripture, pertaining to these recommendations and everything I have discussed in this book, that way, you can allow the Holy Spirit to speak directly to your heart.

Practical Recommendations on How To Receive Your Healing

I will approach these recommendations with 3 major objectives in mind. **Firstly**, I will discuss 2 significant ways that you can position yourself to receive your healing — I call this, "**positioning yourself for the healing**". **Secondly**, I will pose questions to you, that hopefully, you will take some time to honestly search your heart for the answers. I call this, "**evaluating yourself**". It is my belief that an honest response to my questions will do one of two things: (1) cause you to see problematic areas in you receiving your healing, that way you can better position yourself to overcome them in the name of Jesus and receive from God; and/or (2) edify, strengthen, and encourage you that, you are well positioned in the right path to receiving your healing. Then **thirdly**, I will offer some recommendations on how

Receive your Healing: You Can Be Healed Too! (Part B)

to "REST" in the Lord while waiting for the manifestation of your healing. I will discuss the first two objectives in this chapter, then I will discuss "RESTING in the Lord" in the next chapter.

My ultimate goal with these recommendations is to help you to better understand that, "there is nothing new under the sun"— the answer is already available in God's Word. And receiving your healing is not as difficult as you might think. We, human beings, make it very complex, and people attempt to manipulate God's Word and go by formulas, but it is not so! Rather, the key is learning how to position yourself to receive what God has already made available for you on Calvary's cross over 2000 years ago. I also believe that these recommendations will strengthen your faith to receive from God.

Positioning Yourself For the Healing

Since the Lord Jesus has already healed you on Calvary's cross, your role is to learn how to receive it. Hence, it is significant that you know how to align or position yourself in accordance with God's Word, which is His will for you, so as to receive your healing. **You do not have to earn your healing, nor work for it! You just have to learn how to receive it by faith!** So, I suppose the next logical question you may have is this: "How do I position myself to receive my healing?". My testimony in this book provides some answers to this question. Learning from my testimony on how I received my healing provides a classic example for you to draw from. Notwithstanding, below are 2 significant factors I consider essentials, in positioning yourself to receive your healing.

> ➤ *Firstly, and Most Significantly, Evaluate Your Relationship with God Through Christ*

Have you truthfully accepted the Lord Jesus as your personal Lord and Savior? I ask this because unfortunately, there are many people who attend church and various Christian functions, and they are deceived that they are true followers of Christ, but they are not. Church activities, deceitfully calling upon the name of Jesus and even praying in His name without genuine faith in Him will not save you —you must be born again, period! (John 3:1-15). Meaning, you must have (1) honestly acknowledged that you are a sinner in need of a savior; (2) then you must have believed in your heart and confessed with your mouth in all of the claims and works of Christ Jesus; and then (3) you must have invited Him into your life by faith. If you have done so, then, you can confidently call yourself a true follower of the Lord Jesus. If you are not born again, you can change that right now by asking the Lord Jesus to come into your life by faith, and He will do so. Or, if you have received your healing from the Lord during some Christian function/church, and you have not asked Jesus to come into your life as your personal Lord and Savior, I recommend that you do so right now. **While your physical healing is important, your salvation is of utmost importance because you will die soon, and you want to be certain not to reject God's <u>Free Gift</u> of salvation and send yourself to hell.**

Is He Your Lord?

If you have genuinely placed your faith in Christ, have you made Him your Lord? There is a major difference! Sadly, there are many individuals who claim to have placed their faith in Christ as their Savior, but they have not made Him their Lord — personally, I cannot relate to this. Making Jesus your Lord simply means you humble yourself and wholeheartedly obey Him, and submit every area of your life under His Lordship through the power of the Holy Spirit —This is God's will for every true Christian.

The Lord Himself said, **"Why do you call me, 'Lord, Lord,' and do not do what I say?"** (Luke 6: 46). If Jesus is not your Lord, then it means that you are the lord over your own life, and that means you will "mess things up" all of the time, because God did not create you with the supernatural ability and wisdom to rule over your own life. You need His help in order to navigate through this life. If upon an honest evaluation, you can say with certainty that Jesus is your Lord and Savior, then you are in a covenant relationship with God through Christ, and your healing has already been purchased.

To clarify, in a covenant agreement, all parties involved must meet their end of the bargain for the benefits to fully manifest.

As Christians, our covenant agreement is between God and us, with the Lord Jesus in the center. God has already done all of His part through Christ on the cross (2 Corinthians 1:20). On the cross, the Lord Jesus said "It is finished!" (John 19:30). This pertains to our salvation and the thousands of other promises God has given to us in His Word. Our role is to meet our end of the bargain: obedience, studying and seeking to know God more through His Word, walking by faith, serving the Lord, etc, if we want to see His promises manifest in our lives.

As we meet our end of the bargain (i.e., our part in the covenant agreement or relationship) by faith, we will be positioning ourselves to receive God's promises, including healing in our bodies, since He has already done His part. Hope this is clear. Boy! If you can get this, it will save you countless of hours and years of trying to beg God to bless you, when He has already done so! If you are a true Christian therefore, the second most significant thing is for you to focus on your relationship with God through Christ. This brings me to the second essential factor to consider in positioning yourself to receive your healing.

> *Secondly, Do Not Chase the Healing; Rather, Focus on the Healer (Jesus Christ)*

In other words, do not primarily focus or seek after the results (i.e., the healing); rather, make it your primary goal to seek God through Christ with all of your heart (i.e., making certain you have Godly desires), soul (i.e., aligning your thoughts with those of God), and strength (i.e., serving Him) (Matthew 22:37-38). As you do these, the healing will happen as a byproduct of your relationship with God. And as I have said throughout this book, **God is primarily after your heart and a sincere relationship with you, everything else is peripheral, including your physical healing. This sounds simple and easy, but it is the truth, although it may**

not be as easy to accomplish, because we have to fight through all of the unbelief round and about us. But if you sincerely have a vibrant relationship with God, and you are loving Him with all of your heart, soul and strength, He will be certain that He takes care of your needs —This explains why the Lord Jesus said when we seek first the Kingdom of God, God will meet all of our other needs (this also includes the healing of our diseases) (Matthew 6:33). God created us in His image primarily for a relationship with Him first, and everything else is secondary.

This is extremely important to keep in mind because there are individuals whose primary goal is to be healed, and not to develop a relationship with God. In other words, they are purely after what they can get from God, and they are not interested in finding out what God expects from them! I have ministered to countless individuals like these, who go from one Minister/Pastor to another seeking for prayer, inquiring how they can be healed. Such individuals even travel across the country to attend various healing conferences so that a Minister would lay hands on them; and they would read all the books they can lay their hands on about healing. But unfortunately, in spite of all these, they are still unable to receive their healing.

At times, when I have had the opportunity to minister to individuals who are primarily after the healing, **I have had to tell them to stop their "works" — meaning, I have asked them to (1) stop asking for others to lay hands on them; (2) stop reading all of the healing books; (3) stop going to the healing conferences, and just "stay still" , "<u>at the feet of Jesus</u>", and seek God first, wholeheartedly —spending time in His presence, studying His Word, praying and meditating on the Scriptures.** I would often tell them that developing a relationship with God is most important, and then all of God's blessings will flow out of a sincere vibrant relationship with Him—as we live in obedience, stay connected to Christ by faith and depend on the Holy Spirit for strength—this is God's best for us.

Anything we attempt to receive from God apart from

a sincere relationship with Him is considered "works", which is stressful, painful, difficult, futile, and will not last. You need to be grounded in your identity in Christ and in the Truths in God's Word —you will only be set free as you abide in Christ and His Word (John 8:31-32). Not abiding (staying connected, focused) in God through Christ and becoming grounded in His Truths offers one explanation why some people receive their healing when a minister operating in the gifts of miracles or healings lay hands on them and, an observable healing is noted, but later on, the person dies from the same disease.

Although we do not have all of the answers, one possible explanation is simply that, God might have worked through a minister operating in the gifts of the Holy Spirit to effect the healing. But thereafter, if the person who received the healing does not know how to operate in basic Bible faith and walk in that healing, Satan, the Master thief and killer can "attack" the individual at an opportune time. And unfortunately, if the individual is not grounded in his or her identity in Christ and in the Truths in God's Word, he or she will not be able to overcome the lies from Satan, and this may lead to serious consequences and even a worsened physical "attack" in his or her body (John 10:10; Matthew 12:43-45).

Hence, it is essential that we (a) personally have a vibrant sincere relationship with God; (b) know how to receive our healing directly from God; and (c) know how to "walk" in that healing, rather than chronically and/or permanently depend on others. **There is a time to depend on others for help, but a time must come, when each of us must learn to solely focus on Jesus, depend on the Holy Spirit, and trust God.** So if you are one of those people who are primarily seeking after the healing, I recommend that you STOP! Start seeking after the Healer, Christ Jesus, and cease from your "works"— you cannot receive healing through your own futile efforts.

Now that I have discussed the 2 essential factors that must be established as you position yourself to receive your healing, I now proceed to ask you some questions that require that you sincerely search your heart.

Evaluating Yourself in Light of Scripture

As you are being positioned to receive your healing, evaluate yourself in light of God's Word. Because the Scriptures recommend that we evaluate ourselves whether or not we are walking in accordance with God's will, it is critical that we heed to this advice (2 Corinthians 13:5; 2 Peter 1:10-11). In light of this biblical admonition, I pose the following questions to you with hopes that upon an honest evaluation, the Lord will speak to your heart, and your answers will help you to ascertain any problematic areas, that way you can position yourself to overcome and receive your healing.

> ➢ *Do You Really Want to Get Healed from the Lord?*

As already discussed, this question is critical, especially as the Lord Jesus Himself asked this question to the man at the Pool of Bethesda (John 5:1-6). If the answer is yes, then, you are right on track, attached to the "Vine", Christ Jesus Himself (John 15:5), and well positioned to receive from God, because He says that when we ask and seek Him, we will receive. So do not give up, you are well positioned to receive from God (Matthew 7:7-8).

> ➢ **Are you Spending Time in God's Presence, Studying His Word and Meditating on His Truths?**

I have explained how God has already revealed Himself to us through Jesus Christ, and His Word. And as true Christians, we have the Holy Spirit indwelling us to illuminate all Godly Truths and guide our daily lives and decisions. Hence, we cannot know God apart from His Word. This biblical truth is explicit throughout the Scriptures, and I have emphasized this throughout this book. So, now that you, hopefully, are in agreement with this Truth, knowing God through His Word is essential to you receiving your healing. If you are willing and/or, are already beginning to invest some time in God's Word, which is the Ultimate medicine, then you are well positioned to receive your healing!

You do not have to spend as much time studying and meditating on the Word of God as I did. Nevertheless, one way or the other, it is necessary that you rearrange your schedule in order to spend quality and quantity time in God's presence through the art of studying, meditation and prayer. Be determined to know God's Truths about healing for yourself! Meditate on these Truths! Exalt these Truths above and beyond other truths! Allow God's Word to penetrate your soul and change your thoughts, just like it did mine. Allow the Word of God to become your daily medicine; meditate on the healing Scriptures day in, day out, until you perceive its Truths with your spiritual eyes—these Truths will begin to heal your body—they will — it is a promise!

Do not give up on God's Word! — It works! Find what works for you, so that you can have the Scriptures readily accessible at all times. For me, it was a 4 by 4 card, where I had written Scriptures to carry with me. For you, it could be something different. Regardless, use the Word of God as your lifeline, because it is! In preceding chapters, I listed several Scriptures that helped me. Go back and study those Scriptures and allow God to speak directly to your heart through them, and take some time to look up other Scriptures for yourself. Be patient! Remember: **Seed, Time, and Harvest**. The Bible teaches that you will reap a bountiful harvest if you do not give up (Galatians 6: 7-9). Then, as you are standing on God's Word, patiently waiting for the manifestation of your healing, be certain you are not allowing the enemy, Satan, any inroad into your life. This brings me to the next question.

> ➤ *Are There Any Barriers in Your Life Hindering the Release of God's Healing Power?*

I really recommend that you do an honest evaluation in this area. In preceding chapters in this book, I discussed several barriers that will hinder God's healing power from flowing. Have you taken some time to evaluate your internal milieu; meaning your soul, with regards to your motives, the presence of any ungodly emotions of unforgiveness, envy, jealousy, strife, doubt, etc, etc? **You want to be certain you are not harboring any of these demonic emotions that will absolutely prevent the manifestation of God's power in your life?** What about your external milieu; meaning, your relationships, immediate surroundings, etc? Are there any sources in your environment that the enemy may use as an inroad into your life?

These are critical issues to consider. Satan is very clever, although he is stupid and has already been defeated by the Lord Jesus. **Nevertheless, if he cannot get to you directly, he will attempt to gain access through other sources in your life. So be certain you do not allow him any inroad into your life, whatsoever.** You want to be certain there is nothing in the way, preventing God's healing power from flowing in your life. God wants you to receive His healing, so be certain you do not prevent that from happening. Then, as you are doing your evaluation and carrying out the task of eliminating barriers, are you submitting to God by faith and resisting the devil? This brings me to the next question.

> *Are You walking by Faith in Accordance with God's Word and Resisting Satan?*

I believe that your faith walk is where you will be tempted the most by Satan. Remember, just a tempting thought from Satan is not sin; but if you act on the tempting thought, then it becomes a sin. **Also, know that God will test your faith, which for the Christian, will be a good thing, because it is through the testing that we grow and are strengthened. On the other hand, Satan will tempt you unto sin. Keep this major difference straight — God will test you, and Satan will tempt you — God will never tempt you unto sin!** As the Bible teaches, faith without corresponding actions is useless. Again, I must explain that your actions will not cause God to move on your behalf, He has already done so on Calvary's cross. Rather, in accordance with God's laws, your actions have to

Receive your Healing: You Can Be Healed Too! (Part B)

correspond with what you believe in your heart, in order for you to position yourself to receive anything from the Lord.

//

I have heard some Christians say they do not have the faith to receive their healing! This is not true, because every Christian has the measure of faith in their born again spirit (Romans 12:3; Galatians 5:22-23), you just have to use what you have, and God will honor that.

//

It is not about weak or strong faith per se, rather we have to act on what we believe, whether little or big! As you do so, slowly but surely, you will be strengthened to take the next bigger step. It is a step-by-step journey. **When you take one little step of faith, the Holy Spirit will embolden you to take the next one, etc, etc.**

As an example, **if you are believing God for healing, then start to act like a person who is already healed, because God's Word says so, remember? Do not become comfortable with the "sick role". Have a Godly hatred and anger towards sicknesses and diseases, and use your words to curse any disease out of your body, just like I did. Also, if you can, get up and walk around the house, as much as possible, just like a well person would do.** Do your best to live a normal life as someone who is healed. By doing all of these, you will be acting in faith in accordance with your belief that you are healed. Doing all of these will very much position you to receive your healing from the Lord. And as you continue to walk by faith in accordance with God's Word, you will be "resisting" the devil.

By Faith, Lay Hands on Yourself

Some Christians are mistaken to believe that someone else has to lay hands on them, and not themselves, in order to receive their healing. This is not true. You can lay hands on yourself by faith in Jesus name and be healed. I believe the confusion is because, some individuals do not understand the difference between operating in the gifts of the Holy Spirit such as gifts of healings, miracles (1 Corinthians 12:8-10), versus standing on the Word of God and operating by faith in the name of Jesus and effecting the healing. True, the Holy Spirit can flow through any spirit filled Christian who is available, submissive to His promptings and willing to operate in faith and effect healing to manifest. But as a Christian whose faith is in Christ Jesus, you can, by faith, lay hands on anyone who needs healing and believe God for the healing to manifest. Due to space limitations in this book, I am unable to expound on the topic of the gifts of the Holy Spirit (1 Corinthians 12:8-10). For those of you interested in this, I recommend that you obtain my audio CD teaching titled: **What Are the Gifts of the Holy Spirit?** This powerful teaching will teach you how to operate in the gifts of the Spirit.

Recently, I remember explaining this to a lady who called me from out of town and was asking that I pray for a friend who was dying from Brain cancer. After I prayed, I went on to explain that she should proceed to still lay her hands on the person and trust God for the healing. This person was upset, saying, "I believe you have a gift, and I do not! What do you mean I can lay hands on someone?". Boy! It was tough explaining to her the difference between operating in the gifts of the Holy Spirit and simply walking by Bible faith and believing God for His miracles. I hope you understand the basic difference now. So, in Jesus name, I recommend you lay hands on yourself and trust God for the healing, <u>stop waiting for some Minister, please! It will be the Lord working through you, just like He will be working through the Minister</u>.

Additionally, whenever I teach people how to activate their faith and act healed, I am often asked this question: "Should I then stop taking my medications?". The answer is NO, because immediately throwing away your medications is not proof of your faith! Rather, you must be certain in your heart that you have heard from God that, it is time for you to stop your medications. This decision is a personal one —between you and the Lord. Most significantly, God may want to heal you without the drugs, but you may not be ready in your faith walk for that to happen, hence you must wait for His timing. Like in my situation, I continued with medications, and at the right time after I sensed God's direction in the matter, I stopped! So do not try to act "too spiritual" and stop your medications and then die prematurely! I know people who have prematurely stopped taking their medications and died, so be certain to hear from God about this decision. While waiting to discern God's direction, have you considered why you are sick in the first place? This brings me to the next question.

> ### Do You Know Why You are Sick in the First Place?

By asking this question, I am not attempting to offend you, absolutely NOT. But, it is relevant for you to evaluate why you are sick. At heart, many people know exactly why they are sick. Hence in order to help people, it is best to get straight to the "root cause" of the problem, versus wasting time and "dangling" around with futile attempts to fix the symptoms. As discussed in the previous chapters, many people are sick today because of abuse to their bodies and poor lifestyle choices. If this is your situation, then, it is an easier fix! **Start, today, to take better care of your body by eating healthier, exercising, getting at least 7 to 8 hours of sleep, in addition to learning how to manage your emotions, thoughts, appetites,** etc. In essence, learn to be a disciplined person: spiritually, mentally, emotionally and physically, period!

You do not need to even believe God for healing if your disease is due to poor lifestyle choices. Rather, believe God for the wisdom and fortitude to care for your health, ability to be disciplined, and then start changing your lifestyle habits, and you will be healed! These chronic diseases from poor lifestyle habits are the easiest to fix, in my view! **The cause of the problem is very obvious, and a person needs to just act and change their lifestyle, rather than seek God for healing. There are some things we do not even need**

to pray about, rather, by faith, we should just act on them. God says we should exert self control and care for our bodies; when we do this in accordance with His Word (i.e., obeying Him), such diseases will be easily managed and/or you can be healed completely. I have witnessed this happen dozens of times with my own patients.

I can imagine that some of you are blaming your genetics. Well, I am sorry to say that, with regards to chronic diseases, your lifestyle plays a major role in triggering the disease more than your genetics! Did you know that? Personally, I have a family history of the major chronic diseases of Diabetes, High Blood pressure, High Cholesterol, etc, etc, but guess what? I will not develop these diseases, because I am determined to care for myself by eating healthy, exercising, getting 7 to 8 hours of sleep, and living a spiritually, mentally, and emotionally healthy life, as unto the Lord. **So it is possible to have a predisposition to all sorts of genetics, and still be overcoming in Christ Jesus! I am doing it, you can do it too!**

As a true follower of Jesus Christ, you have the Kingdom of God on the inside of you, and you are a citizen of heaven; this earth is not your final destination. Which means that, anything that does not belong in heaven, such as sicknesses and diseases, is not your inheritance in Christ Jesus? So focus on Christ the Healer, fight against sicknesses and diseases, and receive your healing! As you are doing everything within your power to receive your healing, keep in mind that we do not have all of the answers as finite human beings. And a time must come when you must REST, in the Lord! Proceed now to the next chapter to learn how you can "REST" in the Lord while waiting!

LESSONS LEARNED

- Since God has already healed you over 2000 years ago on Calvary's Cross, your primary role is to position yourself in accordance with His will, which is His Word, in order to receive your healing— you do not have to earn it, nor deserve it— Christ Jesus has done it All for you;

- As the Bible teaches, it is necessary that we frequently evaluate ourselves, if we are "walking" in accordance with God's decrees.

**Recommended Resources For Further Studies:
Available At: www.DrRuthTanyi.org**

*All by Dr Ruth Tanyi.

1. The Heart of True Christianity: The Gospel Message of Jesus Christ: Answers to 10 Major Questions Pertaining to Your Salvation in Christ Jesus. **A 5-Part Audio CD Teaching.**

2. *Are You Moving Forward with Jesus? How to Excel In Your Identity in Christ.* ***Also available in Audio CD.***

CHAPTER 26

Resting in the Lord

For all who have entered into God's rest have rested from their labors, just as God did after creating the world. So let us do our best to enter that rest. But if we disobey God, as the people of Israel did, we will fall.

(Hebrews 4:10-11; New Living Translation, NLT).

In context, Hebrews chapter 4 is teaching about ceasing from the legalistic "do's and don'ts" of the Old Testament Mosaic Laws, and instead turning to Christ Jesus, Who has perfectly fulfilled all of those Laws. True "rest" is only found in Christ, and it begins at the time of our salvation and continues for the remainder of our lives as Christians. Which means, regardless of the dire circumstances we might be facing as Christians, we have to learn to "rest" in Christ and trust Him with the outcome.

There are many times when in spite of our best efforts walking in faith in accordance with God's will, we may not be seeing the desired results. In times like this, the only thing we can do is to reevaluate our circumstance(s), and if we have been honestly doing everything as unto the Lord, then we must REST!

By resting in the Lord, I am neither encouraging passivity nor am I implying that you should stop praying, studying the Word, or that you should do "nothing" about the situation and just sit around and "wait" — absolutely NOT. In fact, the true biblical meaning of "resting" in the Lord means that you completely trust Him 100% with no reservation — you wholeheartedly accept whatever the outcome will be, knowing that God knows best. Boy! It is very difficult to get to this place! But it is only when we decide to "rest" that we allow God's miraculous power to manifest. Medically speaking, it is also when we reach a place of "rest" that, our immune system functions the best and our overall health is improved, because there is less fear, doubt, care, anxiety, and stress on the body.

To reach this place of completely trusting the Lord is, in fact, a display of strong/ bold and active faith, because it requires effort (Hebrews 4:1-12). But, as you choose to surrender to the situation while trusting in the Lord, you will realize that you are more focused on Him (i.e., the solution) than on your disease or prognosis. And by focusing more on the solution, you will start to notice His healing power in your life, effortlessly! I really do not fully understand how this works, but this is how it works! Remember my example, when I surrendered and accepted death, I awoke the next morning with a "burst" of new energy and purpose, which refueled my fight!

How To "REST" in the Lord?

Some of you may be asking, "But how do I rest?" You do so by reaching a place of realization and acceptance that there is nothing you can do on your own effort for the healing to manifest any sooner. Thus, you make a heartfelt decision that, regardless of the outcome, God is in Absolute control. He loves you! He is fighting through you and for you! And He sees your faith in action, and eventually, at His perfect timing, He will honor that — This is God's promise to you!

Please avoid the trap of "doing" (meaning acting in faith) without reaching a place of "resting" — There has to be a balance. **Sadly, some spirit filled Christians have the tendency of just wanting to keep "doing", and "doing" (i.e., acting out their faith), without "resting". Doing this is stressful, and it can lead to people trusting more on their "actions", than in God's power. Others want to "trust in faith itself", rather than placing their** faith in God's Word. Be careful —your faith has to be in the promises already available to you in God's Word, and nothing else!

On the other hand, many passive Christians misunderstand "resting" to mean passivity, and as such, they choose to not act out their faith. To avoid these extremes, simply act in faith in accordance with God's Word, spend quantity and quality time in God's presence daily, meditate on His Word, be prayerful, then move on with your life while trusting God's timing —This will be resting in Christ!

I have even had some Christians ask me, "Isn't there anything else I can do besides studying the Word, meditation and prayer?". And I have had to tell them: "No, that is it".

//

God's Word is medicine. In the same way some of you will not stop taking your medications, likewise, why would you want to stop taking God's medicine (His Word)? As Christians, when we start to view and elevate God's Word as medicine, just like we view modern medical treatments, then, we will start to experience Godly benefits, of course, without the side effects!

//

<u>I tell this to my patients straight forward. I tell them, "I prescribe medications, but I will not take them because I trust God's medicine more." This statement is not meant to be boastful, for I am useless without Christ and the Holy Spirit working through me</u>. I say this in humility and honesty, this is where my faith is: God's Word! In fact, I believe that, even if I were to take medications, it will not work for me because I do not trust in them!

Some Reminders While "Resting" in the Lord!

While resting in the Lord, I want you to remember that:

- **God is 100% faithful and consistent! He will honor your faith walk.** Here is how the Bible puts it in Galatians 6:7-9:

Do not be deceived: God cannot be mocked. A man reaps what he sows. Whoever sows to please their flesh, from the flesh will reap destruction; whoever sows to please the Spirit, from the Spirit will reap eternal life. Let us not become weary in doing good, for at the proper time we will reap a harvest if we do not give up.

- **God is fighting this battle with you. He is on your side.** Here is how the Bible puts it in Romans 8:31:

What, then, shall we say in response to these things? If God is for us, who can be against us?

- **God wants you to be well!.** Here is how the Bible puts it in 3 John 1:2:

Dear friend, I pray that you may enjoy good health and that all may go well with you, even as your soul is getting along well.

- **He is always ready, available to help you. Just call upon Him as your lifeline, anytime, anywhere.** Here is how the Bible puts it in Psalm 46:1:

God is our refuge and strength, an ever-present help in trouble.

Remember, regardless of the outcome, all things will, indeed, work out for your good, if you are a true follower of Christ Jesus. Here is how the Bible puts it in Romans 8:28:

And we know that in all things God works for the good of those who love him, who have been called according to his purpose.

- **Remember, regardless of the outcome, God still loves you, unconditionally! You are an overcomer in Christ.** Here is how the Bible puts it in Romans 8:37-39:

... in all these things we are more than conquerors through him who loved us. For I am convinced that neither death nor life, neither

angels nor demons, neither the present nor the future, nor any powers, neither height nor depth, nor anything else in all creation, will be able to separate us from the love of God that is in Christ Jesus our Lord.

*Please take note: All emphasis to Scriptures are author's.

Additionally:

1. Be certain to maintain a **Christ-Centered perspective** (stay focused on Jesus) and surround yourself with strong sisters and brothers in Christ who can fight with you;

2. **Use your mouth as a weapon to curse the disease** and speak faith filled words and Scriptures into your life;

3. Be ready to **fight like a Tiger, and hang-on**! Be patient! It will come to pass!;

4. "**Give healing to others**", go and pray for the sick, lay your hands on them, and trust God with the results;

5. **Do not blame yourself** and allow Satan to torture you with guilt. If you are sick because you have neglected your health needs, then truthfully repent, trust God, and move on. **Do not live in the past. God wants you to move on, let the past be**! You are a new person now! God is dealing with you from NOW onwards, moving forward, so you start to move forward too!;

6. **Do not lean on your own understanding**, be steadfast in trusting God's wisdom, regardless of the doctor's report (Proverbs 3:5). And do not attempt to figure out how things will end up. Remember, God's grace will be available for tomorrow, so do not worry about tomorrow. Deal with today, right now! God's grace is sufficient for NOW. Tomorrow will come, and God's grace will be there as well (Matthew 6:34);

7. **Spend time in praising and worshipping God,** thanking Him in advance for your healing. You are indeed already healed, whether or not you see the visible evidence of it. Praising and worshipping God will cause Satan to flee from you; it will stimulate different hormones in your body which will in turn release powerful chemicals that will promote an overall sense of well-being;

8. **Spend time daily to laugh**, this is good for your overall health;

9. **Maintain a victor perspective,** because you are victorious in Christ. Do not allow Satan or others to deceive you into viewing yourself as a victim —you are not! **Do not allow "garbage" into your soul from others —"guard your soul";** and lastly

10. **Conserve your energy and focus on God's Word**, avoid strife, etc, and view every day as a gift from God. **Do not begin to plan your funeral.** Trust God's report instead and fight! Give God a chance!

Friend, I could go on and on about God's promises to you, but I am sure you get the point. Do not be discouraged! You are not the first, and you will not be the last to undergo what you are dealing with right now. Many of your brethren in Christ have fought the same or similar battles in the past, and they have overcome (1 Corinthians 10:13) — I am a living testimony! — You can be healed too! Allow the peace of God to saturate your soul and heal you (Proverbs 14:30).

Now that you are hopefully encouraged about trusting the Lord as your Healer, proceed to the next chapter and learn about some **"do's and don'ts"** when ministering healing to others. These "do's and don'ts" are also applicable to caregivers, friends, or loved ones caring for anyone facing any disease, especially when the diagnosis and/or prognosis is dire.

LESSONS LEARNED

- As true Christians, we do not have to beg God to heal us, as He had already done so over 2000 years ago on Calvary's cross. Our role is to learn how to align or position ourselves in accordance with God's will, in order to receive our healing;

- Our Godly actions will not enable us to receive our healing, rather, we have to focus on Christ Jesus 100% — Who is our Ultimate Healer.

Recommended Resources For Further Studies:
Available At: www.DrRuthTanyi.org
*All Audio CD Teachings by Dr Ruth Tanyi.

1. Holy Spirit-Led Healthy Emotions: The Fruit of the Spirit and Your Health.

2. *Did God Really Say that? How to Overcome Doubt and Receive God's Promises: 10 Life-Changing Lessons Learned from Overcoming Metastasis Colon Cancer.*

3. 13 Reasons Why People Get Sick: A Biblical Perspective & Remedies.

4. What Are the Gifts of the Holy Spirit?

5. *Faith to Receive God's Promises: How to "Walk" in Biblical Faith and Allow the Blessings of God to Chase You.*

6. Daily Habits For Your Soul: Daily Biblical & Lifestyle Remedies to Prevent Sicknesses and Diseases.

CHAPTER 27

Some "Do's and Don'ts" When Ministering Healing to Others

My dear brothers and sisters, take note of this: Everyone should be quick to listen, slow to speak...

(James 1:19-20; New International Version, NIV).

I was very reluctant to include this chapter in this book. But after much consideration, I concluded it was necessary because this book will not only be read by those with life threatening diseases and a dire prognosis, but even by those who are in good health. Some of you may be caregivers, family members, health care professionals, etc, hence the information in this chapter will be helpful I believe, as you care for others. With this understanding, I will present a general overview of some "do's and don'ts", that I believe will help you (regardless of your role), to assist those who are dealing with any kind of life threatening disease.

It is human tendency to want to say "something," right away to someone who is facing a dire circumstance, disease, or any other calamity.

For some reason, some people erroneously believe that their words will automatically bring comfort to others. Unfortunately, that is not always so! Granted, faith filled words from a fellow Christian, at the right time, can release God's healing power. But the problem is that, many people, even well meaning Christians, do not know the right time to speak, and when to just listen.

Yet, the Bible teaches us to be good listeners (James 1:19-20; Proverbs 18:13), rather than just talkers!

Whether you are a caregiver, minister, family member or a loved one who is ministering healing to others, it is paramount that you understand some basic things about helping a person struggling with any life threatening disease. This is especially significant if it is a disease with a dire diagnosis or prognosis, that way, you could better assist them. I say all of these as a Minister, a Doctor, and as one who has been a patient with a dire diagnosis and prognosis. Below are some common things not to do:

The "Don'ts"

1. **Do not ask someone, "How bad is the diagnosis?".** Or, "How bad is the prognosis?" This question will engender fear. Rather, allow the individual to share that information with you, whenever he or she is ready;

2. **Do not say, " It is God's will that you are sick", or say, "God is punishing you".** These statements are grossly wrong and unscriptural as I have already explained. In fact by saying this, you will be exposing your ignorance with regards to the nature of God;

3. Even when it is obvious that the person has a disease because of poor choices, do not bring it up! **Do not remind them by saying something like, "You see, I have been telling you to start eating right and exercising, etc, etc, this disease is your fault".** If this is the case, the person already knows it, so you do not need to remind them. Doing so can be very discouraging, and it can weaken the person's ability to fight;

4. **Do not say, "This person was/is a good person who served the Lord, love God, etc, and I don't know why God is not healing them".** A statement like this is wrong, unfair towards God and unscriptural, and it reveals that you are looking at the person's "goodness", rather than focusing

Some "Do's and Don'ts" When Ministering Healing to Others

on the Lord Jesus, the Healer. This statement also reveals a deficiency in your understanding of the nature of God, but you can change this;

5. **Do not remind them about the fact that you know people who died from the disease. Do not say things such as, "My aunty Suzie or uncle Dan died from this disease.". You would be amazed at how people do this kind of stuff all of the time. No person facing a deadly disease with a dire diagnosis and prognosis wants to hear such negativity.** Many people say such things without even considering how their words hurt others, please do not do this!;

6. Do not say things such as, **"You are a bad person, that is why you are sick"**. If this is the case, the person already knows that in his or her heart. You do not need to remind the individual of his or her sins! Give the individual the opportunity to talk to you about this!;

7. **Do not say, "You must confess of so and so before God will heal you"**. Boy! This is so common today in the body of Christ. You do not know a person's heart, so do not say such a thing! How do you know whether or not the person has confessed?;

8. **Do not say, "If you just pay all of your tithes, then God will heal you"**. This is wrong and unscriptural — you cannot buy God's miracles with money or your "good works" — we only receive from God by faith because of His grace;

9. Do not gossip about another person's disease. And, **under the guise of a prayer line, do not gossip about others who are sick**;

10. **Do not rejoice because someone you do not like is sick and dying**. This kind of an attitude is not pleasing to God (Proverbs 24:17-18);

11. **Do not assume** that you know how the other person is feeling or what he or she is going through physically, mentally, spiritually or emotionally! You are better off asking than assuming and then acting or speaking incorrectly;

12. **Do not assume a person is a Christian, please ask! Then, if the person is a Christian, do not quickly assume to know where this person is in his or her relationship with the Lord.** You would be wise to ask, because there are many people who call themselves Christians, but for one reason or another, primarily due to disobedience, they are not "walking" with the Lord. Meaning, they have not submitted their lives to the Lordship of the Lord Jesus, and as such, they do not know how to even begin to receive anything from Him — they may need your help, so please ask;

13. **Do not be afraid to be around the sick person.** Most diseases are not easily contagious. If the person has a contagious disease, then you might have to protect yourself with the necessary medical devices. But it is unlikely that you will "catch" a contagious disease by just sitting besides the sick person;

14. **Do not express your fear, doubt or worries when with the sick person.** This will cause the sick individual to become more frightened —rather, display joy, hope, kindness, etc;

15. **Do not repeat to the sick person, his or her negative report** you might have heard from the doctors or others — it will be discouraging;

16. **Do not assume that a person wants you to pray for him or her to receive healing. Always ask!**;

17. Do not tell the sick person that, "<u>**If you just believe and trust God, you will be healed**</u>". It is often not that easy. Only those who have not been in the sick person's situation can make such an incorrect statement. A lot of

sick people are trusting God, but they need help from someone who is strong in the faith to carry them through during this tough time. Alongside this line of thinking is the mistake many people make by saying to the sick person, "<u>You do not have faith, that is why you are not healed</u>". This is wrong and unscriptural, so do not say such a thing;

18. Do not say, "<u>If it is God's will, you will be healed, and if it is not, then, accept it</u>". This is very harsh, unscriptural and offensive. Do not verbalize such unbelief around the sick person, please. Such statements will paralyze them. The sick person needs hope, and not doubtful words.

Even though the list of "don'ts" can be endless, I am convinced that being aware of those I have listed above will make a significant difference in the way you interact with the sick individual. I now proceed to discuss some healthier, encouraging and hopeful ways that I believe you can engender healing when ministering to the sick or when you are around them.

The "DO'S"

The Ministry of Presence

The Ministry of presence simply means that you allow your presence to minister to the sick person without you saying much. Like the Scripture says out of James 1:19-20, we should learn the art of being an excellent listener. **More than anything else, what most sick people need when in that debilitated condition is someone who can just "be there" with them, being quiet, and listening. You do not have to speak! Just hold all of your kind comments, and discern the right time to speak.**

As an example, the right time to speak could be when the sick individual asks you a question. Even before you get into an elaborate discussion, be mindful that the sick person may be too tired to fully engage in a lengthy discussion. Hence, keep it simple, and consider asking his or her permission before offering elaborate answers. Most importantly, if you discern the right time to speak, use your words to engender healing. Here is how Proverbs 16:24 puts it, **Kind words are like honey—sweet to the soul and healthy for the body.** Your words can be a powerful weapon to release healing, encouragement, hope—so put this weapon to use and help others! **Remember, although the Words will be coming out of your mouth, they are God's Words, filled with His power, and you are just the vessel. So proceed and speak faith filled words, trusting that God's Words will not return void (Isaiah 55:11).**

Some Recommended "Do's" When Ministering Healing to Others

1. **Pray and ask God to use you as a vessel** to bring healing to the sick person. Do not be afraid to minister healing to others. Primarily, God is looking for those who are ready, willing and obedient. You do not have to be a professional Minister before God will use you. Rather, be willing to trust Him to use you, and He will;

2. When you are around the sick individual, **be fully present,** giving the person your full attention. Let the person know you are glad to be there with them. **Be calm! The sick individual can tell by your bodily gestures and language whether or not you want to be around them.** While with them, share fond memories you have shared with the individual in the past. And as you listen to the sick person, take note of what the individual is saying;

3. **Ask the person's permission to touch him or her, holding his or her hand**, if appropriate. Medical research shows that touch is very therapeutic. Offer yourself to help with whatever they might need;

4. Also, with the person's permission, **read aloud Scriptures** over the individual's body daily, and sing praise and worship

Some "Do's and Don'ts" When Ministering Healing to Others

music. Even in situations when the individual might be unconscious, his or her spirit and soul are still alive and aware of what is happening, so continue to minister to them. <u>We have many medical reports of people who were unconscious and comatose, and upon awakening from that state, have told stories how they remembered exactly what was happening around them.</u> You know why? Because the spirit and soul are always alive, even when a person cannot physically function.

Just recently, I was asked by a family to minister to a relative who was dying with advanced Kidney cancer. The family members were uncertain about his position with Christ. Before going to the hospital, they warned me that he was unconscious, and I reassured them that he will be able to hear me still. While I was ministering to him, I asked him to squeeze my hand to indicate a Yes, if he has accepted the Lord Jesus as his personal Lord and Savior. Boy! That man, who was comatose and had no energy, squeezed my hand so tightly, right in front of his family, and he would not let go; everyone there started to cry. It was an amazing experience. Then about 3 or 4 hours later, they called and informed me that he had died, but the family was very reassured that he had accepted the Lord. So Yes, even in a comatose state, you can still minister to people;

5. **Reassure the person, that you are in agreement with him or her**, and you are standing in the "gap" interceding for him or her;

6. **Do not give up! God answers prayers, in His perfect timing. And, whatever you do, please <u>trust God's report more than medical science</u>, do not give up!**;

7. If there are obvious sins and/or noted barriers you have perceived in the person's life that are hindrances to the individual receiving his or her healing; then, I recommend

you ask the Lord to embolden you so that you can gently address this in grace and love, pointing the individual to relevant Scriptures. **But please, do not ignore to address sin** in a person's life if you have the opportunity to do so. You may be the only opportunity God has to reach this person who needs help. If you disobey and ignore this, God will hold you accountable for this wrong;

8. Ask permission, and then pray for the person, that way, both of you will be in perfect agreement about his or her situation.

//

Know God's will, which is evident in the Bible that He wants us well, then pray a prayer of faith, agreeing with God's Word, that He has already healed the person.

//

What Is a Prayer of Faith

A prayer of faith simply means that you know God's will regarding the matter you are seeking Him for, then you pray in accordance with His will. Doing so will position you to receive the answer, in God's perfect timing (1 John 5:14-15). Since we know that it is God's will for us to be healed, you can pray with confidence knowing that you will be praying in accordance with His will, as you pray for healing. And as you do your best to walk in true Bible faith and overcome barriers that will prevent the flow of God's healing power, trust that in God's perfect timing, you will see the visible results. **Below is a sample prayer of faith**:

*Dear God, in Jesus name, I thank You that You have already healed { **place the person's name here, e.g., Rose**}. And I thank You for the power and authority I have inherited in the name of Jesus. Holy God, in the name of Jesus, I curse [**name the disease here, e.g., Diabetes; Cancer**], and I command it [**the disease**] to leave [**name the person's name**] body right now! By faith, it has been done. We come* *in agreement, and we believe that Your healing power is restoring* **[insert the person's name here]** *right now, and she/he* **[insert the person's name here]** *is receiving that healing, right now. We thank You God, for we have prayed in accordance with Your Word, and we know, by faith, You have answered us, and because You are faithful, we are expecting to see the answer, in Jesus name, Amen.*

The length of your prayer is not significant to God; rather, it is the sincerity of your heart as you pray in accordance with His Word, which is His will. After praying a prayer of faith like stated above, thank God daily for answering your prayer. Use your mouth to speak aloud Scriptures and release life into the person's body, praise and worship God for the deliverance. **Remember, as Christians, true Bible faith is first believing in your heart, and then receiving God's promises by faith before actually seeing the physical evidence.** So by praising and thanking God in advance before even seeing the manifestation, you will be operating in true biblical faith, and God will take notice of this. **Please, do not waver in doubt or fear. God will honor your faith! He is faithful! He is consistent!**

As a caregiver, a minister or a loved one believing God for another person's healing, a time must come when you too must "REST", in the Lord! While I could have added more "do's" on the above list, I believe what I have shared in this chapter will help you when helping the sick individual. But most significantly, keep in mind that your ability to give the sick person your undivided attention will be most appreciated! With this thought, I now turn to the next chapter with some concluding remarks.

LESSONS LEARNED

➤ The Ministry of presence is what most individuals facing a life threatening disease mostly desire;

➤ When ministering to the sick person, our primary role is to allow God to flow through us, as we minister to the individual.

**Recommended Resources For Further Studies:
Available At: www.DrRuthTanyi.org**

1. *Are You Moving Forward with Jesus? How to Excel In Your Identity in Christ.*

2. *Who is the Real Jesus? Answers to 25 of the Toughest Questions About the Real Jesus: Simple & Straight forward to the point answers that will change your life!*

3. Faith to Receive God's Promises: How to "Walk" in BIBLICAL FAITH and Allow the BLESSINGS of GOD to Chase You.

CHAPTER 28

MOVING FORWARD WITH JESUS: CONCLUDING REMARKS

for everyone born of God overcomes the world. This is the victory that has overcome the world, even our faith.

(1 John 5:4; New International Version, NIV).

To us, Christians, testimonies of God's work in our lives are potent "faith builders" that enable us to overcome hardships and the evil one, Satan himself, in this dark world. For this reason,

I have shared my testimony in this book with hopes that you will be encouraged, edified, and be strengthened to know that what God has done in my life, He can do for you likewise, because God is no respecter of persons (Romans 2:11-16), meaning He does not favor any particular person.

Rather, anyone who walks by faith in accordance with God's Word will absolutely position him or herself to inherit His promises. **At the end of the day, it will come down to your faith and ability to trust God 100%, period!**

As I come to the conclusion of this book, I hope my story has done one of three things: (1) encouraged, edified, and strengthened you to firmly look upon the Lord Jesus as your Ultimate Healer; (2) enabled you to perceive some common barriers that can prevent you from receiving your healing, in addition to showing you ways to overcome these hindrances; and/or (3) offered some recommendations on how to receive your healing.

In spite of all of our hardships in this present life, we as Christians are already overcomers through Christ Jesus, because He has overcome the world for us (John 16:33). Hence, regardless of what you are going through right now, you have already won the battle whether or not you perceive the physical results. Do you believe this? While this biblical Truth might be very difficult for anyone to accept in the middle of a trial, it is, indeed, the Truth, which was not easy for me to come to grasp with during my crisis. Nevertheless, whether or not we accept it, God sees us victorious through Christ. Hence, we would be wise to perceive ourselves likewise.

I Am a Living Testimony

Today, I am a living testimony that the Word of God works, 100%, all of the time! The issue is never God. For His Word as encased in the Bible is flawless, alive, and powerful— It works — if we apply it correctly! (Proverbs 30:5; Hebrews 4:12). However, it is us, His children, finite human beings, who do not fully understand how to apply His Word into our lives and expect Godly results. As emphasized throughout this book, you cannot separate God from His Word. Therefore, to receive God's medicine for your spirit, soul, and body, you must know His Word and spend time in His presence. **The Word of God is truly the best medicine anyone can ever ask for —and we have this medicine readily available to us, if we choose to "take it" (meaning, apply it into our lives) faithfully.** And, the Bible is very instructive that only those who practice the Word of God will experience Godly results and are blessed (James 1:22-25; Luke 6:46-50).

As you have read in my story, **I was healed through the Ministry of the Word, and no one laid hands on me, and no one anointed me with oil.** The Word of God was my primary medicine, and I took it daily, several times a day, as you would take prescription medicines from a doctor. Just like most people are faithful in taking their prescription medications, I chose instead, to be faithful in taking God's Word, and it worked, and is still working today in my life! **If you recall, one of my goals for choosing the Ministry of the Word was that, I wanted to be well grounded in God's Word, that way I will be well prepared for the long fight with cancer, and to learn how to overcome and "walk in divine" health daily. Well, <u>I have accomplished my goal, as today, after 9 years, I continue to walk in "divine health" daily, using the Word of God</u>.**

It has been over 9 years, and I am 100% Cancer Free, healed by the Stripes of Jesus. I have no disease in my body, and I continue to fight a fight of faith, not to allow any disease entrance into my body! I am not special in God's eyes. Rather, **I received my healing because (a) I believed God's report more than any other report; (b) I applied biblical principles of healing into my life, and (c) I stood by God's Word with unwavering faith — I wish the same for you.** You do not have to do exactly what I did, but you can learn from my story and modify it to meet your personal needs.

I remember what one lady told me one day. She said, "<u>Well, Dr Ruth, I am not you. I am not strong enough in faith to do what you did to receive your healing</u>." **I informed her that it was the Holy Spirit working through me, and not my own efforts. Likewise, do not be intimidated by my courage and faith; instead, be encouraged, and know that it was the Holy Spirit and not me. Thus, be dependent more on the Holy Spirit for strength, and who knows, you may have a similar testimony as mine someday!**

Moving Forward With Jesus

Today, I am serving God fulltime as a Minister, sharing my story with all those who are interested in listening. Whenever I share my testimony in a crowd, or one-on-one, I witness people's immediate reactions of joy, hope, and in many instances, I have perceived faith in people's eyes because of my testimony. Just recently, I shared my testimony with a lady who was on hospice care (i.e., given less than one year to live), diagnosed with the exact same diagnosis and prognosis I had received. **Upon hearing my testimony, she immediately cancelled her hospice end of life care, and instead chose to fight the cancer!** I hope my testimony has given you much hope as it continues to do to others who have heard my story face-to-face.

In the last 5 years since I started sharing my story publicly, I have seen many people implement some of the recommendations I have explained in this book, and they have received healings from all sorts of diseases, such as Diabetes, Anxiety, Arthritis, etc, and have been set free from all sorts of bondages. **My testimony has given hope, revelation, and strength to countless individuals. I hope it has done the same for you. I have, and continue to teach these same principles to others during our Ministry's healing events/ meetings, and I have witnessed many individuals receive their healings from all sorts of diseases, including cancers.** I have laid hands on countless amounts of individuals, and I have seen them healed! Even as a former Prayer Minister with Andrew Wommack's Ministries during Andrew's Gospel Truth Seminars, I have prayed for countless people, taught them these same principles in this book, and seen them healed from all sorts of dire diseases —It works!

Whether or not you have a disease, these principles I have shared in this book will help you to overcome any trial or tribulation you are experiencing right now. **These principles work! They have worked for me and others, and they will work for you as well, if you decide to put them to practice —because God is no respecter of persons!**

The 3 Most Significant Scriptures

In the last several years, several people have frequently asked me to share the 3 most significant Scriptures on the list of my favorites during my battle with cancer. While all of the Scriptures I have listed in this book were significant, but by far, here are the three that were on top of the list during my fight with cancer, and they remain just as significant to me, today (1) **Isaiah 53:3-5** [Because of the Absolute Truth that the Lord died for my physical healing too!]; (2) **Romans 12:2** [Because of the Absolute Truth that to receive my healing I had to change my thinking to be consistent with God's Word]; and (3) **Romans 8:28-29** [Because of the Absolute Truth that regardless of the outcome, all things would work out for my good].

Lastly, as you have received from the Lord through this book, share with others. I now close this book by reminding you that

//

only God, through the Lord Jesus and the empowering of the Holy Spirit can make you "WHOLE"! The Word of God is your best medicine! —Take it several times daily! —Live it out in your life by faith! —and then pass it onto others! You will be blessed and God will be glorified, in Jesus name, AMEN!

//

I leave you with these powerful words from the Bible:

For the word of God is quick, and powerful, and sharper than any twoedged sword, piercing even to the dividing asunder of soul and spirit, and of the joints and marrow, and is a discerner of the thoughts and intents of the heart **(Hebrews 4:12)**, (emphasis author's).

*The Word of God is indeed, your **best medicine!***

LESSONS LEARNED

- You can be healed too! God is no respecter of persons! Do not give up!

Recommended Resources For Further Studies:

Available: www.DrRuthTanyi.org

Biblical Principles For a Blessed Life: An Audio Podcast teaching across the entire Bible, from the Book of Genesis to Revelation.

ABOUT JESUS
ACCEPT THE LORD JESUS NOW!

Jesus answered, "I am the way and the truth and the life. No one comes to the Father except through me. If you really know me, you will know my Father as well. From now on, you do know him and have seen him."

(John 14:6-7; New International Version, NIV).

As much as receiving your physical healing is important to God, He is most concerned about your salvation. Because it will not profit you if you receive physical healing in this life, but then later die and send yourself to hell (i.e., separation from God in all eternity). God is patient, wanting for no one to send him or herself to hell, but rather, for people to spend eternity with Him (2 Peter 3:9). **But He has given each of us a choice to choose Him and then spend eternity with Him when we die, or reject Him, and send ourselves to hell.**

God is love in His very essence. And in His love, He has made the provision for you not to go to hell. For the Bible teaches us that: ***For God so loved the world that he gave his one and only Son, that whoever believes in him shall not perish but have eternal life*** (John 3:16), (emphasis author's). God Himself in the person of the Lord Jesus came into this world, died on Calvary's cross, and then 3 days later He was raised from the dead—He did this all for you, so that you will live in this present world and overcome the evil one (Galatians 1:4), and then upon your death, you will spend eternity with Him — **This is the Gospel Message — The Good News we proclaim!** —**The love of God for us, His Creation!**

Jesus Christ, God Himself in the flesh lived a sinless and perfect life (1 Peter 2:22) and fulfilled **All** of the prophecies of the Messiah (i.e., Savior of the world) perfectly, something that no other human being in the history of the world has ever done, and will ever do (Matthew 5:17-20). He came to save you from your Sinful Nature, which every human being born by a woman inherits at the time of birth, because our common ancestors, Adam and Eve transgressed God's Law and sinned against Him. Ever since that sin by Adam and Eve, every human being is born into this world as a sinner, in need of a Savior to deliver him or her from that Sinful Nature inherited at birth (Romans 3: 23). The Lord Jesus is that Savior, Whose death and resurrection has paved the way for you to receive salvation (i.e., deliverance from that Sinful Nature and from the kingdom of darkness, belonging to Satan).

There is no other name given unto us, Mankind, by which salvation must come, except the name Jesus Christ, because He is the Messiah (Acts 4:12). The Bible teaches that if you believe in your heart in all of the claims of the Lord Jesus and in all of His works (i.e., His miracles, testimony, etc), and you confess that with your mouth, you will be born again and be saved (Romans 10:9). Every one experiences a physical birth, but to become a follower of Christ, a second birth in the spiritual realm (i.e., being born again) is necessary (John 3:1-15).

Once you genuinely acknowledge to God that you are a sinner in need of a Savior, and then you invite the Lord Jesus into your heart, **He will instantly forgive all of your sins: past, present and future sins**. Then, that darkened spirit which you inherited at birth as a result of the sin from Adam and Eve will be instantly illuminated (meaning, given the life of God; restored, and revived), and God Himself in the form of His Spirit will come and live in your heart by faith (Revelation 3:20).

Receive the Life of God Now!

Are you ready to invite the Lord Jesus into your life? Today is the day of Salvation! Tomorrow is not guaranteed to anyone. Before you close this book, you want to be certain what will happen to you upon your death? If you are ready, sincerely say the simple prayer below aloud. Keep in mind that the prayer is not what will save you; rather, you will be saved because you believe in your heart in the claims of the Lord Jesus, and you will be saying the prayer aloud as a confession of your belief or faith. **Below is the prayer:**

Dear God. I acknowledge that I am a sinner. I ask You to forgive me of all of my sins knowingly and unknowingly. Today, I believe in my heart that Jesus was/is God Who lived a sinless life, died on the Cross, and was raised from the dead on the third day. Right now, I receive His forgiveness of my sins, and I am asking You, Lord Jesus, to come and live in my heart. By faith, I believe You have accepted me. Today, I denounce all false ways to You, God, and I declare I will follow You, Jesus, for the remainder of my life. I thank You God, for accepting me, in Jesus name, Amen.

Then, I want you to say the simple prayer of faith below, in order to be filled with the Holy Spirit.

Heavenly Father, I ask You to fill me, right now, with Your Holy Spirit so that I can be strengthened and emboldened to live as a Christian and witness to others about the Lord Jesus. By faith, I believe I am being filled, right now! Thank You God, in Jesus name, Amen.

Friend, if you said the above prayers, based on the authority of God's Word, I declare you are a true Christian, filled with the Holy Spirit. **Next,** start studying your Bible. Any modern translation of the Bible will suffice. **Except, do not get the Jehovah's Witnesses Bible called New World Translation (NWT), because it is a falsified translation. Also, do not get the Church of Mormon's Book of Mormon, this too is falsified.**

Once you **obtain a true Christian Bible, begin with the Gospel of John,** then study the Gospels of Matthew Mark, and Luke. **Thereafter, begin studying the book of Genesis.** Very importantly, **find a Bible believing and practicing** church in your local area and start attending regularly. Get involved in ministry there and serve God wholeheartedly, and I promise you, He will take you places you can never go through your own efforts.

Recommended Resources For Further Studies:

Available: www.DrRuthTanyi.org

All teachings by Dr Ruth Tanyi.

1. The Heart of True Christianity: The Gospel Message of Jesus Christ: Answers to 10 Major Questions Pertaining to Your Salvation in Christ Jesus.

2. Are You Moving Forward with Jesus? How to Excel In Your Identity in Christ. ***Also available in Audio CD format**.

3. Can I trust the Bible as God's Word? How do I Know? What Is the Evidence?

4. Who is the Real Jesus? Answers to 25 of the Toughest Questions About the Real Jesus.

5. Faith to Receive God's Promises: How to "Walk" in BIBLICAL FAITH and Allow the BLESSINGS of GOD to Chase You. ***Also available in Audio CD format**.

6. Biblical Principles For a Blessed Life: An audio Podcast teaching across the entire Bible, from the Book of Genesis to Revelation.

CONTACT US

Please let us know if you have accepted Christ Jesus as your Lord and Savior, so that we can send you **FREE materials** to help you grow as a Christian. Welcome into the Kingdom of Light, God's Kingdom.

About Jesus: Accept the Lord Jesus Now!

Our Bible Teaching Series

We have a Bible Teaching Program called: **Biblical Principles For a Blessed Life.** This is a teaching across the entire Bible, from the book of Genesis to the book of Revelation: Book by book, chapter by chapter, verse by verse, teaching you how to apply biblical principles into your life daily and expect Godly results. You can listen to the teachings on the go, at your convenience, 24/7.

Here is How You Can Subscribe to the Bible Teachings

Visit: www.DrRuthTanyi.org, then go to the tab that says Bible Teachings, Listen to some **FREE** Teachings there, and then you can Subscribe.

Healing Conferences

If you are interested in attending one of our **healing or other conferences,** visit our website, (www.DrRuthTanyi.org), check out our Events page for details, and sign up there.

We Want To Hear About Your Testimony

We would like to hear from you. Please let us know how this book has helped you.

Email: Info@DrRuthtanyi.org

Write: Dr Ruth Tanyi Ministries, Inc;

P O BOX 1806; Loma Linda, California; 92354; USA

To Invite Dr Ruth to speak at Your Church or Event

Email: DrRuth@DrRuthTanyi.org or call (909) 383 7978.

Appendix A
Comments From Nurses at
Loma Linda University Cancer Center

"Dear Ruth: Nice knowing you. Congrats, stay strong and we don't want to see you here again." Nurse K.

"Good luck and stay healthy." Pharmacist T.

"Oh my gosh!! Congrats! I will miss your smiling face! Keep in touch and stay healthy." Nurse L.

"Dear Ruth, Congratulations! You are wonderful! May God bless you always. We'll miss you." Nurse S.

"Dear Ruth: So happy for you, congrats... Best wishes and will keep you in my prayers. Stay healthy and God bless." Nurse D.

"Ruth, So happy to have met you... May God keep you cancer free... you are incredible! Best wishes." Nurse M.

"Ruth, I'm so glad I got to be your beginning and end. It's been a ball knowing you! I'm proud of you... No more spitting! God bless you and keep you, love." Nurse D.

"Will miss your smile and laugher...Hope you come to visit!" Nurse C.

"You are such a champion, I love your smile & positive attitude, love." Nurse M.

"Ruth you did it! Its so great to know you and your contagious smile and laughter!" Nurse D.

"Congratulations! Survivor! Best wishes." Nurse G.

"Great job! You did it!" Nurse C.

Some of the nurses who cared for me at Loma Linda Cancer Center

BIBLIOGRAPHY

Bibliography

1. James Strong & John R. Kohlenberger 111, John. The New Strong's Expanded Exhaustive Concordance of the Bible: Red-Letter Edition. Nashville: Thomas Nelson.

2. W. E. Vine, Merrill F. Unger, William White, Jr. Vine's Complete Expository Dictionary of Old and New Testament Words. Nashville: Nelson, 1996.

MINISTRY RESOURCES

OTHER BOOKS BY DR TANYI

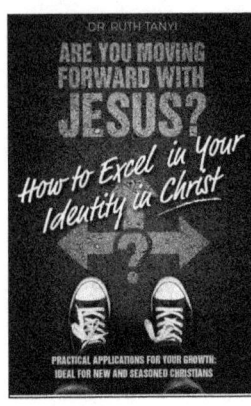

Are You Moving Forward with Jesus? How to Excel In Your Identity in Christ

Can I Trust the Bible as God's Word? How do I know? What is the Evidence?

Faith to Receive God's Promises. How to "Walk" in Biblical Faith and Allow the Blessings of God to Chase You

Walking with Jesus Personally Answers to 6 Questions About "Walking" with Jesus Christ Daily

Your Path to Knowing the Only True Living God. Life-changing Answers on the inside!

Who is the Real Jesus? Answers to 25 of the Toughest Questions About the Real Jesus: Simple & Straight forward to the point answers that will change your life!

MINISTRY RESOURCES

OTHER BOOKS BY DR TANYI

COMING SOON

13 Reasons why People Get Sick! A Biblical Perspective & Remedies

Did God Really Say that? How to Overcome Doubt and Receive God's Promises: 10 Life-Changing Lessons Learned from Overcoming Metastasis Colon Cancer.

AUDIO CD TEACHING LIBRARY

Faith to Receive God's Promises: How to "Walk" in Biblical Faith and Allow the Blessings of God to Chase You

The Heart of True Christianity: The Gospel Message of Jesus Christ: Answers to 10 Major Questions Pertaining to Your Salvation in Christ Jesus

What Are the Gifts of the Spirit?

Holy Spirit-Led Healthy Emotions: The Fruit of the Spirit and Your Health

How to Overcome Doubt and Receive God's Promises

13 Reasons Why People Get Sick: A Biblical Perspective & Remedies

AUDIO CD TEACHING LIBRARY

Unforgiveness and Other Toxic Emotions: How to Walk in Forgiveness

Live Above Your Fears & Overcome Sicknesses and Diseases

Be Anxious No More

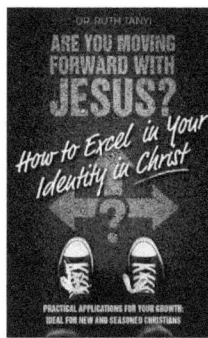
Are You Moving Forward with Jesus? How to Excel In Your Identity in Christ

The Book of Genesis: An Expository Teaching! Chapter by Chapter, Verse by Verse

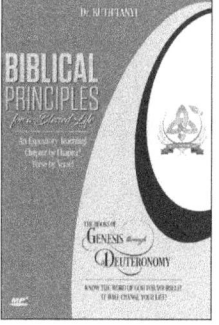
Biblical Principles for a Blessed Life: An Expository Teaching! Chapter by Chapter, Verse by Verse: The Books of Genesis Through Deuteronomy

Daily Habits for Your Soul: Daily Biblical & Lifestyle Remedies to Prevent Sicknesses and Diseases

OTHER TEACHINGS BY DR TANYI

Discipleship Bible Teaching Series

Biblical Preventive Health with Dr Ruth ® Magazine

13 Reasons Why True Christianity is Different: A Wall Mount Poster
A Call to Action Poster

Visit **Dr Ruth Tanyi Ministries YouTube Channel** and watch our FREE Devotional Teachings, Plus Other FREE Teachings at your convenience, 24/7. Subscribe to our YouTube Channel and start enjoying our Free Teachings Today.

Visit www.Drruthtanyi.org/blog and watch our FREE Devotional Teachings.

Obtaining Ministry Resources

To get more information about the above ministry resources, please visit our Website: **www.DrRuthTanyi.org**

Contact Information
You Can also Email or Contact us:

Dr Ruth Tanyi Ministries, Inc
P O BOX 1806
Loma Linda, CA, 92354, USA
Email: Info@DrRuthtanyi.org

Obtaining Ministry Resources Outside the USA
Visit Amazon.com to obtain Dr Tanyi's books if you live outside the USA

About The Author

Dr. Ruth Tanyi, DrPH, NP; ACSM HFS, CNS, MA, Ministry

Dr. Ruth Tanyi is a Bible Teacher, Doctor of Preventive Care/Integrative Medicine, Board Certified Nutritionist and Exercise Physiologist. She is the founder/CEO of Dr. Ruth Tanyi Ministries, a non- denominational Christian, non-profit ministry located in San Bernardino, California, with primary focus on spreading the uncompromising Gospel of Jesus Christ; sharing God's unconditional love and grace, while concurrently teaching others how to integrate Bible-based principles with medical lifestyle practices in order to prevent and overcome diseases.

Even before being healed by God from Metastasis Colon cancer and other diseases in 2009/2010, Dr Tanyi felt called by God into Ministry. However, since her healing and experiential knowledge and revelation of the love and grace of God, she has become an ardent student and teacher of the Word of God. Dr Tanyi is also actively involved in the Body of Christ via her involvement with other ministries in advancing the Gospel of Jesus Christ, and in espousing the necessity of knowing God's Word. For almost 9 years, Dr Tanyi faithfully served as a volunteer at her local church: Abundant Living Family Church (ALFC) in Rancho Cucamonga, California, under the leadership of Pastor Diego Mesa; and while there, she counseled and taught individuals about the interconnectedness between God's Word and medical lifestyle practices, and witnessed many transformed lives.

She has also served as a Prayer Minister with Andrew Wommack Ministries under the leadership of Andrew Wommack, during his 2016 and 2017 Gospel Truth Conferences, where she prayed for countless individuals and witnessed their healings and deliverances from all sorts of diseases and bondages. Dr Tanyi's recent appearances on Television as a guest Minister with Fr. Mike Manning (now deceased) on a series called Catholic Insights, continues to educate the public on the major differences between Protestants and Catholics' expressions of true Christianity; this TV series, which originally aired on TBN's Church Channel is still broadcasting in various Christian Networks, and it continues to change countless lives.

Dr Tanyi is a public speaker and author, and offers a CD and DVD teaching library in addition to books on various topics ranging from the essential doctrines of true Christianity, to teachings on the very essential connection between God's Word and Medicine. Dr Tanyi has a daily Audio Podcast Bible Teaching Series called Biblical Principles For a Blessed life (available through iTunes, Podbean, USB flash drive and other media), which is an in-depth teaching across the entire Bible, from the Book of Genesis to Revelation, focusing on how to apply God's Word practically and expect results.

Dr Tanyi has authored over 7 books pertaining to the Christian lifestyle. She has also published numerous academic peer-reviewed journal articles and research papers. She is still pursuing her academic research in the area of lifestyle practices in preventing and overcoming depression. She has been nominated and selected in WHO IS WHO IN AMERICA and in WHO IS WHO IN Medicine and Healthcare. She is in private practice in San Bernardino, California, and lives in Southern California.

For more information visit www.DrRuthTanyi.org, or to contact Dr Tanyi to speak at your event, church or non-Christian event, email her at: DrRuth@DrRuthTanyi.org, or call (909) 383 7978.

www.ingramcontent.com/pod-product-compliance
Lightning Source LLC
Chambersburg PA
CBHW032031150426
43194CB00006B/233